Whistle Stops

Whistle Stops

Adventures in Public Life

Wilson W. Wyatt, Sr.

THE UNIVERSITY PRESS OF KENTUCKY

Frontispiece: Wilson W. Wyatt, Sr., campaigning

Photo Credits
Photographs in this book are from the author's personal collection
except as indicated, by page number, below: Frontispiece, Lin
Caufield; 11, 19, 119, 170, 211, 217, *Louisville Courier-Journal*; 38,
Ankers Capitol; 46, 57, Acme; 139, United Press International/Bettmann
Archive; 200, United States Information Service–Tokyo.

Scholarly publisher for the Commonwealth,
serving Bellarmine College, Berea College, Centre
College of Kentucky, Eastern Kentucky University,
The Filson Club, Georgetown College, Kentucky
Historical Society, Kentucky State University,
Morehead State University, Murray State University,
Northern Kentucky University, Transylvania University,
University of Kentucky, University of Louisville,
and Western Kentucky University.

Editorial and Sales Offices: Lexington, Kentucky 40506-0024

Library of Congress Cataloging-in-Publication Data

Wyatt, Wilson W. (Wilson Watkins), 1905–
  Whistle stops.

  Includes index.
  1. Wyatt, Wilson W. (Wilson Watkins), 1905–
2. Diplomats—United States—Biography. 3. Kentucky—
Lieutenant-governors—Biography. 4. Mayors—Kentucky—
Louisville—Biography. 5. United States—Foreign
relations—1945–   . 6. United States—Politics and
government—1945–   . 7. Kentucky—Politics and
government—1951–   . I. Title.
E748.W97A39 1985   976.9'04'0924 [B]   85-15066
ISBN 0-8131-1537-X

For Anne, my complete partner

Contents

Illustrations

Chapter 1

A Conversation
with Trygve Lie

"Vat is dis business about private practice of law?" asked Trygve Lie in his deep Norwegian guttural. The Secretary-General of the United Nations was on the telephone trying to persuade me to take a position described by him as "the under secretary-general of the United Nations." It was January, 1947, and I had just that day returned to Louisville to resume my law practice after spending five years away from it—first as mayor of Louisville for four years and then as President Truman's National Housing Administrator and Housing Expediter. I had exhausted my savings and was convinced that a more extended departure from my profession could well mean the loss of it. Nevertheless, I responded to his urging by agreeing to turn right around and fly back East to talk out the situation with him. The United Nations building in New York had not yet been built and the headquarters was then at Lake Success, just outside the city on Long Island.

Trygve Lie was a large man whose cordial self-assurance matched the size of his body. With jovial charm he tried to persuade me that my training in the law, my service in local government as the elected wartime mayor of a major war production city, and my national experience in the appointed quasi-cabinet post under President Truman in launching the postwar housing program all constituted the ideal background for the position he was urging me to take. I demurred and explained what I felt was the financial necessity of my returning to the practice of law. In addition, I told him, it was my philosophy that public service is improved by periodic return to private life. A public official should feel free to do what he deems to be right and best,

With Trygve Lie at the United Nations

whether or not those actions will be most apt to maintain him in office. Because such independence sometimes requires unpopular actions, the official must be willing to risk losing his office and having to return to private life—and that makes it necessary to have a private career to which one can return. I am also convinced that uninterrupted public office tends to lessen a person's objectivity and leads often to an unhealthy separation from the life, the thinking, and the needs of private citizens. Although I salute those who follow an uninterrupted public career, and acknowledge that continuing years of service often develop special expertise, I also think there is benefit to the public for at least some people to serve only on occasion, in special circumstances.

I temporized by telling Trygve Lie that, in any event, he would need the approval of our government before we could consider the proffered position seriously. He responded that he had already obtained that approval from the secretary of state. He proceeded to make the position very challenging. He explained that while there was no such office, technically, as Under Secretary-General (only the several assistant secretaries-general, one of whom is an American), he would create the special circumstances that would result in the de facto position. He took me to the window of his office and pointed down to the official guest house on the grounds, a charming white residence surrounded by a picket fence. He said significantly, "You and your family will live there. No other assistant secretary-general will have an official residence." Then he added that whenever he left the New York headquarters on various official missions over the world (and this occurred often) he would always designate me the acting secretary-general. "Everyone will soon get the idea—that you are indeed the under secretary-general." I would have had no trouble turning down the administrative post of assistant secretary-general—but the unique post he proposed to create was admittedly most tempting. In those years the U.N., by the exercise of its good offices, was often able to prevent war, maintain the peace, or terminate conflict in many places around the globe. The spectrum of challenge in the international field was unlimited. But acceptance, I was convinced, would have spelled the end of my professional career, which was my anchor of financial independence. With genuine regret, I reached the conclusion that for my own future freedom I had to decline and return to Louisville to reestablish myself as a lawyer.

This decision on the U.N. post was a turning point in my life. Had I accepted, I would probably have served in public positions the rest of my days. As it is, out of my more than fifty years at the bar, I have spent a total of some ten in public life, and the remaining forty or so in private life, in the practice of my profession and in various extra-curricular civic activities. It is about the adventures of those ten public years—those periodic whistle stops in the public arena—that I now write.

Chapter 2

The Home Front

From my earliest recollection I have always felt the challenge of public life and the conviction that the most important activity of mankind is to participate in the betterment of each generation—expressed in the oath of every Athenian youth "to leave his city better than he found it." Biography, especially of political leaders, was an early boyhood fascination for me. I had read with avid interest those biographies of public figures in Lord's "Beacon Lights of History." By the time I was nine or ten I had already decided I would like to be a lawyer, as the legal profession offered the combined advantages of an interesting career and relative freedom to participate in public life.

The Louisville public school system in my childhood was extremely good, especially the Louisville Male High School, where I acquired an excellent basic education in classical studies—including Latin, English, mathematics, history, and the sciences—and graduated as valedictorian. Male High had a faculty that would have done credit to a college. After a year at the University of Louisville I met the necessity of self-support by going to work at the Louisville and Nashville Railroad. And I enrolled at the Jefferson School of Law, a private night school maintained by a group of outstanding Louisville lawyers who taught all the classes. Only two years were required to obtain the degree in law, but with work for a living each day at the L&N and classes and study each night and weekend the two years were strenuous. At twenty-one I graduated (again fortunately as valedictorian), passed my state examination and was admitted to the bar in October in 1927.

It was an early beginning—but where to start? I resigned my salaried job with the L&N and applied to every large law firm in

Louisville, but there was no opening. I finally was successful in finding a place to hang out my shingle in a cubbyhole office with Garnett and Van Winkle, a fine two-man law firm where I was given the opportunity to escape overhead expenses by doing research and miscellaneous chores for the firm, but there was no salary; I was on my own. I described my arrangement as no overhead in consideration of no compensation, and later compared it to Puerto Rico's Commonwealth status of no taxation in consideration of no representation. It gave me a full realization of the value of every single client and every item of professional employment, however small. I supplemented my meager and uncertain income by teaching night courses at the Jefferson School of Law and at the American Institute of Banking.

Toward the end of my first year of practice I met Anne Kinnaird Duncan, who was one of Louisville's debutantes that season. After a rapid courtship we were secretly engaged on February 10, 1929. But economics delayed our wedding. That was the year of the historic stock market crash and the beginning of the great depression. I felt it was unfair to Anne for our engagement to be announced until I had completed one full year of practice with a net income of at least five thousand dollars. By the spring of 1930 this was narrowly accomplished and we were married on the 14th of June. In our happy innocence you could almost have convinced us that the flags that bedecked the streets that Flag Day were in honor of our long-awaited wedding.

I was attracted early to the Democratic party. Even in my school days I was impressed by the philosophies and idealism in the writings of such party heroes as Thomas Jefferson and Woodrow Wilson. Despite the approaching landslide for Herbert Hoover in the 1928 presidential race I strode jauntily down Fourth Street with Al Smith at the head of the Young Democratic Club parade—all four hundred of us sporting our brown derbies, the emblem of the Smith campaign.

The Democrats had been out of office in Louisville for sixteen years, but the Roosevelt victory of 1932 changed things. A group of us from the Young Democratic Club endorsed Neville Miller for mayor of Louisville. As the young dean of the University of Louisville law school, he was an attractive new type of candidate. When he was elected in 1933 he urged me to take the post of director of law for the city. Although it was tempting to a lawyer still in his twenties I declined, since my private practice was growing and I did not want to risk leaving it. I did agree, however, to handle the trial work for the city

The 1928 Brown Derby parade in Louisville. *From left,*
Wilson Wyatt, Lebanon lawyer (later Congressman) Frank Chelf,
presidential candidate Al Smith, Pike County lawyer John A.
Runyon.

in order to gain valuable experience in the courtroom; this could be
done without leaving the private practice. A few years later I accepted
the offer of a junior partnership in one of Louisville's larger law firms,
which then became Peter, Heyburn, Marshall & Wyatt. My particular
responsibility with them was the representation of the Louisville
newspapers and the defense of their litigation, an extremely attractive
assignment.

In 1937 the mayor and other key leaders of the local Democratic
party urged me to run for mayor of Louisville. Their endorsement, in

those days, was virtually an assurance of election. I was flattered and tempted, but I was thirty-one and just getting well established in my profession. The salary of the mayor of Louisville was only $5,000, and I had no nest egg to supplement that income or to tide me over, let alone to give me a cushion for the period it would take to reestablish my practice after the end of the mayor's term. After much soul searching I declined, but the decision haunted me in the four years that followed. As Hitler rose to power and spread his lethal reach across the continent of Europe, I was increasingly troubled in my conscience by remaining in private life while the world was in such turmoil.

My friend Mark Ethridge, then publisher of the Louisville papers, arranged for me to meet President Roosevelt at the White House to ask his advice about coming to Washington in some full-time position. He encouraged me to enter public life and told me there would be a place for me (just what, I didn't know) in the administration if I would come to Washington, but he left to me the choice between that and running for mayor of Louisville, which he also recommended. It was a fascinating session and my first visit to the Oval Office. The president had just held his press conference on the budget, which he described to me as his "annual seminar for the press." The major issue at the session was whether Congress would be willing to raise the debt limit to a total of $48 billion (about 3 percent of today's debt limit) to accommodate the new defense expenditures. He told me he had pretended ignorance of budgets and had said it was immaterial to him whether Congress increased the debt limit, since an act of Congress that authorized expenditures was just as much the law of the land as a technical measure about debt limits—so he would just leave the matter to Congress. He was confident. He was very friendly and a buoyant spirit.

Out of a conviction that democracy begins at home, in local government, and that this was where I could be more immediately useful, I decided to announce for mayor and make the race. Furthermore, it seemed to me important to learn the lessons of the elective process, as a prelude to any further participation in public life. With another four years of practice I had been able to accumulate a reserve of about $50,000; in the economy of those days it was enough to give me comfort. My wife and I, as always in every important decision involving our family life and my career, had talked it over endlessly and were in complete accord. Partners and close friends with whom I conferred about the decision were somewhat baffled, but wished me well.

The primary did not present a problem in view of the announced support of party leaders. The primary did, however, give me an opportunity to get better acquainted with the political organization and to encourage several very worthwhile people to join the ticket. This was especially important as to the candidates for aldermen, the County Fiscal Court (in Kentucky the governing body of the county), and the state legislature. I knew I would need their help and cooperation in carrying out my program and that close work with them in the primary and election would strengthen our relationship.

Throughout the primary and the summer, I worked hard on developing a program for the fall campaign. I read endlessly about urban affairs and spent several days in Chicago with the municipal experts at the Public Administration Service and their related organizations, including the American Municipal Association; these were then the center of the best prevailing wisdom about the various aspects of local government. I discussed my program with the Kentucky governor, Keen Johnson, as well as with key candidates on the ticket. These early discussions proved to be very important, as they led to a sense of partnership among the officials whose help I would need.

When we launched the fall campaign in early October, 1941, we had hammered out a specific twelve-point program that called for the most extensive overhaul of local government since the granting of Louisville's current charter sixteen years earlier. There was, of course, no television in those days. All four of the Louisville radio stations were used for major speeches in the explanation and exposition of the program. Despite urging by many of the old hands to enliven the race with something more vigorous, we confined the campaign to the affirmative unfolding of the twelve points.

Our most important issue was national defense, and the next most important was post-defense planning—for the later conversion period back to peacetime pursuits. The productive power of the United States had become indispensable to England, France, and the allied powers, fighting for their survival against the onslaught from Hitler's Germany. We had become the arsenal of democracy. Although we were still at peace the allied cause had become our cause. Among the strictly local planks, we pledged consolidation and streamlining of local government by eliminating overlapping city-county functions, rightful representation in the legislature through redistricting, equalization of salaries between men and women and between blacks and whites, and a lightening of the local financial burden by several specific proposals for state action. We also were committed to support two amendments to the Kentucky constitution: one would permit modern voting machines, in the interest of honest elections; the other would set aside ten percent of the state's education funds for use in needy districts. The latter would be at the expense of Louisville but was equitable and would raise the educational level of the state. Support from Louisville would show Louisville's unselfish concern for the rest of the state.

With these themes, our campaign was a quiet one devoid of any mudslinging or bombastics from our side, despite continuous provocation from our opponents, who charged that I was a corporation lawyer, that I was the candidate of the *Courier-Journal* (since I was one of their counsel and a member of their board of directors), that I would be dominated by the banks and the utilities (I was a director of the First National Bank, our firm represented the Louisville Gas & Electric Co., and my father was vice president of the Louisville Railway Company), and that I was the candidate of the Birth Control League. To support the last charge (calculated to alienate Catholic Democrats) they asserted erroneously that my wife, Anne, was president of the Birth Control League; in some way they had confused this with her position as president of the Louisville Junior League. One Sunday morning, as election day neared, the opposition stationed workers near Catholic churches throughout the city, to distribute cards carrying these charges, especially about the Birth Control League. But their negative campaign failed—it may even have backfired. On election night Louisville elected its youngest mayor in this century (age thirty-five) in a landslide vote.

The ballot box had justified my conviction that an affirmative campaign on issues of substance would be successful. For sixteen years Louisville had elected Republican administrations. Then things changed with Roosevelt's election in 1932, and Louisville elected Democratic mayors in 1933 (Neville Miller) and 1937 (Joseph D. Scholtz). But the majorities, either way, tended over the years to be rather close.

Upon my election I decided to sever all ties that might involve any real or apparent conflict of interest. I ended my partnership in the law firm of Peter, Heyburn, Marshall & Wyatt and resigned from the boards of the newspapers, *Courier-Journal* and *Louisville Times*, and the First National Bank group of companies. As I was the youngest

member of the bank boards and the only outside director of the
Bingham (newspaper) companies, I took these steps with genuine
regret but out of a strong conviction that to continue in these positions
might give rise to public perceptions that could handicap the proper
fulfillment of my duties as an impartial mayor.

On the first of December, about an hour before the inauguration
ceremony was to begin, I closed the door on my law office and walked
a block to the City Hall, where the inaugural platform had been erected.
As I started up the side steps into the City Hall, two policemen
stationed there blocked my entrance with the caution, "You can't go in
there, Bud, they're swearing in the new mayor today." A little
embarrassed (I am not sure whether it was for them or for me), I
explained I was to be the new mayor. When several of the gathering
crowd started laughing at the police officers, they decided to take the
chance, so, though still dubious, they waved me in.

When I was administered the standard Kentucky oath of office
(which includes an elaborate disavowal, required by our 1891 constitution, of participation in duels by deadly weapons), my daughter,
Mary Anne, a wee youngster, raised her right hand and solemnly held
it upraised throughout my repetition of the lengthy oath, while my
other daughter, Nancy, just learning to talk, kept loudly calling
"Daddy, Daddy." Her message came out all too clearly over the radio.

Since 1941 preceded television, we had been spared this expensive
medium in the campaign. Heavy election expenditures were not
thought to be either necessary or appropriate, and the final report
showed that the fall campaign had cost a total (for the entire Democratic ticket, not just the race for mayor) of only $26,400.79, including
advertising, direct mail, precinct workers, radio—the whole works.
Not a single candidate was asked for, or made, a contribution, and four
or five thousand dollars remained as a small surplus, which was later
spent for the first local public opinion polls (by Elmo Roper) on issues
that arose during our term of office.

One of my first acts was to name a new chief of police, carefully
chosen from the ranks of the professional and non-political civil
service. This was a definite departure from a time-honored practice of
appointing a political loyalist to head the police force. I had intended
to take the step later in the week, but the rumor of the appointment
circulated before the inaugural ceremonies were concluded, and I
decided I should act at once to forestall the political upheaval the rumor
was beginning to generate. The old-line politicos objected strenuously

Inauguration as mayor of Louisville, 1941. *At left*: Anne D. Wyatt
with daughters, Nancy K. and Mary Anne, and parents Mary W. and
Richard H. Wyatt; *right*, outgoing mayor Joseph D. Scholtz.

but the appointment stuck—in fact, it set a precedent that has been
followed ever since. The professional civil service was relatively new
in those days, and the selection of the police chief was a clear signal
that politics would not be tolerated in law enforcement or in the ranks
of the police force.

The first week in office was a constant round of appointments of
new people, conferences to launch new programs, preparation of bills
for the legislature to implement the twelve-point program on which I
had been elected, sessions with the governor and our local legislative
delegation to review the approach to the new General Assembly, and
meetings with the Louisville Board of Aldermen and the Jefferson

County Fiscal Court to cement the moves toward consolidation and streamlining. Things were off to a speedy start.

On Sunday, the 7th of December, Anne and I motored to Indianapolis to relax by watching Sonja Henie perform gracefully in her ice show. On the way back to Louisville, late that afternoon, we turned on the car radio and heard the shocking, the almost unbelievable news of the Japanese bombardment of the American fleet at Pearl Harbor.

We arrived home to a ringing telephone, and calls continued until late in the night. I was warned by the War Department that guards should be posted at once on the four Ohio River bridges and at all other strategic points because of the danger of sabotage. Since what could not have been predicted had just happened in the Pacific, Washington was desperately concerned as to what might happen elsewhere. Nor was it known what action Germany might be about to take. Extra guards were ordered for all of the war plants in the area. Louisville was one of the eighteen most significant arsenals of defense in the United States. There were the powder plant at nearby Charlestown, the chemical plants in Rubbertown, the Naval Ordnance Plant, the shipyards on the Ohio, the Curtiss-Wright plant (later to become International Harvester), the bomber squadron at Bowman Field. The country's entire gold reserve was stored a few miles away, and thousands of men were training at the Armored Forces Headquarters at neighboring Fort Knox.

On the following day, Roosevelt made his historic address to the joint session of Congress, and a state of war was declared with Japan. Three days later, Germany and Italy declared war on the United States. From that Sunday of Pearl Harbor, well over half of my time was devoted to matters of defense and war production.

As mayor, I organized the Louisville Metropolitan Area Defense Council and served as its chairman. It was our first functional consolidation of the area and included not only Louisville and Jefferson County but the Indiana regions of New Albany and Jeffersonville, as well. I issued an immediate call for 500 auxiliary police, 500 auxiliary firemen, and 1,000 air raid wardens. To emphasize nonpartisanship, I recruited a former Republican mayor, William B. Harrison (he had also been a Republican candidate for governor), to serve as director of volunteers. The response to the appeal was electrifying—5,926 volunteers. Ultimately, some 50,000 citizen-volunteers were engaged in the various activities of the Defense Council. The war emergency generated a spirit of close cooperation. The area functioned as a single unit in responding to the multitudinous demands that were made of it—boundary lines seemed of little or no importance. My duties as chairman of the Area Defense Council were my first priority throughout the war, which was virtually coincident with my four-year term as mayor.

When the legislature convened at Frankfort the 1st of January, all of our Louisville bills were ready for introduction. They had been reviewed with Governor Keen Johnson and I was assured of his assistance. I scheduled a regular luncheon each Saturday in Louisville with our entire Jefferson County delegation of twelve in order to canvass the progress that had been made and to meet, early on, any objections or problems that were being encountered. Because of the landslide victory at the polls, the public familiarity with our program, the advance clearance with the governor as well as with our own delegation and county officials, and the early preparation of the proposed laws, most of our program passed both houses very smoothly. Three measures, however, presented special problems.

For years, the towns and cities of Kentucky had sought without success to have the state highway department make local grants for street building and repair. It was possible to recognize the boundary line of almost any Kentucky city in those days by riding blindfolded on any highway leading into town—the city boundary had been passed when the bouncing and the bumping commenced. In 1942 we took a new approach. The state had been reluctant to transfer funds away from its own control, and there was a serious constitutional question whether it had the right to do so. We met both points by advocating a law—statewide, of course, in its application—that would authorize the state highway department, itself, to expend its funds in improving and repairing any city street that was a part of the state highway system or a feeder to it, provided the affected city made an official request and turned over to the state the traffic control of that portion of the street. Through the Kentucky Municipal League we obtained the backing of all the urban centers of the state, and although the state was then still predominantly rural and agricultural, the urban areas, acting jointly, constituted a substantial power bloc. The advance approval of the governor and his highway commissioner removed, or at least muted, most of the objections from the farming areas. What had not been possible before now became law. Kentucky cities entered a new era. The road work started on a limited basis in 1942 and was phased in with larger expenditures each year. Louisville's potholes started disappearing and soon a dilapidated street structure was transformed into modern urban highways. This bill alone has brought millions and millions of dollars of relief to Louisville's budget over the years, and at the same time has repaved our streets and made us a vastly better city. And the same has been true across Kentucky's city landscape. Interestingly, one of the few early objections was from those within the cities themselves who were not willing to surrender traffic control over these highways to the state.

Another bill that promised financial relief provided for the refund to Jefferson, Kenton, and Harlan Counties of 100 percent of the fees collected by the sheriffs' and clerks' offices. In all of the other 117 counties, the full amount of these fees had always been returned to the counties for their own use. But an exception had been made by law as to these three counties because of the large amounts of their fees, and 25 percent designated as "excess" had been retained by the state. The governor declined to urge the passage of this bill but agreed to keep hands off. With that much accomplished and the help of the officials of the other two affected counties, we organized support from various members of the assembly and when the support was sufficient we brought the bill up for passage. It became law—to the governor's great surprise—but the bill was fair, and we had organized the support. Governor Johnson laughingly said this had taught him a lesson on the danger of legislative independence. This was an important benefit to Louisville, as I had already secured the agreement of the Jefferson Fiscal Court that, if I could get the legislature to pass the bill, the county would apply the refunded 25 percent to the benefit of the city through jointly supported agencies.

The benefit of these two financial bills was immediately equal to 14 percent of Louisville's total real estate taxes—and much more in the years since.

Of the eleven "Louisville Bills" eight passed both houses without a single dissenting vote, one had two negative votes in the house, and one had one negative vote in the senate. I have never felt metropolitan Louisville faces a problem with the General Assembly—provided we present a sound program on which we have achieved a consensus in Jefferson County in advance. It is only when we have failed to do our own homework and when our delegation has failed to present a united front that we have fared badly at Frankfort.

But on one bill we met with surprising problems, not from the rest of the state, but from our own people. Again it was evident that division at home makes life difficult in the legislature. As one of the several city-county consolidation moves, I had pledged to merge into a single unit our separate city and county health departments. Thus far, there was no objection. But as the legislation was developed, it seemed equally logical to merge two other units into the new city-county Board of Health—the City (General) Hospital with its separate board, and the Waverly Hills Tuberculosis Sanitorium, with its separate board. The latter was the sticking point. The members of the Waverly Hills board were outstanding citizens who had built a special constituency for tuberculosis and, even though they had been appointed by the mayor and county judge, they sincerely believed that they were not "political"; the new city-county health board, though it was to be appointed by the same mayor and the same county judge, *would* somehow be political. They also feared that their singular emphasis on tuberculosis would be diluted if "their" sanatorium passed into a consolidated health unit.

The objections became so pronounced that the legislature was disturbed and, finally, the senate took the unusual step of deciding to sit as a committee of the whole for a lengthy and very spirited public hearing. Prominent Louisville citizens and doctors spoke on both sides. The dispute had become very acrimonious. Against the charge of "politics" I responded that I was "not impressed by the unreasoning and emotional opposition to this program because of sentimental attachment to one disease." When it finally came to a vote, it was approved 54-27 in the house and 32-3 in the senate. Since there were prominent opponents I was doubly grateful for the support of the League of Women Voters and, among others, of William A. Stoll, the president of the Board of Trade, and of Dr. Irvin Abell, who was president of both the American Medical Association and the American College of Surgeons. Just as I heaved a sigh of relief that this important step of government streamlining had been accomplished, seven of the ten members of the Waverly Hills Board resigned in a mass protest. I was shocked but I accepted their resignations and immediately appointed the new board on which, fortunately, I was able to obtain two former presidents of the Jefferson County Medical Association along with other prominent civic leaders. Again it was brought home to me that change is almost always resisted, no matter how much for the better. There is always a vested interest in the status quo. It was a source of great satisfaction that the new health board received a national award for excellence a couple of years later.

Another bill in our program created the Louisville and Jefferson

County Planning and Zoning Commission—the first such city-county agency in the United States.

In order to meet the increasing need for automobile parking, we secured legislative approval for the city to own and operate parking lots and garages and to issue bonds to provide the necessary funding. This 1942 legislation has served Louisville well in the 1980s, in the creation of parking facilities needed for our downtown modernization program.

A bill with sweeping significance passed with hardly a murmur of complaint—our Urban Rehabilitation Act, the fourth such bill enacted in the United States, even before Congress passed the companion federal law. It is satisfying to realize that this bill, passed during World War II as a tool for the postwar era, has indeed made possible the new downtown Louisville with its Belvedere development on the riverfront, the Commonwealth Convention Center, the Galleria, garages, hotels, office towers, and now the Broadway Project.

Our election system was greatly improved, both as to honesty and efficiency, by authorizing modern voting machines for the first time in Kentucky, doing away with the archaic paper ballot, and instituting the requirement of the comparative signature to prevent chain balloting. Jefferson County made immediate use of the new authority and installed voting machines. Eighteen years later, in 1960, when I became lieutenant governor, we applied the 1942 law to the entire state and now have voting machines in every precinct of Kentucky's 120 counties.

In order to obtain passage of our entire legislative program I went to Frankfort for at least part of almost every day the legislature was in session, with the result that I was nicknamed the "39th senator" and "Assistant Floor Leader". In fact, I was given a "welcome home to Louisville" party when the legislature adjourned.

All the while the legislature was in session our civil defense activities were proceeding at an increasing pace. Under the Defense Council we launched regular scrap drives to aid the war effort, conducted a continuing tin campaign that shipped carload after carload of tin cans to the smelting plants, carried forward a rubber program, an aluminum program, and paper drives, promoted the sale of war bonds, and launched a combined War Fund to embrace not only the Community Chest but the U.S.O., the Defense Council, and other war-related agencies. At the request of Washington we had practice blackouts under the direction of our air raid wardens. As mayor and chairman of the Defense Council of the area I was asked to nominate the members of our citizen rationing boards for tires, cars, gasoline, and food. As the result of these nominations we had blacks (then referred to only as Negroes) on our rationing boards, serving alongside white civic leaders. This worked exceedingly well. As mayor, I did not receive a single complaint against the membership of the boards, although when it was first learned that I was about to name "mixed" boards I was warned it would cause "the walls of the City Hall to come tumbling down." Much to my surprise, I learned near the end of the war that Louisville was the only city south of the Mason-Dixon Line with "mixed" rationing boards. There was even an inquiry from Detroit (which had no black members on its ration boards) as to how this had been accomplished in Louisville, a city of the South. In addition to placing blacks on the rationing boards, I appointed the first black member of the Board of Equalization, the first black member of the Library Board, and Louisville's first Interracial Commission; doubled the number of blacks on the police force; and elevated the first black policemen to officer rank.

The Louisville Metropolitan Area Defense Council functioned so effectively that it was twice awarded the Citation of Merit. In January, 1944, *Life* magazine held one of its "Life Goes to a Party" functions in Louisville to photograph and celebrate nationally the success and cooperation of our local rationing boards on their second anniversary. This was held at the famous old Brown Hotel and was made especially memorable by the presence of the black board members at the banquet—the first black guests in the Brown's ballroom.

Louisville was a soldiers' town, with some sixty-thousand troops in training nearby. As part of our close cooperation with Fort Knox and Bowman Field, we organized the first Soldiers' Club in the country. At this club, on downtown Fourth Street, soldiers had a home away from home and were entertained by Louisville people.

An air raid siren system was built. Victory gardens were encouraged. More than a million pounds of steel streetcar rails were removed from the streets with the cooperation of organized labor and consigned to war production. We inaugurated a vice squad as part of our drive against prostitution and venereal disease. Work shifts were staggered throughout the area to accommodate traffic and public transportation. A joint Louisville-Jefferson County priorities screening system was inaugurated—later duplicated elsewhere as the "Louisville Priorities Plan." This became extremely important as almost all essential items (trucks, cars, tires, plumbing, fire and police equipment, appliances) were in short supply during the war and could be obtained only by the issuance of a priority after essential need was duly established. Every single war drive exceeded its goal. Early in the war I put away the official limousine and either rode the public transit system or walked.

There was a serious question as to what should be done about the running of the Kentucky Derby. Many racetracks were closed down for the duration of the war. Colonel Matt Winn, the ever innovative impresario of the Derby, invited me to help him plan to keep Churchill Downs running and to continue the tradition of the Derby by converting it into a "streetcar derby" for local people, discouraging the use of automobiles and visitors from out of town, and devoting a large part of the proceeds of the racing meet to the War Fund. The infield was occupied by tanks and exhibits from Fort Knox. The flavor was so completely changed that it became almost a civic and patriotic duty to go to Churchill Downs.

In June, 1943, I requested and received from the local leaders of the American Federation of Labor and the Congress of Industrial Organizations a pledge against any strikes throughout the war, and this pledge was faithfully kept (although there was one close call when I had to referee a labor dispute that was about to cause a walkout at the packing plants).

When we were preparing for our first practice blackout, in order to avoid the disorder and confusion that had occurred in a few other cities, it was agreed that I should go on the radio to explain the purpose of the practice, the time it would occur, the boundaries of the area which would be blacked out, and exactly what was expected in the way of citizen cooperation on the occasion. Louisville's four radio stations agreed to carry the blackout speech at various hours, to be certain that everyone would be able to hear it. I made a transcription, which was then broadcast several times by each of the four stations. It seems elementary now, but the transcription method was a first in Louisville. When one of the transcriptions was played on the Sunday afternoon before the blackout, I decided to turn on the radio at home to hear how it sounded. I closed my eyes and sat back in an easy chair to listen. Just after the speech started, my wife and several friends entered the room. They laughed and accused me of putting myself to sleep by my own speech. That week at the Rotary Club I told the story on myself with an interesting result: a reporter embellished it to make it still more interesting and turned it over to the Associated Press. It went out over the AP feature wire and appeared all over the United States—mostly on

Wartime no-strike pledge with Louisville labor leaders, 1943. *At left:* Fred Whitehouse and Henry Beatty, CIO; *right,* Edward H. Weyler and Harold Colvin, AFL, and Samuel Despeaux, CIO.

the front pages. *Time* dramatized it still further and gave it the headline "Spellbinder." Their item read, "In Louisville Mayor Wilson Wyatt made an electrically transcribed speech, played the record back to himself to hear how he sounded, fell asleep before the finish."

A Boston paper made it into a cartoon strip, depicting me as a short, bald, potbellied politican. *Reader's Digest* ran it in all of their editions. And *Time* found it so irresistible to have a story about a politician putting himself to sleep with his own speech that, at year-end, in picking the calendar of the twelve monthly news tidbits of the year, they repeated the story as the choice morsel for the month of May. I couldn't complain—initially I told the story on myself, and though it was considerably distorted in its final version it was at least founded on a certain amount of fact. Anyway, the practice blackout was a complete success.

The day after the 1942 General Assembly adjourned, the governor called the legislators back into special session to redistrict the state. It was his response to my campaign pledge to attempt "rightful representation" for Jefferson County. I had pointed out that Kentucky had continually violated the 1891 constitution that mandated redistricting every ten years, that 158,000 people in our metropolitan center were without representation, and that citizens not represented in government were "required to submit to taxation without representation." Quoting from the Court of Appeals I argued that "it was this kind of oppression which inspired that great struggle for freedom which began on Lexington Green in 1775, and ended at Yorktown in 1781." Governor Johnson told me that this special session was, by all odds, his "hottest political potato." This was years before the "one man, one vote" decision of the Supreme Court; the legislature was acting only under executive pressure. The bitterness was pervasive. In the end, they did not do a particularly good job for the rest of the state, but they legislated a 33-1/3 percent increase for Jefferson County—from four to five in the senate, and from eight to eleven in the house, raising our total from twelve to sixteen legislators. That made Louisville's representation one of the fairest in the nation. At the same time, locally, we redistricted the city's wards so as to make all of the aldermanic districts equal.

Frequent out-of-town trips were required on official business—to Washington on all manner of city-related missions (legislation pending in Congress, obtaining priorities for city equipment, including Louisville's first automated garbage trucks, and multitudinous defense and war-connected projects), to New York on a variety of urban concerns (including board meetings of the U.S. Conference of Mayors), and to Chicago (giving the Walgreen lectures at the University of Chicago, appearing on the Chicago Round Table, a national radio program, and meetings as president of the American Municipal Association and the American Society of Planning Officials, both of which were headquartered there).

In Washington I usually made my government appointments through Senator Barkley. On one such trip Barkley called me out of a conference at mid-morning to ask if I would like "to have lunch over Washington." I asked in surprise, "You mean in a plane?" (Travel was by train in those days.) He asked me to come by his office to ride with him out to the airport. At his office I met his fellow senator, Harry S. Truman, who was joining him. Senator Barkley was late, and Senator Truman, out of friendly consideration for the majority leader, turned to me and said, "Mayor, Alben is late so often that his colleagues are beginning to complain, so if you don't mind (you are from out of town and it won't hurt you) let me tell the others that we were waiting for you and that will excuse him." I readily agreed. It developed that our "lunch over Washington" would be in the first Constellation, the new plane that dominated the news that morning for its pioneer flight by Howard Hughes from the West Coast to the East Coast in a transcontinental record for speed—six hours and fifty-eight minutes. And to make it more interesting, Howard Hughes would be our pilot. When we arrived at the field a group picture was taken with Hughes and we boarded with box lunches. During the hour flight each of us was invited to the forward cabin to take a brief hand at the dual controls with Howard Hughes as our personal instructor. This lean, lanky, very remarkable, and very rich young man, later to become such a mysterious recluse, was patient and pleasant with each of us. His great new plane was turned over to the govenment the following day for use in the war. One of my recollections of Hughes was that his coat sleeves stopped well above his wrists, giving him an Ichabod Crane sort of appearance. My later law partner, Gordon Davidson, when he heard the story, commented jokingly that I should refer to this incident as "flying in World War II with Howard Hughes as my co-pilot." At all events, Hughes is the only flying instructor I have ever had.

In early 1943 I was asked by the Office of Strategic Services, now the C.I.A., and the Board of Economic Warfare to take a leave of absence from my duties as mayor for a wartime emergency mission overseas. Both interested me, as I had the understandable desire to be closer to the scene of action. I met in Washington with Colonel Bill Donovan, the colorful director of the O.S.S., and Vice President Wallace, who headed the B.E.W. This culminated in my appointment as special representative of the Board of Economic Warfare and leaving for Algiers on March 21, 1943. As North Africa was then a theatre of military operations, my original travel orders were to fly to England and there to await military transportation to Algiers. But I was told that if I chose, I could leave the American plane at Lisbon (a stop on the way over) and maneuver my way from Lisbon directly to Algiers, without going up to England and back to North Africa. In Washington they emphasized that I would be on my own but that it probably would be speedier.

As only four planes were then flying passengers across the Atlantic, their use was limited to priority personnel. These Boeing Clippers travelled at about the same speed as the old DC-3, around 170 miles per hour. The week before I left, one of the Clippers had cracked up on its landing at Lisbon, from unknown causes—some thought accident, others sabotage. That left three. It was on one of these that I left New York. Refueling stops were required at Bermuda, then the Azores, then Lisbon. At Lisbon I was met by Gilmour Nunn, of Frankfort, Kentucky, who was then attached to the State Department. He arranged for me to board a Portuguese plane the next day for Tangier. The plane taking off from the Lisbon airport just ahead of mine was German, carrying a large enemy swastika on its side, bound for Rome. As Portugal was neutral, Lisbon was the center of much intrigue, with representatives from the various enemy countries very much in evidence. I crossed the Strait of Gibraltar by ferry from Tangier to Algeciras, Spain. From the hotel where I lunched, Germans with field glasses were giving close scrutiny to the American and English vessels in full view in the Gibraltar port across the harbor. I proceeded by another ferry across to Gibraltar and from there caught an American military plane to Algiers. It seemed strange to see so many ships in such plain view in the Gibraltar harbor but, for reasons best known to the Germans, they were never attacked at that location. Even at night, the work on the fleet proceeded under bright illumination.

After being on my own from Lisbon to Tangier to Algeciras to Gibraltar to Algiers, I felt much more secure on landing in Algiers, even though it was a theatre of operations and still subject to sporadic enemy bombing attacks. My christening came quickly. On our way from the airport into Algiers, enemy strafing caused us to leap from the bus and hit the ground until the planes passed over. Rommel's forces had been defeated but Tunisia was still to be taken and the invasion of Europe was in preparation. One night during an enemy air raid over Algiers I saw a Junkers 88 shot down in flames a couple of blocks away. The next day a Kentucky soldier, learning of my presence, brought me a tag plate from the downed plane as a souvenir of my first real air raid. I rewarded him with a key to the City of Louisville.

My mission included specific asignments with reference to "the procurement and development of strategic materials required by the United Nations" from North Africa. In addition, I was to determine certain specific needs (such as for spare parts, cargo clearance, trucks, etc.) and to evaluate the work and the personnel of the BEW as a part of the North African Economic Board (NAEB), which was the economic section of General Eisenhower's Allied Force Headquarters, then in Algiers. After this work in Algiers, I had somewhat similar charges to perform at Casablanca in Morocco and at Dakar in West Africa. And beyond my specific charges I was to exercise good offices toward improving the cooperation among the North African field personnel of Lend-Lease and Economic Warfare.

One item on my list was the question of the continued need for green tea, which was being flown out of China, over the hump, and halfway around the world for the civilian Arab population in North Africa. This program arose from the belief that Arabs not only preferred green tea as their habitual drink but were so completely dependent on it that they would become restless, difficult, and prone to uprising if they were deprived of it. The green tea procurement, with all of its costs and risks, was carried forward in the conviction that it was producing greater cooperation from the Arabs behind the lines and therefore was very helpful to Allied troops, which were then preparing for the invasion of Europe.

Through an interpreter, I interviewed the turbaned caid of Casablanca in his beautifully carpeted Arabian villa. Not only he, but General Wilson and others with whom I conferred told me that while green tea was indeed the local Arabian preference, black tea was an acceptable substitute; even coffee would do if both teas were unavailable. So I cabled Washington that green tea was unnecessary for the Arabs in North Africa. The cable caused great consternation in Washington, as it called for the ending of a significant, dangerous, and expensive program. Long afterward, I was told that in Washington at the BEW offices they debated into the night whether they should peremptorily dismiss me and order me home or comply with the cable and discontinue the green tea flights from China. Fortunately for me — and for the country as well—they decided to go with the cable.

Robert Murphy was chief of the economic operation of the NAEB and was very pleasant to work with. I found that John Cowles of the Minneapolis Publishing Company was there for Lend-Lease on a mission somewhat similar to my own for the Board of Economic Warfare. At that early stage of the war, communications were so difficult by cable and State Department pouch that personal representatives had to be relied upon to fill many of the gaps.

Because of the severe weight limitations in war travel at the time, I had to limit myself to the suit and the shoes I was wearing in order to take with me two books, Webster's *Collegiate Dictionary* and the

World Almanac. Each proved to be an important addition to the Algiers economic headquarters. The former settled one jurisdictional dispute between Lend-Lease and BEW over responsibility for development in North Africa, and the latter became an important source book for all manner of needed information. I was both pleased and amused when on my return to Washington I saw a cable from Algiers requesting ten more copies of the *World Almanac* for the NAEB. It was an interesting commentary on the lack of informational sources at outposts in the war.

When I concluded my official assignment I flew back on an American bomber from Dakar to Natal and thence to Belem, Miami, and finally Washington, returning to City Hall on May 17, 1943. I had removed myself from the city payroll while away on the mission but had received $22.22 per day from the BEW, plus the munificent sum of $6.00 per diem for living expenses in Washington and $7.00 in Europe and Africa. In addition to whatever I had been able to accomplish for the war effort, I returned with a deeper understanding of the problems our country was facing overseas.

On returning to the City Hall I learned that some of the Republican leaders had considered filing a lawsuit to declare that I had vacated the office of mayor by going to North Africa. But they had decided against it, on the grounds that the court would probably decide against them as a matter of law, and that such a move, even if successful, would be badly received as I was overseas on a war mission.

Early in the administration I realized the need for creating a new position, an assistant to look after the day-to-day administrative chores otherwise incumbent on the mayor. My first choice was Roy Owsley (who later served Louisville under succeeding mayors), a Kentuckian with all the necessary municipal background, but as he was in the military service and unavailable I went to the Public Administration Service in Chicago. They recommended and I employed Gus Schneider, a trained urban professional who stayed with me until lured to New York by the Port Authority. His service made possible many efficient and orderly approaches to the management of city government. For example, he was of great help in carrying forward a complete survey and reorganization of the public education system—a program I initiated with the cooperation of the Board of Education. It was a tribute to the ability and judgment of Dr. George A. Works, the Chicago educator who directed the comprehensive survey, that every recommendation was put into effect, to the great betterment of Louisville's public schools.

As we approached the 1943 gubernatorial race, Happy Chandler, senator and former governor, urged me to run for governor against Lyter Donaldson, who was backed by Governor Johnson. I well recall his intoning to me those lines from *Julius Caesar*: "There is a tide in the affairs of men, which, taken at the flood, leads on to fortune." He was very enthusiastic and very persuasive. I was still in my thirties and admittedly the prospect was tempting. But I felt a moral commitment to cooperate with the governor, who had so superbly cooperated with me in carrying forward the Louisville program, and I knew Keen Johnson hoped (he never asked) for my support of his highway commissioner, Lyter Donaldson. After all, the legislature, with Johnson's powerful persuasion, had passed our entire legislative program with all of its sweeping changes, and had redistricted the state for the particular benefit of Louisville and Jefferson County. It is probably fair to say that neither before nor since has the General Assembly done so much in one session for the benefit of the Louisville area. So, I announced my support for Donaldson.

It was not a happy race, nor did it have a happy outcome for the Democratic party. The Republican candidate, Simeon S. Willis, was a highly regarded, attractive public figure, a former chief justice of Kentucky's highest court. He ran on a very appealing pledge to repeal the state income tax. Although this later proved impossible of fulfillment, the pledge had special attraction in Louisville, where such a large proportion of the income taxpayers lived. Donaldson was a fine man but an unappealing candidate and suffered from having served as patronage chief for the governor. In addition, out of conviction, he declined to match the income-tax repeal pledge. The result was a close race but a narrow Republican victory, which carried with it the aldermen in Louisville, where the voters were eager for the promised income-tax repeal. I now had a Republican Board of Aldermen.

Before the dust settled on the election, I invited the new Republican aldermen to my home to dinner and extended the olive branch of cooperation. Their group elected Judge Arthur E. Hopkins as president. It was not the same as the very close relation I had enjoyed with Andrew Broaddus, who had led the Democratic board, but we were able to put together a quite satisfactory working relationship, which lasted until Judge Hopkins's untimely death the following year.

In the 1944 session of the legislature we secured a law authorizing the consolidation of city and county functions. Under its umbrella, all welfare was later passed over to the county from the city. Initially I had hoped to effect a complete city-county merger, but concluded that the idea was so novel and revolutionary that it was not possible at that time. The course on which I then embarked was consolidation of various functions in the hope (a hope I still have) that, in due time, with more and more functions consolidated, it would be determined that a simple merger would better serve the needs of the area. The issue of city-county consolidation is one that continues to plague many of the major cities of the country. As I look back on these beginnings of forty years ago I am again impressed that governmental improvement is a slow process, but I am also consoled with the thought that that fact is not all bad.

At this time the city's adviser on utilities, the Chicago firm of Alvord, Burdick and Howson, reached a dramatic conclusion in its analysis of the gas and electric situation in Louisville. Under the Public Utilities Holding Company Act, the federal government had just ordered the Standard Gas and Electric Company to divest itself of its subsidiary, the Louisville Gas and Electric Company; the consultants recommended that the city should purchase and operate the local company. Because of the saving of income taxes under municipal ownership, the city could pay the $85,000,000 purchase price with 2 percent, twenty-year bonds and still net an annual income equal to half of all the taxes then collected by the city. When the bonds were paid, the income to the city would obviously increase greatly. The recommendation held great promise. Had it been successful, the city would probably never have been required to enact the occupational license tax. The city's experience with ownership of its other local utility monopoly, the Louisville Water Company, had been most success-ful—so much so that since its acquisition in 1856 its divestiture has never been seriously considered. In addition, the water company's steady income has been a major factor in causing Louisville's credit rating to be outstanding and its bonded borrowing costs proportionately low.

I shared the Howson recommendation with the Republican Board of Aldermen through Judge Hopkins. He studied the situation very carefully and reached, as did I, the decision that the city should undertake the purchase. After all, it was not different in principle from ownership of the water company, and some two thousand other cities in the United States owned their local utilities.

In keeping with our relationship, I never took a step in the negotiations without the full concurrence—and usually the personal presence—of Judge Hopkins. In turn, he secured the written approval of ten of the other eleven Republican aldermen. We met with the top officials of the holding company owner and were assured the purchase by the city could go forward. We reached agreement on price. We employed Blythe & Co. and Lehman Bros. of New York as our investment advisers to set up the bond issue for the purchase. The necessary financing was arranged. We conferred with the SEC and Federal Power Commission. At last, when all systems were go, Judge Hopkins, as president of the Board of Aldermen, and I as mayor made a joint public announcemnt of the plan. The Louisville Gas & Electric officials—who, interestingly, had never been informed of the negotiations by the holding company parent—were irate and launched an all-out opposition with their stock and bond holders as well as with the general public. Committees of civic leaders, for and against, were organized. The public controversy was intense. The newspapers, the *Courier-Journal* and the *Louisville Times*, gave the purchase their wholehearted approval. They labelled the proposal "one of the most important steps in the history of Louisville and of utmost importance to the future of Louisville." The editorial support continued; "It is hard to think of any single achievement in the realm of the practical and attainable which could be as momentous in its favorable effect upon the programs of this locality as a place to live and work in." They added, "The proposal is dictated by hard facts of economics with special reference to taxation."

Despite all the controversy, there was every reason to believe that the deal would be successfully consummated, when Judge Hopkins suddenly became ill and, on September 30, died of what was thought to be a spider bite. His death put the entire transaction on hold.

Judge Hopkins had been the leading candidate for the Republican nomination for Congress, but had been persuaded to withdraw. The press reported that Jouett Ross Todd, a Louisville Republican who was national treasurer for the Tom Dewey presidential compaign, "was said to have told Hopkins that it would be embarrassing to him (Todd) to solicit utilities for contributions to the National Republican Campaign fund when Todd's candidate, Hopkins, was advocating munic-

ipal ownership." After Hopkins's death the Republican party leadership played a strong hand with the aldermen. The one alderman who
had not signed the written concurrence in the utility purchase was
elected president to succeed Hopkins, and the majority of the board
changed their positions from favoring to opposing the purchase; instead
of being 11 to 1 for, the board was now 8 to 4 against. Tom Dewey lost
the election to Roosevelt, but an indirect result of the Dewey campaign
was the loss to Louisville of the utility purchase and the financial
stability it would have assured. It was a situation that will probably
never recur, since the whole transaction grew out of the legal compulsion that the holding company dispose of various subsidiaries.

During the last year of my term, Louisville's Republican aldermen
had at best a stand-off relationship with my administration. But since
my twelve-point program was now in full swing, I did not need any
new authorizations from the board and our differences were more
irritating than significant. Furthermore, by that time the Louisville
Area Development Association, a major new organization for Louisville's future, was solidly established and was preempting most of my
time and energy, as well as that of a great many of Louisville's most
effective civic leaders.

The previous fall (in 1943) I had become convinced that the time
had come to develop a postwar plan. I felt a triple compulsion:
primarily as mayor of Louisville, but also as president of the American
Society of Planning Officials and as chairman of the Post-War Planning
Committee of the United States Conference of Mayors. It was not
enough to advocate that something should be done throughout the
country; it seemed imperative that I put the concept into actual
practice—and in an exemplary way—at home in my own community.
I reviewed everything that was then under way elsewhere in the United
States and conferred with various experts in the field. In addition, at
that time, I was vice president of the American Municipal Association
(now the National League of Cities) and shortly scheduled to become
head of that organization. I was extremely anxious for Louisville's
approach to the problems and opportunities of the postwar period to be
so effective that it might not only serve our own area well, but become
an example that could be emulated and applied elsewhere.

First, I was convinced it should result in action and not become
just another plan to gather dust in the archives. Next, it should embrace the entire area in its scope and not stop its work at the city
boundary. In addition, it should be nonpartisan and have its separate

existence outside of the city hall and, in fact, outside of government. Consequently, it should be financed mostly from nongovernment funds. Similarly, it should involve a wide cross-section of our interested citizens. It should be a unique fusion of the private and the public. I selected the name Louisville Area Development Association—the word "area" to emphasize (as we had in the Defense Council) that the activity would not be limited to the city, and the word "development" to connote action, not just planning. I developed a budget of $100,000 as sufficient (in those noninflationary times) to pay the staff, rent the headquarters, provide for publication of reports, and meet the general expenses for a two-year period. The city and county put up $25,000 and the remaining $75,000 came from private corporations, except for $10,000 that came from labor unions. Labor was pleased to be asked to be an integral part of the work (then unprecedented) and was convinced that it would be a direct beneficiary as well. I shared my plan with George Buechel, a leading merchant and businessman. He was most enthusiastic. The two of us solicited financial commitment for the entire budget before the organization was publicly announced. The spirited acceptance the general plan was to receive was brought home to us the morning we invited the president of a large Louisville bank to come to the mayor's office for a conference. The vice president who accompanied the banker later told me the story. They both had suspected the probable purpose of the visit, but not its scope. On the way to City Hall the president confided to his vice president that a previous mayor had asked him "for $500 for some committee for some kind of future planning and if this mayor asks me for something like that, I'm just not going to do it—nothing came of the plan and the money was wasted." Not knowing this discouraging background, I unfolded the plan to him with the great promise I knew it would have for our metropolitan area and concluded by asking his bank to put up $10,000 (twenty times what he had just told his vice president a few minutes before they would not give). He became almost as enthralled with the possibilities as I was, agreed completely with the plan, assured me he would recommend it to the board, and called me two days later with the final approval. The newspapers and a handful of other interested companies pledged the rest.

In October, 1943, we launched the organization—already fully funded—publicly with a dinner attended by some three hundred civic, business, labor, and government leaders. The absence of a need for a general fund-raising enabled everyone to concentrate, from the outset, on the work to be done. And concentrate we did. We secured an able, full-time executive (Dr. K.P. Vinsel) to direct the work. A task force of interested citizens was appointed to canvass and propose action for every phase of community life—the population trend, economic development, education, sanitation, arterial highways, agriculture, culture and entertainment, finance and taxation, government housing, smoke abatement, labor, parks, recreation, public works, safety, utilities, welfare, zoning, and all forms of transportation. The appropriate person from government was attached to each committee. A staff person assisted each committee. Women, labor, and minorities were involved from the outset. The governing board of the LADA (as it came to be known) included, in addition to the mayor and the county judge, nine outstanding civic leaders (among them the head of organized labor). It was planned to include significant Republicans as well as Democrats and Independents. At the Board's insistence I served for two years as its president.

Throughout 1944 and 1945 the work went forward aggressively. The population report was especially interesting. The thinking in most cities, including our own, was that when the war was over the painful conversion back to peacetime pursuits would bring unemployment and a shrinking urban population. For this reason most cities were planning a shelf of public works to give work to the coming unemployed. Two out of every five in the Louisville work force were then engaged in war production—40 percent of our labor pool. On our population committee—and this was typical of our approach—we called on local business to lend their best experts gratuitously. We employed almost none from the outside. To the surprise of everyone the population committee reached the conclusion that although the Louisville area in the preceding two years had leaped forward with 50,000 more people because of its war production and had crossed the 500,000 mark for the first time, we should expect to expand much more as soon as the war ended. Our problem would be to obtain enough workers, not to handle the unemployed. Our local experts had done their work well; time proved them absolutely right as our population has since almost doubled. The population conclusion became basic to the work of all the other task forces and reversed the negative thinking that would otherwise have guided Louisville's plans.

Because of the active cooperation of most of Louisville, we were able, almost without cost, to tap the abilities, the knowledge, and the facilities that would otherwise have cost an enormous sum, if indeed they had been available at all.

Out of the work of the LADA organization many far-reaching improvements were effected. Douglas Nunn, the director of urban studies at the University of Louisville, later concluded in his report, *Louisville Perspective*, "There was hardly any aspect of community life that did not come under LADA's scrutiny." He wrote that the LADA originated "the concept of an earnings tax that was to become—under the name of 'occupational license fee'—the means by which Louisville, and later County Government and the public school systems, would stave off bankruptcy as post-war developments strained community resources to the limit." The Metropolitan Sewer District was brought into being with a system for funding its many millions of dollars of work, and with it came the extension of the sanitary system (previously confined to the city) into the built-up areas of the county. This in turn opened up large areas for both residential and industrial development. Our arterial highways were planned and located, even though more than two decades would be required to complete them. Parking meters, previously rejected because of the opposition of the Automobile Club, were installed to alleviate the area's parking problems. New schools were built.

Innumerable facets of community life were enriched from the plans made through the LADA—plans made for the area by the citizens of the area. Central to the whole idea of the organization was that almost every citizen would like to be the mayor—at least just a little—and would welcome the chance to participate if assured that forthcoming suggestions would be dealt with seriously and made effective. The organization of the task forces harnessed this spirit by selecting the right people to cooperate on a given project, by giving staff assistance to each committee, and by associating the appropriate government personnel in the development of each proposal. Louisville became the architect of its own future.

The organization was widely copied, in full or in part, in many other cities. After the *Harper's* "museum piece" article in 1937 about Louisville as "the city of let well enough alone," it was a welcome relief to see glowing articles about Louisville in *Fortune, Life, Reader's Digest*, and other national publications.

At the end of my term as mayor, when I went to Washington to launch the postwar housing program, the LADA continued its work for four more years. Then at the request of the Board of Trade and the

Retail Merchants Association, the three organizations were merged into the Louisville Area Chamber of Commerce—and the merger was proposed largely to obtain the benefit of the LADA organization.

I think nothing impressed me so much, in my four years as mayor, as the constant and repeated willingness of people to cooperate when requested to do specific things as a part of a specific plan. Their cooperation was an inspiration. When we explained the need and called for volunteers for air raid wardens and volunteer police and firemen, the response was immediate and abundant. And so it was with our regular periodical collection of scrap for the war, money for the War Fund, and the purchase of war bonds.

And perhaps most dramatic of all was the cooperation of Louisville people during the 1945 flood, our second-worst flood in the history of the city. The memory of the 1937 flood (ten feet deeper than in 1945) was still indelibly impressed in the minds of thousands of Louisvillians who had lost their belongings eight years before. They were not going to be caught flat-footed again. As the Ohio River flooded higher and higher and rains continued, it became clear that some 200,000 people were about to flee the area, determined not to be flooded out a second time. I obtained the best information possible from the Corps of Engineers and the Weather Bureau as well as from George Armstrong, then vice president of the Louisville Gas & Electric Company and an expert on the Ohio River and its flood history. At the City Hall we prepared a detailed topographical map of the entire area and applied the flood information to each street. In this way we were able to predict each day exactly which street, and which part of which street, would be inundated, and to what depth. This detailed information was prepared continuously throughout each day, in light of upstream flow and the Ohio River readings. First daily, and finally three times each day, I would take to the radio and broadcast this specific information. I urged all people to remain where they were unless our mapping indicated that water was about to enter their area, in which event we dispatched trucks and crews (both volunteer) to move them and their belongings. The cooperation was unbelievable. From near panic it became a very peaceful "truck flood." No one was caught unawares. Thousands who had felt threatened did not have to move at all. At one point the Indiana Telephone Company reported that the Jeffersonville and New Albany exchanges were jammed by excessive and unnecessary use, with the result that emergency calls could not get through. They asked me to explain that on my next flood broadcast and request that telephone use be limited to the most urgent and important calls. I did so. The telephone company reported that within ten minutes the lines were clear again and back to normal. It was another example of beautiful cooperation, as no offender could have been detected. Of course, I often thought that if my flood information and my all-too-specific predictions had at any point been inaccurate I would have had to leave town.

As the result of the 1945 flood and with work done through the LADA, Louisville's flood wall was planned, located, and commenced. Our first issue of bonds for the flood wall were sold before the end of the year to a syndicate headed by J.P. Morgan and Company—25 year serial bonds bearing an interest rate of 8 tenths of 1 percent—the all-time low rate on municipal bonds in the United States. The average rate of municipal bonds in the early 1980s is some twelve times as high. The low rate in 1945 reflected not only a different economy but the excellent credit rating of the city and the benefit of the ownership of the Louisville Water Company.

Never once did I call on the citizens of Louisville for help or co-operation in a project for the public interest that I did not find their response immediate and complete. Over the years Louisville has had a wonderful tradition of public service by its outstanding citizens. For example, Henry Y. Offutt, a leading banker, while serving as president of the Sinking Fund, pioneered a computerized system for amortizing Louisville's various bond issues, so as to create an orderly pay-as-you-go system for liquidating the city's bonded debt. As the result Louisville started the regular discharge of its bonds as they came due, whereas earlier the maturing debt had customarily been "rolled over" and continued. The first issue paid off under the new program, interestingly, was for the building of City Hall some seventy-three years before. When that "rolled over" issue was paid off in 1943, the interest over this extended period had quadrupled the original cost.

My four years as war-time mayor were abundantly rewarding. With Pearl Harbor happening just a week after I took office and with VJ Day in August of 1945, some three months before the end of my term, it was a time that challenged all of us to do our very best. It was a rare day that was not packed with twelve to sixteen hours of demanding work, whether for the war effort, the management of the city, or the planning for the period to follow. By the end of my term, most of my personal backlog of savings had been exhausted to supplement the $5,000 salary as mayor. But I didn't regret a day or a dollar of it. In fact, it was one of the most satisfying periods of my life.

Chapter 3

The Great American Lottery

To paraphrase Churchill's oft-quoted statement about democracy, a national political convention may not be the ideal way to choose a nominee for the powerful office of President of the United States, but it is certainly a lot better than any other method that has ever been devised. These quadrennial institutions miraculously crystallize a decision out of the rough and tumble of political turmoil. Several thousand locally selected delegates gather from every part of the nation. Endless speeches are intoned—some historic, many dull. Bands play; leaders confer; cameras roll; reporters quiz; banners are waved; delegates demonstrate and march in the aisles; committees draft rules, decide contested elections, articulate the principles that will become the platform of the party; and judgments are formed—sometimes influenced by oratory from the rostrum, often worked out in conferences and caucuses. By the end of the week this great American circus, out of all its seeming chaos, has fashioned a sense of order, selected the nominees for president and vice president, and enunciated the platform. It is really a most remarkable occurrence. It is a veritable kaleidoscope, in which every turn produces a new and often surprising design.

It has been my good fortune to participate in seven of these conventions as a delegate-at-large from Kentucky, and in one as Kentucky's national committeeman as well. Since there is never an advance script, each has produced its special interest and surprises.

My first was in 1944 when, as mayor of Louisville, I attended the Democratic National Convention in Chicago. I went with no anticipation of playing any role except to cast my vote along with my fellow Kentuckians for Franklin Delano Roosevelt for his fourth term and for Alben W. Barkley for vice president. Our delegation had decided on this course by unanimous vote. While our country was winning against Hitler, we were still in the throes of World War II. A fourth term was utterly without precedent but so were the circumstances of the free world, and so was the need for unbroken leadership. Although Henry Wallace was serving only his first term as vice president and most people assumed that Roosevelt would tap him for renomination, there were many, especially in Kentucky and the South, who felt he was too pro-Russian (even though Russia was then our ally in the war with Germany) and that our own Barkley would make a better candidate and a better vice president. There were growing reports that Roosevelt was yielding to the pressure of public opinion, which was being reflected through the "bosses"—Edward J. Flynn of New York, Frank Hague of New Jersey, Mayor Edward J. Kelly of Chicago and the others—and that, in the end, Wallace might be passed over.

Our Kentucky hopes were enlivened on the 3rd of July, some two weeks before the convention, by Roosevelt's request for Barkley to make the nomination speech for his historic fourth term. Barkley was not only the majority leader of the United States Senate, but a great orator. Although he had consistently supported Roosevelt's New Deal with loyalty and fervor, he had also become popular with the conservative South because of his spirited speech against Roosevelt's veto of a major tax bill—a speech he concluded by resigning dramatically from the majority leadership position for which he had been virtually handpicked by Roosevelt. In fact, even with the aid of Roosevelt's arm-twisting, Barkley had won that post over Sen. Pat Harrison of Mississippi by the scant margin of one vote. He was clearly regarded as Roosevelt's man. Consequently, his impassioned denunciation of the president's veto and his simultaneous resignation as majority leader constituted a Barkley declaration of independence—all of which endeared him to his colleagues, who often squirmed under Roosevelt's cavalier dominance. The Senate had immediately and resoundingly reelected Barkley majority leader and had thereby clothed him with the toga of the Senate's Man, rather than the President's Man.

Barkley was obviously pleased to be the one selected to place Roosevelt in nomination. Reports from Paducah carried stories of Barkley's work on the historic nominating speech. There was even one press picture of Barkley practicing his speech—although practice was never needed by this natural orator.

It was widely thought that if Roosevelt decided to ease Wallace out and submit a list of acceptable candidates, such a list would include Alben Barkley, Harry Truman, and Sam Rayburn (Speaker of the House), with Barkley first.

On the 18th of July, as the convention prepared to open, Senator Barkley was elected chairman of the Kentucky delegation and, among the convention assignments, I was elected to the Platform Committee. On the same day the Gallup Poll reported that while Wallace, as the sitting vice president, was first choice with 65 percent support, Alben Barkley was next with 17 percent, Rayburn third with 5 percent, and Harry S. Truman tied with William O. Douglas for sixth place with only 2 percent.

The convention opened with a welcoming speech from Chicago's Mayor Edward J. Kelly, who was also the boss of the powerful Chicago machine. The keynote address was given by an attractive new orator figure in the party, Robert S. Kerr, the governor of Oklahoma. As usual, the parliamentarian was the crusty congressman from Missouri, Clarence Cannon. Interestingly, already exhibiting his national political ambition, Lyndon B. Johnson, the young House member from Texas, served as deputy sergeant-at -arms. The attractive young chairman of the Democratic National Committee—who was to play a very important role—was Robert E. Hannegan of Missouri, just elected to that post in January, six months before the convention.

FDR (no doubt to demonstrate the need for uninterrupted leadership in the White House in the form of a fourth term) was at the time busy inspecting war plants around the country and did not even attend the convention. He sent an historic letter to Indiana's Senator Jackson, the permanent chairman, under date of July 14, 1944, but it was not made public until July 19, when Senator Jackson read it to the convention. In it he wrote (referring to Wallace), "I personally would vote for his renomination if I were a delegate to the convention," but added these words—words that were to assume considerable significance the following day: "At the same time, I do not wish to appear in any way as dictating to the Convention. Obviously, the Convention must do the deciding. And it should—and I am sure it will—give great consideration to the pros and cons of its choice."

While attending a cocktail party at the Ambassador East on the night of July 19, at the end of the convention's first day, I was told by

Franklin D. Roosevelt, Sam Rayburn, Alben W. Barkley

my friends Barry Bingham, Sr., and Mark Ethridge, president and publisher, respectively, of the Louisville papers, that Senator Barkley—on this, the night before the nomination was to be made— had just withdrawn his nominating speech from the press and report- edly had abruptly decided that he would not place Roosevelt in nomination.

On that same evening the report circulated that a second Roosevelt letter had been written that day to Bob Hannegan: "Dear Bob: You have written me about Harry Truman and Bill Douglas. I should, of course, be very glad to run with either of them and believe that either one of them would bring real strength to the ticket. Always sincerely, Franklin D. Roosevelt." Barkley's name was not even mentioned. FDR never explained why he had omitted Barkley but it is known that he thought Barkley too old (he was then nearing his sixty-seventh birthday) and that he had been offended by Barkley's denunciation of his tax bill veto. It is probable that both of these reasons contributed to the omission of Barkley's name from Roosevelt's significant second letter.

The reason for Barkley's withdrawal of his renomination speech was clear: Barkley thought—in fact he was convinced— that Roosevelt had agreed that if he did not tap Henry Wallace for renomination he would keep hands off the convention and thereby give Barkley a full opportunity to run for vice president. As a matter of fact, Barkley later told me he had been so assured by President Roosevelt when Roosevelt asked him to make the nominating speech.

Bingham and Ethridge thought (and I agreed) that Barkley should be persuaded to change his position and go forward with his scheduled nomination of Roosevelt. They urged me to undertake this mission at once. I was very doubtful that I was the one to do it, but finally yielded to their persuasion. It was midnight and timing was critical. I caught a cab immediately to the Blackstone Hotel where Barkley was staying, took the elevator to his floor, and knocked on the door of his suite. As the attendant who greeted me had never seen or heard of me, he very properly left me standing in the hall while he went to Barkley for assurance that it was acceptable to admit me to the strategy conference that was still in progress. I found that indeed Barkley had been advised by some of the Democratic moguls of the time to withdraw his speech from the press—and that he had already done so. Among the group of a dozen or so who were in the room advising Barkley were James A. Farley, the longtime chairman of the Democratic National Committee and the mastermind of the earlier Roosevelt campaigns; Les Biffle, the sargeant-at-arms of the Senate and the political confidant of leading Democratic senators; several of Barkley's fellow senators; and other major leaders of the party. They looked to me like—and they were— a very formidable group.

As this was my first national convention and as I was a neophyte in the national political arena, I felt quite presumptuous to be presenting a view opposed to the conclusion these older and very experienced leaders had already reached. They were all close friends of Barkley's and were offended that Roosevelt had passed him over, especially after asking him to make the nominating speech. They thought Barkley should strike back by refusing to place him in nomination. One or two may even have had the wild hope that such action by Barkley would cause the convention to nominate him for the vice presidency despite the lack of Roosevelt's approval. I clearly recall Jim Farley making the comment (he had once entertained the hope that he would be tapped by Roosevelt) as I entered the conclave, "Alben, you have been double-crossed by the boss—just as I was." These seemed to me very caustic words about the president of the United States, who was one of the two acknowledged leaders of the Free World, and who was obviously about to be nominated for a record-breaking fourth term in the White House. Nevertheless, Barkley very graciously asked me to speak my piece in the presence of the group. I told Senator Barkley that I felt his action would be completely misunderstood by his admiring Kentuckian constituents, that it would look like sour grapes, and that I felt strongly that he should proceed with the nomination the next day as he had previously agreed to do. I pointed out also that the fact of his nominating speech, even a photograph of his rehearsal of the speech, had resulted in wide publicity across the nation and that his last-minute withdrawal, on the heels of the apparent Truman selection, could never be explained in a way that would be complimentary to Senator Barkley. It was not a matter of being fair to Roosevelt, but of not being unfair to himself.

It was a brief presentation and I must admit a somewhat nervous one. It was an argument against a postion that had already been taken by a senior group of the party, who must have regarded me as a youthful interloper in their conference.

At the end of my brief statement Jim Farley, in a surprising reversal, and to my great astonishment and relief, said "Alben, the mayor is right." I could hardly believe that such a major decision, so recently made, and by such a responsible senior group, could be so quickly reversed. But the Farley approval of my argument seemed to cast the die. Jim Farley was regarded as the great pro of all time. His name was synonymous with political professionalism. Senator Barkley immediately agreed. The others in the group acquiesced. I had survived my political baptism at a national convention.

The discussion of the group, interestingly, then proceeded as to how they would explain to the press that the speech had been suddenly withdrawn and then as surprisingly reissued, unchanged. One of the suggestions made from the group was that they would say it had been withdrawn in order to make some typographical and editing changes. That was rejected as lacking credibility and being, in fact, untrue. It was finally decided to make no explanation—simply to reissue the speech.

All of this happened around midnight before the day on which the nomination was to be made. Fortunately the event was too late to hit the morning press (there was no television in 1944) and therefore the withdrawal and reissue, which took place between editions, of this historic nominating speech went largely unpublicized. On the following day Alabama yielded to Kentucky and Senator Barkley made a

With Alben W. Barkley, about 1943

rousing speech for the renomination of FDR for an unprecedented fourth term. He extolled FDR's courageous and innovative launching of the New Deal to meet America's depression crisis and heralded FDR as a great leader of the Free World in the embattled days of World War II. The speech was delivered with such fervor that no one would have guessed that, just a few hours before, an angry decision had been made not to deliver it at all. The enthusiasm of the convention took over and swallowed up what had promised to be a very dramatic and embarrassing change of events. Had Barkley refused to make the nomination, the withdrawal of the speech would have made boxcar headlines throughout the world and might have had who knows what effect in causing a split with Roosevelt and quite possibly with Truman as well, with whom Barkley was to run for vice president four years later.

Through other reporters Drew Pearson (the widely read "keyhole" reporter of the time) learned of the events of that midnight caucus and published them in his syndicated column. Senator Barkley, in the fashion of diplomacy, denied the Pearson story and said he had "merely called in some friends, including Mayor Wyatt, to help me revise my speech and delete those parts that had already been covered

by (Governor Robert S.) Kerr and (Senator Samuel D.) Jackson."
Needless to say, I said nothing.

I doubt that Roosevelt ever knew of Barkley's midnight withdrawal
and reissue of the speech of nomination. Furthermore, what is threatened but doesn't happen is often forgiven or at least forgotten.

My duties on the platform committee proved not the least bit
taxing, unlike the situation when I served on the same committee
twenty-four years later. When I returned to the Ambassador East after
my session with Barkley and his advisers, Paul Porter (a fellow
Kentuckian) had just arrived from Washington where he was then
serving as the director of the publicity division of the Democratic
National Committee. He read to Barry Bingham, Sr., Mark Ethridge,
and me the draft of a brief proposed platform. After general comments,
we started making suggestions for what we thought would be improvements—all the time thinking it was merely Paul's working draft to be
suggested to the committee the following day. Paul ended the discussion very politely but quite clearly when he interrupted our suggestions
by saying, in effect, "You're too late. This is President Roosevelt's
draft—and he's given it his final approval." It may well be the only
time a platform has been completely drafted outside the convention
process. We, the platform committee, dutifully adopted it—unchanged—and it was made official by the convention following
Barkley's speech.

Next came the balloting by the convention on the presidential
nomination. When the delegates completed the roll call a few hours
after Barkley's speech, Roosevelt was the easy winner on the first
ballot: FDR 1,086; Senator Harry F. Byrd (a conservative Democrat from Virginia) 89; and James A. Farley 1. Senator Jackson notified the president of his nomination by telegram and FDR, who
always enjoyed doing the unusual, accepted the nomination from his
train at a West Coast Naval Base in a speech to the convention by
radio.

On the third day of the convention the vice presidential nomination
and balloting developed into a dramatic "battle of the letters"—
Roosevelt's letters of the 14th and the 19th. Sixteen candidates were
placed in nomination but clearly the two main contenders were Wallace
and Truman. The CIO and other supporters of Wallace argued the first
letter and the fact that President Roosevelt wrote officially to the
convention that if he were a delegate he would vote for Wallace.
Hannegan and his fellow "bosses" argued that even the first letter

disavowed any effort to dictate to the convention (as Roosevelt had done in Wallace's behalf four years before), and that the second letter stated Roosevelt's real preference. In fact, they reported that in telephone conversations Roosevelt had so stated to them. They also emphasized the words in the second letter—that Truman "would bring real strength to the ticket." Justice Douglas's name was hardly discussed. The Hannegan group greatly preferred Truman and spent an intensive twenty-four hours, around the clock, pressing Truman's candidacy. Hannegan was widely given credit for the success of the entire strategy.

On the first ballot Wallace led with 429½ votes, but less than a majority. Truman was second with 319½, Alabama's Senator John H. Bankhead was third with 98, Illinois Senator Scott Lucas fourth with 61, and Barkley fifth with 49½. As soon as the official tally was announced the roll was called for the second ballot. It was very confused and spirited. Every delegation was lobbied by the Wallace and Truman forces. The Roosevelt letters were cited and interpreted by each group according to its purpose. Before the changes and switches started, the tentative second ballot gave Truman a 4½-vote lead—477½ to 473 for Wallace. Then Maryland switched its vote from its favorite son to Truman and started a landslide. Senator Bankhead withdrew his name as a candidate and cast Alabama's 22 votes for Truman. Other states switched. Senator Barkley changed Kentucky's 24 votes from Barkley to Truman. At the end of the polling and canvassing and switching, the official tally of the second ballot was announced: Truman, 1,031 to Wallace's 105.

Senator Barkley, with his usual good sportsmanship, campaigned vigorously for both Roosevelt and Truman.

As Roosevelt was concerned with his own renomination but very little with the vice presidency, it is interesting to speculate on the course history might have taken had Hannegan not been so active and so effectively persistent in behalf of Truman. It seems entirely possible that Wallace might have been renominated and reelected vice president, and thus have succeeded to the presidency on FDR's death the following year. The thought is not comforting when we recall that Wallace led a third party in 1948 with views and surrounding advisers all too tolerant of Soviet Russia. Comparing what actually happened with what might have been, and Truman's strong presidency with Wallace's ingenuous nature, may put the power-brokers of the "smoke-filled rooms" in a more favorable light. The give and take of the conference room, with the opportunity to consider all developments up to the time of the convention, often produce a sounder consensus than that of separate primaries held over a period of many months. It seems clear that neither Truman nor Stevenson (two of our very best) would have been nominated under the present primary system.

Following the adjournment of the 1944 convention in Chicago I returned to Louisville to resume my duties as mayor and as president of the Louisville Area Development Association. Between the 1944 and the 1948 convention, several things happened to affect the course of events when the Democratic delegations again convened, this time in Philadelphia, to formulate a platform and select their nominees. By reason of my election as president of the American Municipal Association (now the National League of Cities), I had a close working relationship with the mayors of the other cities in the country. Then in 1946 came my year in Washington as President Truman's housing administrator in launching the postwar housing program. As this was the hot seat in government at that time, the housing post brought me into close contact with the congressional leadership as well as the officials of state and local governments throughout the nation. In January, 1947, when the Americans for Democratic Action was organized I was elected its first chairman, with Hubert H. Humphrey and Franklin D. Roosevelt, Jr. as vice chairmen. The ADA was often referred to as the "government in exile," since so many of its organizers were New Dealers who had been active with President Roosevelt—among them Governor Herbert H. Lehman of New York, Averell Harriman, Ben Cohen, Dr. Reinhold Niebuhr, Arthur Goldberg, Phil Murray, Ted Sorenson, Arthur Schlesinger, Jr., John K. Galbraith, Chester Bowles, Joseph Rauh, Adolf Berle, Walter Reuther, and Eleanor Roosevelt herself. As a matter of fact, she was a member of the group that asked me to serve as the founding chairman.

The ADA supported the Truman Doctrine and the Marshall Plan, which saved Europe from Communism, and the Point Four Program, which gave freedom and free enterprise a foothold in the emerging new nations of Africa and Asia. It supported the battle for equal rights at home and abroad, regardless of race, color, or creed. It supported the freedom of labor to organize and bargain collectively. It supported Social Security, health care for our senior citizens, decent housing for all Americans, and parity of income for the American family farmer. The dominant original purpose of the organization was to shore up the philosophy of Roosevelt's New Deal, which had been placed in jeopardy by the Republican landslide of 1946. In fact the ADA was often called the conscience of the Democratic Party. All of these doctrines are now well accepted (Eisenhower embraced them fully as "the American way" in the 1952 campaign) but they caused sparks of friction—and often, flames of emotion—in those pioneering days when ADA was first formed.

In early 1948 President Truman asked me to be chairman of the National Jefferson-Jackson Day Dinner which was then the principal fund-raising gathering of the clan each year in Washington. The occasion was so successful that, for the first time, we had to divide the dinner between two hotels, the Mayflower and the Statler. President Truman was, of course, the principal speaker at both hotels. During the course of the dinner Truman commented to me on the parallel between certain current political events and a situation in ancient Greece; he was an avid student of history and in conversations often compared current with historical situations. I asked him how he could manage to read so much history while being burdened twenty-four hours a day with endless foreign and domestic problems. He answered—quite sincerely—that he was president and could control his own time. On another occasion I asked him how he managed always to appear so buoyant and how he could be up for an early morning walk almost every day when he was preempted by conferences and decisions throughout the day and then by the many documents which accompanied him from the office to his private quarters each night. He said it was because he took a nap after lunch. And he added, "I don't just lie down on the couch—I take off my clothes and put on my pajamas and go to sleep." He commended the same practice to me—advice which, I regret to say, I have never followed—but he added smilingly, "It would be harder for you to do, Wilson, since you are in private life, but as president, I can get by with it."

Parenthetically, it is typical of Truman's loyalty and personal thoughtfulness that in early 1949, following his surprise victory over Governor Thomas E. Dewey, the president called me and said "since you were nice enough to serve as chairman of the Jefferson-Jackson Day Dinner in 1948, when everything was gloomy and *no one* wanted to serve, I would like for you to be chairman again in 1949, now that we've won and *everyone* wants to serve." Again I accepted, each time

Presiding at the Jefferson-Jackson Day Dinner, Washington, 1948. *Right*, Majority Leader Alben W. Barkley and President Harry S. Truman.

with Perle Mesta (Washington's "hostess with the mostest"), as my co-chairman. These dinners not only supplied the financial support for the Democratic party but served as an annual get-together of the party leaders from the entire country.

In February, 1948, at an ADA convention I denounced Henry Wallace and his third party movement, the so-called Progressive party, and along in the spring I declined personal requests from FDR, Jr. and James Roosevelt to join their abortive attempt to draft Eisenhower as the Democratic candidate to replace Truman.

Against all this background Carlton Kent, in his *Chicago Times* column, reported that Albert M. Greenfield, a Philadelphia financier and chairman of the host city convention committee, was heading a group willing to "rake up $500,000 to spend on Wyatt's campaign" if he should be chosen for vice president as a way of keeping the Democratic liberals from leaving Truman for Henry Wallace and his third party. This was the first time I had heard my name mentioned for vice president (the office some have called "The Great American Lottery") and, while I must admit it was very pleasing, I did not entertain any thought that it was a realistic possibility. The *Kentucky Irish-American*, a Democratic weekly published in Louisville, reported the story and the *Courier* carried an item that said Hubert H. Humphrey and I were being mentioned as possible running mates with Truman. Leon Henderson, the first head of the wartime Office of Price Administration, and some of the labor leaders publicly made the same suggestion. At the convention Humphrey suggested my nomination. I appreciated the compliment but responded: "I am one person in the United States who is not a candidate for any office."

As a matter of fact, I was carrying heavy professional responsibilities at the same time that I was active in the forthcoming Democratic convention. It was at the Philadelphia convention that I learned how well one can achieve complete privacy in a crowded room. As counsel for the aluminum companies I had a deadline to meet; I needed to complete and file a brief in support of the aluminum industry. Although I had done the basic work, the formulation of the final brief had to be made while I was in Philadelphia at the convention. I tried to prepare this brief in the privacy of my Adelphi Hotel room but the number of calls and callers kept me from having any opportunity to work with the concentration that was necessary. For this reason—and also because I was anxious to keep in touch with the convention proceedings—I went to the convention floor with my briefcase and while sitting there as a delegate proceeded to draft my brief, writing it out in longhand on a pad in my lap. Every now and then, I would hear some friend pass by and, instead of interrupting, say, "Let's not bother him; he's working on his speech." In this way I was able to complete my draft without interruption, go to a telephone on the edge of the convention floor, telephone my brief to my secretary in Louisville, and have the brief completed and in final form by the time the convention was over. The privacy I had not been able to achieve in my room at the hotel I had obtained by entering the maelstrom of the convention.

Barkley had been selected to make the keynote speech at Philadelphia. He was one of the ablest natural orators in the party and could be counted upon to raise the hopes and enthusiasm of the delegates. He had still not become accustomed to the time constraints of the electronic media, but that would not be a factor before the convention delegates. I recall one occasion when, concerned about his tendency to overstay his audience, he asked Anne, my wife, who was seated by him on the podium, to give him a three minute warning and then a one-minute warning by a slight tug on his coattail. She complied punctually as Barkley had requested—and then when, carried away with the enthusiasm of his speech, he ignored both signals, she finally but reluctantly gave him a third tug of his coattail. Barkley—who had completely forgotten his request for the warnings—merely paused, shrugged his large shoulders, adjusted his tie, and, to Anne's embarrassment, said to the audience, "I don't know what's wrong but Anne Wyatt keeps pulling my coattail." In due course, however, Barkley adapted completely to the scheduled timing of radio and then of television.

On July 6, less than a week before the Democratic convention was scheduled to convene in Philadelphia, Governor Earle C. Clements called me from Frankfort and asked if I would go to Philadelphia in advance to assist in bringing about the nomination of Barkley for vice president on the ticket with President Truman. I readily agreed, as I had a high regard for Barkley, the dean of the Democratic party in Kentucky and the long-time majority leader of the United States Senate.

On arriving in Philadelphia on the morning of the 9th, I started organizing a Barkley drive on a methodical, state-by-state basis. By 1948 I knew personally one or more leading members of most the state delegations. I telephoned or talked in person with those delegates to try to get them to influence their state delegations to vote for Barkley for vice president. Whenever I met with reluctance I pointed out that Barkley would be making the keynote speech on the opening night of the convention (the 12th) and urged them to have their delegations at least take to the aisles and march in tribute to "the grand old man" of the Democratic party at the conclusion of his oration. I could assure them very truthfully that Barkley would make a rip-roaring political speech that would be well received in any event and that, therefore, it would be a fine tribute for everyone to join in giving enthusiastic recognition to such an important party stalwart.

Almost without exception I was able to get agreement on the second score—to join in the demonstration—even though in many states I was unable to get agreement on the support of his candidacy, particularly because of his age (he was then seventy). My feeling, obviously, was that if there could be a sufficient demonstration of convention enthusiasm even the states that were reluctant to join in nominating Barkley would be influenced by the "spontaneous" and overwhelming show of support, and as a result might be willing to accept him as the nominee.

During the afternoon of the 12th, as I was nearing the end of my work for the Barkley demonstration and nomination, a member of the national press corps opened the door and came into the hideout room where I was working alone on the telephone. He said in effect, "I've been looking for you everywhere—you're it." I asked "It? For what?" He said, "You have been tapped for the vice presidency. Justice Douglas has just turned Truman down." It had been widely reported that Truman was trying to persuade Bill Douglas to resign from the Supreme Court and run on the ticket—shades of 1944 when Roosevelt approved both Douglas and Truman for the vice presidency. My response to the reporter was, in effect, "I am hard at work organizing the Barkley drive." My die was clearly cast, but I was intrigued by this startling development.

Shortly I left my hotel to go to another building where David Lawrence, then mayor of Philadelphia, Ed Prichard of Kentucky, and I were to be on a national CBS discussion program about the convention, unity in the party, and the vice presidential selection. Prich and I were strongly for Barkley and it was our purpose to make use of the national interview to promote the Barkley candidacy. Prich was well known in top party circles as he had been active as one of Justice Frankfurter's prodigies and had served as general counsel to Fred Vinson when Vinson was secretary of the treasury.

Going up on the crowded elevator in the Bellevue-Stratford Hotel, where the broadcast was to originate, I saw George Allen, with whom I had had an interesting but, at times, quite divergent relationship when he was head of the Reconstruction Finance Corporation and I was in charge of postwar housing. I was very surprised to hear him call across the crowded elevator, for all to hear: "I am a Wyatt man!" I then connected Allen's greeting to the reporter's appearance a short while before at my convention hideout. George Allen was close to Truman as he had been with Roosevelt, and as he subsequently was with Eisenhower. In fact, George Allen always prided himself on being able to maintain his own "status quo" regardless of the political quicksand. (He wrote an amusing book about it, under the title of *Presidents Who Have Known Me*.) Because of all of this, I knew I could attach significance to his very nonconfidential profession of being "a Wyatt man." He would certainly not have made such a public statement without knowledge of Truman's position.

Nevertheless, I proceeded to the radio session, and Prich and I did all we could to advance Barkley for vice president. Then came the Barkley speech that night—a real convention-rousing oration that stirred delegates to great enthusiasm.

In his thunderous voice, Barkley called out "what is this New Deal?" and then he pounded out the answers: "It is the gainful employment . . . of more than 61 million American workers compared to 15 million 16 years ago.

"It is corporate profits . . . of more than $17 billion.

"It means increased production to a level exceeding $230 billion per annum, and an annual income to the American people of more than $210 billion last year compared to only $38 billion 16 years ago.

"It means prosperity . . .

"It means an increase in the sale of goods . . .

"It means an increase in our exports . . . " and he roared on through the whole litany of New Deal accomplishments. He was interrupted repeatedly by applause and cheers. It was the oratorical red meat for which the delegates hungered.

When Barkley concluded almost every state delegation took to the aisles to march in tribute. My organizing efforts, and those of Earle Clements and Lawrence Wetherby, proved to be seed planted in very fertile ground. I had arranged for amateurish-looking signs to be carried by some of the marchers, indicating support for Barkley for vice president. The march in the aisles was tumultuous. So many states joined the demonstration that it became virtually unanimous. I think everyone at the convention—and the reporters the next day in the press—interpreted the demonstration as the equivalent of a nomination of Barkley for vice president. Barkley's magnificent performance, and the four days of intensive organizing efforts in his behalf, dealt a complete death-knell to any move in my own behalf.

I had further confirmation of Truman's reluctance about Barkley when Perle Mesta, a devoted friend and supporter of Truman, came to me at the convention and protested that Barkley, seven years Truman's senior, was too old and should not be nominated.

Later Bob Hannegan, for four years the chairman of the Democratic National Committee and a person with whom I had worked on a very friendly and cooperative basis when I was housing administrator two years before, told me what had happened. He said that immediately after Bill Douglas had declined to run, Truman consulted him about the vice presidency. Hannegan met at once with several of the king-makers of the day. They included Mayor Edward J. Kelly of Chicago, "Boss" Frank Hague of New Jersey, Ed J. Flynn and Frank Walker, both former chairmen of the Democratic National Committee, Clinton Anderson, former secretary of agriculture, and two or three others. Undoubtedly, they were the most significant power-brokers of the convention. And in those days—long before the primaries changed all this—the power-brokers carried great authority in a Democratic National convention. Hannegan said that when he had proposed my name for vice president all of the group agreed, but one said, "How does he stand with Truman—you remember he resigned as housing administrator and we had better be sure how he stands with 'the Boss'." Bob Hannegan said that he then telephoned President Truman, direct at the White House, told him of their discussion and asked the president how he felt about me for the vice presidency on the ticket. He said Truman's response was, "He's okay in my book—shoot the works." Had Douglas acted a day earlier, the Truman decision, implemented by the political power-brokers under the skillful guidance of Bob Hannegan, might have had a different result. In the main they were the same group who had successfully launched Truman for the vice presidency in 1948, four years before. But this was happening at the very time that the Barkley speech and the great demonstration for Barkley were taking place, certainly assisted by the commitment I had obtained from almost all the states to join in the riotous tribute. The *U.S. News & World Report* wrote: "The Senator's keynote speech that evening brought him a big ovation (stimulated by careful planning by the Kentucky delegation). . . . The question of his age could be offset by his general popularity and speaking ability."

Even Hannegan was quoted by the Associated Press on the 13th saying that it looked to him as though the demonstration "has decided the issue" for Barkley. The AP added:

Hannegan and others had been reported seeking a younger and more New Dealish candidate to run with the President. The demonstration even had its effect on Hague, cast as one of the diehards still looking around for another candidate. . . . Present plans are for Wilson W. Wyatt, former Mayor of Louisville and former Federal Housing Expediter, to make the Barkley speech when the time comes. An odd thing about the Kentucky situation is that a group of big city Democratic leaders has rallied behind Wyatt as a candidate (without Wyatt's consent) instead of Barkley.

On the morning after the Barkley speech Governor Clements came to me and said that while ordinarily the governor of a state would be the one to place in nomination a person from his home state, he felt under the circumstances that this was an honor that I should have and therefore asked me to nominate Barkley for vice president. We arranged for seconding speeches to be made by Jim Farley and Adlai Stevenson. In reality, the convention by its enthusiastic ovation had already "nominated" Barkley and our speeches, made at about 1 o'clock in the morning, merely gave technical authorization to what the convention had already emotionally committed itself to do.

I recall very well Stevenson's response when I asked him to make a seconding speech. He remonstrated that nobody really wanted to listen to him and that while he was for Barkley and would like to support him, he didn't see the need for him to speak. Reluctantly he acquiesced and made one of the seconding speeches. He later wrote me, "I had hastily prepared for about five minutes and when I was introduced Sam Rayburn (the convention Chairman) said 'not over a minute'. It scared me to death and I have no idea what I said. In all events, I am enclosing a copy of what I intended to say."

One of the most exciting phases of the convention, the fight over the civil rights plank, was taking place on the afternoon of the third day while I was writing my Barkley nominating speech. Hubert H. Humphrey, the young mayor of Minneapolis, championed a strong minority plank in opposition to that proposed by the platform committee and the fight became so bitter as to threaten the already dismal chances of November success. Humphrey denounced the more moderate plank and shouted to the applauding delegates, "My friends, to those who say that we are rushing this issue of civil rights, I say to them, we are 172 years late." He urged the "Democratic Party to get out of the shadows of states' rights and to walk forthrightly into the bright sunshine of human rights."

Strom Thurmond, then a Democrat and the governor of South Carolina, led the southern states' rights delegates and threatened to bolt the party if the minority plank should be adopted. It was an electrically bitter battle, but when the roll was called the Humphrey forces triumphed by the vote of 651½ to 582½. Alabama and some of the other southern delegates announced a walk-out from the convention.

That evening Truman was placed in nomination and a discouraged and badly divided convention duly chose him over Georgia's Senator Richard Russell by the vote of 947½ to 263.

In the meantime I had finished writing my nominating speech in my hotel room. I saw that it was raining outside but didn't realize what this would do to transportation in a city crowded with thousands headed simultaneously for one building—the convention hall. I had been offered an official car to drive me to the convention but in a mistaken act of modesty I told them not to bother, that I would simply take a taxicab. I went down to the front of the hotel to grab a taxi but found there was a large crowd waiting ahead of me and virtually no taxicabs available for anyone.

In desperation, I was finally able to negotiate with two or three women clerical employees, who had scheduled a taxi to come for them, that I would happily pay their taxi fare and go with them to each of their destinations if they would then turn the cab over to me. But for this arrangement I think I would never have been able to make it to the convention that night. We even had to detour to a department store to pick up one of their girlfriends but, finally, after all of them had been deposited one by one at their several destinations, the taxi took me toward the convention. We were stopped two blocks from the convention hall; police barricades turned us back. The president of the United States had arrived. No automobile traffic was permitted any closer. I left the taxicab and half walked, half ran, in the rain to the convention hall—but without benefit of umbrella or raincoat.

When I arrived there the first person I saw whom I knew was Charlie Farnsley, then the mayor of Louisville. Charlie told me, "Don't worry. You might as well go back to the hotel; they have guards on all the doors; the place is packed and jammed. All the doors are locked. And they're not permitting anybody to enter." I replied, "But Charlie, I am to nominate Barkley for vice president." Charlie said, "Don't worry, he's really already been nominated so nominating speeches aren't necessary." And except for protocol he was about right.

I knocked on door after door, trying to get some police guard on the inside to open for me, but without success. Finally, I went to a police officer on the outside of the convention, explained to him my plight and asked if he would take me backstage to where the president and Senator Barkley were. He looked at me very dubiously and said, "I'll take you back there, but if the president doesn't recognize you, you're in big trouble." Fortunately, when the police officer got to the backstage area, there was President Truman, and he came forward immediately and gave me a very cordial greeting. With that, the police officer smiled, turned, and left. He had delivered me.

I was soaking wet through and through. The ones in charge of the program took me backstage and arranged to have my clothes dried out so that I could make a more presentable appearance when the moment for the vice presidential nomination arrived.

It was after midnight when Arizona yielded to Kentucky for a vice presidential nomination, and I launched into my Barkley speech: "On Monday night, in this Convention, a great American . . . sounded the battle cry of Democracy in a great keynote address . . . He gave the call to arms, the call to wage the fight. You answered that call quickly, noisily, enthusiastically. In fact, of your own free will, spontaneously expressed, you nominated the next vice president of the United States—Alben W. Barkley."

I continued: "Who fought the battle for the farm program and the Wagner Act? Alben W. Barkley.

"Who fought the battle for Social Security so that we might have reality in that phrase 'freedom from want'?

"Who fought the battle to guarantee our bank deposits and for a minimun wage law? Alben W. Barkley."

And even though Barkley was already the acknowledged nominee I continued to list for the record all of the other programs for which he had fought—human rights, education, health, Reciprocal Trade Agreements, Veterans Emergency Housing, European Recovery, the World Bank, and the United Nations, and concluded, "he has always fought the battle of progressivism and liberalism on the front line where the bullets are the thickest and the flame of conflict is the hottest."

All the way to the convention hall I had been worried that my delay in getting a taxi and then delivering the various passengers might result in my arriving after the nomination point had already been reached and passed; fortunately, the delays of any convention—particularly a Democratic convention—are such that I need not have worried. I had time in abundance. I was thoroughly dry, the conventioneers thoroughly tired, and nobody much listening when the moment for Jim Farley's, Adlai Stevenson's, and my speeches arrived in the wee small hours of the morning. When the roll was called James Roosevelt also seconded Barkley's nomination, as did Senator Millard Tydings of Maryland, who pointed to the "tremendous and spontaneous demonstration" brought forth by Barkley's speech.

There was further evidence of the Southern revolt when George Wallace of Alabama, in placing Senator Richard B. Russell in nomination for the vice presidency, paraphrased William Jennings Bryan and declared that Russell was the "man who will see that the South will not be crucified upon the cross of so-called civil rights." Senator Russell withdrew his name and Alben Barkley was nominated by acclamation.

It was almost two o'clock in the morning when President Truman was introduced for his acceptance speech. He proceeded to arouse a tired and despondent convention by perhaps the finest speech he ever made—certainly the most telling. He launched his campaign against what he labeled the "do nothing Republican congress" which had resulted from the postwar 1946 landslide. He gave chapter and verse on each issue on which the Congress had failed to enact his requested legislation. He recited the bright promises the Republican platform had just formulated in late June for Governor Dewey's campaign, and then dramatically announced "I am therefore calling this Congress back into session on the 26th of July." He said that he would ask them to do all those things they had promised in the Republican platform—and that way they could get them done before the election. Cockily he said, "They could do this job in 15 days if they wanted to do it." The delegates were jarred from their despondency and their complacency; they now had a new-found enthusiasm and a new-found hope.

Truman called the special session. The Republicans failed to enact the program. Truman had new fuel for his campaign theme song—the "Do Nothing Congress."

Strom Thurmond made good on his threat and ran for president on a states' rights splinter ticket. Henry Wallace also bolted the party and led a so-called Progressive ticket. With two major leaders bolting the Democratic party, New York's Governor Dewey campaigned with cool confidence in anticipation of a certain Republican victory. He campaigned as though he were already elected. Even the respected Gallup Poll predicted a Dewey victory.

Truman and Barkley made a strong team and crisscrossed the country with their message. Still, very few really believed Truman could win. The outstanding exception was Truman himself. I took an active part in the campaign and spoke in Kansas City, Grand Rapids, and other cities. But there were two events that stand out in my memory. On the way up to Grand Rapids I overheard two Republicans in the parlor smoking car discussing the coming election. One said he liked the manner in which Dewey spoke, that he didn't always pay attention to what he said—he just liked the way he said it. In other words, it was Dewey's form he liked, rather than any substance. I told the story in the course of my speech and the audience cheered and cheered. It was their response that impressed me—they obviously regarded Dewey as a candidate of form, not substance—something that the Republican wit Alice Longworth epitomized when she called him the "little man on the wedding cake." The incident convinced me that Dewey was so self-confident, so smooth, so cool and collected that he was not getting through. But Truman, the cocky underdog, was arousing the voters. When he was labeled "Give-em-hell Harry," he happily responded that he just gave them the facts and they thought it was hell.

The other incident occurred when Truman came to Kentucky a month before the election. I was with him a good deal of the time, as I was in charge of his Kentucky arrangements. At one time when the two of us were alone he said, "You know, Wilson, when I was nominated I think I was the only one in the country who believed I would win—now look how different it is!" I didn't have the heart to tell him that even then most people still thought Dewey would win. But Truman was sincerely and completely confident. He showed that spirit that led so many—including Republicans—to admire him.

Truman was a real family man and very proud of both his wife Bess and his daughter Margaret. One day during the election he told me that, the night before, Margaret was out with several young friends in New York when the group decided to go to El Morocco, a prominent night club. Although there was certainly nothing improper about going, his daughter declined to join them as she concluded that the opposition might try to make something negative out of her going to a fancy night spot. She wanted to make sure she didn't do anything to hurt her father in the campaign. His warm affection and deep appreciation showed clearly as he told me the story.

Even election night most commentators, including the redoubtable H.V. Kaltenborn, were still predicting Dewey's victory. But the following morning it was a different story—even though Strom Thurmond and Henry Wallace had each polled over a million votes, Truman was the winner with 303 electoral votes to Dewey's 189. Truman and Barkley had confounded the experts.

A few days later President Truman asked me to be the chairman of his inaugural ball and I happily accepted. Truman was no longer in Roosevelt's shadow—he was now president in his own right.

Robert S. Allen reported in his newspaper column (and later in his book *Truman Merry-Go-Round*, written with William V. Shannon) the

With President Truman and daughter Margaret Truman

series of vice presidential happenings in those eventful hours on the late afternoon and early evening of July 12: Douglas's refusal of Truman's invitation to be his running mate, the Hannegan group last-minute recommendation of my candidacy, President Truman's approval, and the Barkley speech, followed by the massive demonstration which assured the Barkley nomination. Allen wrote, "Barkley was not the President's choice after Supreme Court Justice Douglas declined to run. Young, liberal Wilson Wyatt of Louisville, former Housing Administrator, was the man Truman really wanted. He considered Barkley, who will be 71 in November, too old." And the events were reported, on occasion, in the Louisville newspapers and elsewhere. But the majestic sweep of events at the convention carried all before it. Truman's expressed preference for me never had a chance to surface.

To those relatively few who knew of the developments, I've always responded that I won—that I got my man Barkley on the ticket just as I had hoped to do when I went to Philadelphia.

Chapter 4

Washington Hot Seat

My term as mayor of Louisville had ended in December, 1945, and I was winding up my affairs without benefit of staff in a temporary hideaway office on the third floor of City Hall. One morning while I was talking on the phone with a friend in New York, a young lady from a nearby office called in to me that I had a long distance call on another phone. I told her I was on long distance and would call back if she would take the number. After completing a leisurely conversation, I stepped into the next office and asked her who had called. Nervously she said, "It's the president of the United States, but I told him you were on long distance." A little embarrassed, I called the White House at once. President Truman cheerily asked me to come to Washington the next day to see him. He did not explain the purpose of the visit, but I assumed it would concern some post in the administration. I was not interested in moving to Washington, as I was anxious to return to my profession and reestablish my finances, which had been sorely depleted by my four years as mayor of Louisville. I felt so sure of this decision that I arranged with Arthur Grafton (who happened to be in Washington that day) to spend the evening planning our new law firm.

Shortly before this, Abe Fortas (then the under secretary of the interior) had urged me to take his place, and Secretary Ickes, who was soon to retire, encouraged me to believe that I would soon thereafter succeed to his post in the cabinet. I was flattered but declined. Harold D. Smith, the director of the Bureau of the Budget, had earlier urged me to come to Washington to succeed him. But neither the interior nor the budget seemed to me to be my forte. In addition, I had been sounded out on a wide variety of other posts. After such a diverse assortment I knew there was nothing that could tempt me away from determination to resume my law practice.

On the evening before meeting with the president, my prospective partner and I stayed up until the small hours laying out floor plans for our new law firm in Louisville and deciding on associates to be employed. The next morning at eleven I went to the White House in the belief that I was merely fulfilling a courtesy. President Truman opened the conversation by telling me he was glad I had turned down these other positions since he had something more significant to discuss. He said that the most important and difficult problem facing him, now that World War II had been won, was the housing problem; that the country had underbuilt for years before the war and almost no homes had been built during the war; that millions of servicemen were being demobilized and would be needing places to live; that in fairness they should have housing; that the problem needed the same kind of dynamic action that had enabled us to triumph over Germany and Japan; that it really was another vital phase of the war effort itself; and that he proposed to create a housing position that would be the first government "czar" since the war. And then he said, very pointedly, "Wilson, I need you to do this job. How can I be expected to do my job if I can't get fellows like you to help me?"

Dismayed but impressed, and in fact inspired by President Truman's sincere urgency, I knew I had lost, but merely agreed to think it over and get back to him in a few days.

The next week I returned to the White House, and when I entered the Oval Office I said simply, "Mr. President, I have come to surrender. I can start the first of January." I told him I had not had a vacation for more than two years and that I would first like to spend ten days in Florida with my wife and three young children over the Christmas holidays. On New Year's Day I would be back in Washington.

My post was created by presidential Executive Order as Housing Expediter in the Office of War Mobilization and Reconversion, known by its initials as OWMR. The President's appointment included the sweeping power to issue directives to any official of government in order to eliminate red tape, break bottlenecks, and accelerate residential construction.

The president told me I need not "staff up" as I was momentarily to be appointed also as administrator of the National Housing Agency which had some 20,000 employees and included the Federal Home

Courtesy of Herbert Block, *The Washington Post*

Loan Bank System, the Federal Housing Administration, and the Federal Public Housing Authority. I was to attend all cabinet meetings dealing with the postwar economy in general and housing in particular. I was told my immediate station, pending the NHA appointment, was to be across from the White House in the Washington Building overlooking Lafayette Park, in the offices occupied during the war by Bernard Baruch. That was a rather grandiose way to describe two rather bare offices.

As housing was a totally new field for me, my first need was to become immersed in the facts of the housing industry and to confer with every government official identified with it—John W. Snyder, director of OWMR, the then administrator of the National Housing Agency, John B. Blandford, and the commissioners presiding over his three constituent units; my fellow Kentuckian Fred M. Vinson, then the secretary of the treasury; Harold D. Smith, the director of the Bureau of the Budget; Marriner S. Eccles, the chairman of the Federal Reserve System; the administrators of the wartime agencies, Chester Bowles, the Economic Stabilization director, John D. Small, Civilian Production administrator, and Paul Porter (another fellow Kentuckian), the head of the Office of Price Administration; Lewis B. Schwellenbach, the secretary of labor; General Bradley, the head of the Veterans Administration; Stuart Symington of the War Assets Administration; Tom Clark, the attorney general; Robert Patterson, the secretary of war; Clinton Anderson, the secretary of agriculture; Oscar Chapman, secretary of the interior; and many others.

As all housing-related matters were being consolidated under my jurisdiction I needed to know what was already under way in the government. At the same time, I launched a series of conferences with the various housing elements of business, labor, and industry. This included the Producers Council, the National Association of Home Builders, the National Association of Real Estate Boards, the AFL, the CIO, the U.S. Chamber of Commerce, the American Institute of Architects, the five national veterans groups, and the various organizations representing all the building materials and components, such as lumber, plywood, brick, cast iron soil pipe, plumbing fixtures, pig iron, paint, nails, motors, etc. In addition, I met with representative mayors and governors since local and state cooperation would be essential.

In all, I met with some thirty nongovernment groups in those early days. It was a cram course. To prepare a program it was necessary to learn where we were, where we wanted to go, and how we might get there. Eighteen-hour days were routine and Sunday was just another day. The absence of a regular staff was not a problem at the outset as my time was spent conferring, reading, and planning. I had at the beginning only one full-time assistant, but I borrowed part-time help from the OWMR. Permanent staffing awaited my appointment as administrator of the NHA. (Incidentally, I never became accustomed to the Washington bureaucratic custom of being addressed as Mr. Expediter or Mr. Administrator—titles that sounded to me like Gilbert and Sullivan.)

From day to day I anticipated my appointment as administrator and with it the assistance of the personnel of that large agency. Fifteen days after my official arrival in Washington I had a call from Jack Blandford, who was still serving as administrator. He invited me to join him for a drink at the Cosmos Club that afternoon. I felt sensitive about his cordiality since I knew—but he didn't—that President Truman from the beginning had planned for me to take Blandford's place. In the press of his many other problems the president had simply not gotten around to telling Blandford, and the situation was becoming sticky. Early in the conversation Jack (I had known him pleasantly for several years) came directly to the point. He said that it was increasingly obvious to him, from the president's public statements about my position and his sweeping executive order vesting all housing authority in me, that Truman meant to put one person in charge of the total housing front, that he appreciated the wisdom of that decision, and that it was clear to him that I was intended to be that person. Accordingly, he proposed to resign and arrange for a cooperative transition. His was a sensitive and very decent attitude and he harbored no grudge against Truman for his unfortunate oversight in failing to inform him at the outset. It was the result of poor staff follow-up at the White House and Blandford had served in the capital long enough to realize how such things not only can, but do, happen. Visits with the president and the White House staff smoothed things out and the balance of my dual appointment (as administrator of the NHA as well as expediter in the OWMR) was publicly completed.

While preparing my program under these rather frenzied circumstances, and prior to the NHA appointment with its accompanying staff, I looked one evening at a table stacked high with mail that kept arriving in abundance in the absence of a permanent and concerned secretary, and asked my sole assistant to open and read all of it that night—and it did take most of the night. The next morning I asked him if anything vital had escaped attention and, bleary eyed, he said, "Yes, one is a little embarrassing. A week ago, Mrs. Evalyn Walsh McLean (the owner of the Washington *Times-Herald*, and then a leading capital hostess) wrote you a longhand invitation to a dinner she was having at her Friendship Mansion last Friday night." I was mortified and called her at once to apologize and explain. Coolly (and I didn't blame her for being cool), she said it was just a small dinner attended by two members of the Supreme Court and a few others but, she added with a touch of sarcasm, she knew I must have been very busy. Shortly thereafter she published a full-page open letter in her daily newspaper (then very potent in Washington) addressed personally to me as the housing expediter and calling my attention to a particular housing problem in the District. Needless to say, it got my attention. Out of that awkward beginning, Mrs. McLean in due course, became a warm friend. I attended many of her later functions, and from time to time she invited Anne to bring our children over for a swim in her indoor pool. At her traditional Easter luncheon her carefully arranged place cards put me at a table just opposite Senator Taft, the Republican leader in housing. She explained that it was her custom to bring possible opponents together in a social atmosphere. Later that year after one of her dinners she showed me her famous Hope Diamond. In view of its mythical reputation as the harbinger of bad luck, I jokingly declined to touch it. She then put it around Anne's neck and Anne proceeded to disprove its reputation by winning at bridge with Chief Justice Vinson as her partner and General Eisenhower as one of her opponents.

The housing crisis had been nearly twenty years in the making. First there had been the long Depression years, and then the war. Not since the late twenties had there been a really good housing year. In 1941 we crossed 600,000 units for the first time since 1928, but that beginning was aborted by the war. The two previous years had averaged only about 200,000 units. So there was—wholly aside from demobilization—a huge pent-up demand for houses resulting from nearly two decades of under-building. Already more than a million families were living doubled up in quarters meant for single families, and with the advent of peace they were seeking homes of their own. Now, demobilization was going forward at a rapid rate. Servicemen returning from the war would be marrying and establishing new family units. Not only did the country have an enormous need for new housing but it needed housing within the economic range of the typical veteran.

A survey of the 11,800,000 discharged servicemen showed 4,000,000 would like to build, rent, or buy a home within a year. That would require almost twenty times as many as were built the year before. The survey also showed that on the average the veterans could afford only $43.00 a month for rent, and only $5,500 for the purchase of a home. These figures seem startling today, but even in 1946 they were rather forbidding. It is a dramatic commentary on the extent of the postwar inflation that we could fashion a credible program to meet a great part of the housing need of 1946 at figures that typical veterans could afford.

Materials represented an enormous problem. The country was engaged in a major shift from war production to peacetime uses. The economy was still operating largely under a system of wartime controls—priorities, set-asides, price and rent controls. A wartime order (known as L-1) that curtailed or prevented all but the most essential commercial and industrial construction had just been lifted with the result that building materials were being drawn, as if into the vortex of a whirlpool, into business structures and away from residential construction. And such houses as were being built were the more expensive ones, which were, of course, more profitable to the builder but beyond the reach of the average veteran. It was discouraging to realize that even if we were able to double, triple, or quadruple the volume expected at the outset of 1946, the shortage would still be worse at the end of the year than when the program started, because of the rush of returning veterans eager for homes of their own.

Housing was indeed the hot seat in government in 1946. I well recall the very blunt comment from Mayor Kelly of Chicago when I met with him and a group from the U.S. Conference of Mayors, "Sure, we'll cooperate. But remember the problem is yours, not ours. Don't try to put it on our shoulders."

Toward the end of January I reached my conclusions, formulated a plan, and took it to the president. He had enjoined me "to make no little plans." At first blush John Snyder, both as the head of OWMR and as the president's close adviser, was shocked almost breathless by the enormity of the plan. He said the press would be hostile and that Congress would never pass it. The President turned to Charlie Ross, his wise and philosophical press secretary. Ross said the press would, in his opinion, be very favorable; they would welcome it as a bold attempt to solve a critical national need. Mr. Snyder then suggested I take it to my friend, Alben Barkley, the majority leader of the Senate, in order to assess the legislative chances. He was confident Senator Barkley would set me straight. That night I met with Alben Barkley at his apartment and reviewed the program with him. At the end of the review, he said he felt that Congress would buy it, and that I could so report to President Truman. He added a piece of advice. "Be prepared to compromise. Congress doesn't like subsidies. Since you are seeking (as one step in the total program) a sum for subsidizing the rapid speedup of production of building materials, ask for more than you need, as Congress will probably cut you down. Remember, in Washington, it's just like Kentucky, and you'll need to do a little old-fashioned horse trading." The result was that I asked for $400,000,000 for "premium payments for production" while needing perhaps half that amount.

I returned to the president and his advisers with Barkley's favorable report and the president (then with John Snyder's concurrence) decided to give the program his complete and enthusiastic blessing. It was put in final shape in a report to the president on February 7 and released by him on the following day with a strong message:

When I called Mr. Wilson Wyatt to Washington, I gave him only one instruction: to "make no little plans."

For five weeks Mr. Wyatt has been hard at work preparing his plans in consultation with all government agencies concerned and with the principal business, labor and veterans groups involved.

He has recommended a Veterans' Emergency Housing Program which is bold, vigorous and eminently practical. It has the complete and unqualified support of the Administration. All agencies of the government are directed to use every resource at their command to fulfill this program. The Budget Director has of course been asked to review the budget recommendations in the light of the new housing proposals.

I urge the Congress to enact promptly the legislation necessary to carry out the program.

I call upon every public-spirited organization to muster its forces behind the program. I ask each community leader, each citizen, to do his utmost to make the plans a reality in his community.

I asked the president if he did not think it would be well for him to call Majority Leader Barkley and Speaker Rayburn and send me to the Hill to preview the program with the congressional leadership in advance of the public release that evening. He readily agreed and I spent the rest of the day in conference with the leaders of both houses

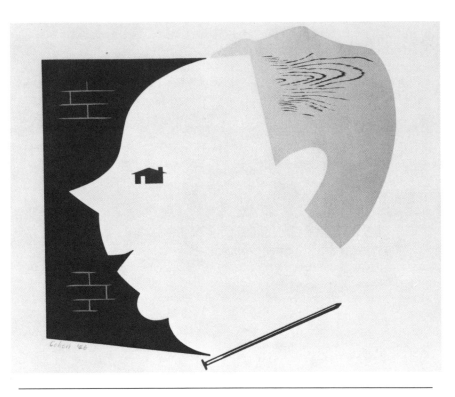

"The Housing Czar," gift of the artist (an agency staff member), 1946

and on both sides of the aisle. Senator Barkley wisely said to Sam Rayburn at the outset: "We're for it. Let's have him talk to the Republicans. Get Bob Taft on the phone." It was a good strike, as Senator Taft was a strong voice in the Senate and gave considerable support throughout the difficult days that followed.

Charlie Ross had been right. The press, for the most part, welcomed the program. *Fortune* and *Architectural Forum* each turned over almost an entire issue to the program and the issues involved. *Business Week* and *U.S. News & World Report* made it their cover stories. It was off to a good start. The program set a breathtaking goal: 1,200,000 units in 1946; 1,500,000 in 1947. This called for six times as many in 1946 as the average of the two preceding years. It called for an eight-fold expansion of the 1945 levels of building materials. It asked for modernization of building codes, price ceilings on land and houses, cooperation of labor through acceleration of apprenticeship training, priorities to channel materials to housing selling under $10,000 (including the lot), and for rental units at $80 a month or less, with the aim of having half under $6,000 or $50; premium payments and price adjustments to speed up production of building materials; federal loans for plant conversion and expansion; lease or sale of surplus war plants for housing material; a two-billion-dollar authorization for 90 percent loans to builders at 4 percent interest; continuation of rent control; reimposition of the "stop order" to curtail all nonessential or deferrable commercial and industrial construction; sales and rental preferences for veterans; expansion of prefabricated housing; the launching of factory-built housing as a new industry; guaranteed markets for the latter; priorities and allocations to homebuilders for equipment and material; funds for access roads to open up new forests on federal lands; and community housing committees to break local bottlenecks.

I had called the plan "the Veterans Emergency Housing Program," first, because it accurately described the program, and, second, because it contained three persuasive words: veterans, emergency, and housing. In the language of lawyers the name of the program amounted to res ipsa loquitur. After the first warm glow, however, the clouds began to gather. The AFL feared factory-built housing would take work from the building trades. Low-cost producers viewed subsidies with apprehension since they would bring high-cost producers into competition. Everyone who had planned a postwar commercial or industrial expansion (and, unfortunately for me, almost every magazine and newspaper had done so) objected to a limitation order on nonresidential construction after four long years of waiting to build. People generally were just plain tired of wartime controls. Builders disliked the emphasis on low-priced houses and apartments. Labor was apprehensive about speedup of apprentice training. Nonveterans did not want to stand aside for veterans to have first choice. And so it went. My friend Harold Smith, the budget chief, reviewed the program with me and then commented laconically but sympathetically that although I had been in Washington only a few weeks I had succeeded in unbalancing the budget by a billion dollars.

Legislation was hastily prepared and sent to the Hill. Hearings were commenced by Congressional committees. Helpfully for me, the House Banking and Currency Committee, where housing legislation must originate, was chaired by a sympathetic Kentuckian, Brent Spence of Covington, and the Senate committee by a strong supporter of housing, Senator Robert Wagner of New York. Still, many predicted the legislation would not be passed until fall at the earliest, and even then greatly altered. After all, the Wagner-Ellender-Taft General Housing Bill had been pending long before my arrival, and was still under consideration. Chairman Spence moved my bill rapidly through hearings by the committee and to the floor. Enough opposition had developed by then that it was no longer assured of passage. After all, it was a war-type bill in a postwar period. As I was scheduled to address the homebuilders at their national convention in Chicago at the very time that the bill was nearing a vote, I sought the counsel of Speaker Rayburn. He strongly advised against my being away from Washington as the bill seemed "touch and go." On the other hand, on that very day a committee of the homebuilders in their convention at the Stevens (now the Sheraton Plaza) Hotel came out with a resolution in opposition to the program, and the president of their association publicly labelled it "socialistic." I was scheduled to be their banquet speaker. Under the circumstances, not to go—to back out at the last minute and while under attack—seemed to me unthinkable. Mr. Sam finally said, "Okay, but go at your own risk. You are needed on the Hill." Filled with foreboding, I took the train to Chicago. It was a damned if you do and damned if you don't situation.

Just as I was to leave my hotel room to go downstairs to the huge Stevens Hotel ballroom for the banquet, an official of the homebuilders called me (with some glee I thought) to say that they had just cancelled their floor show entertainment, at considerable cost to the association, so that they could devote the entire evening to me; following my speech they would also have an open session for questions from the floor. I felt they were substituting a Daniel in the lions' den as their replacement entertainment for the Roman populace.

The hall was jammed. Extra chairs were brought into the balcony to accommodate those who could not be seated on the main floor. More than 3,000 builders were eagerly waiting. Even though their officialdom had become very negative, I was convinced (I have always been an optimist) there were many members friendly to the program. I needed to reach them.

I started by throwing away my prepared speech. I told them that if they were against the program it could only be because they didn't understand it, and if that were the case, then the fault was mine for failing to make it clear. Therefore, I would like to explain the entire program, right then, off the cuff, in a direct and straightforward way.

But first I wanted to tell them a story. I referred to the fact that their president (seated near me, on the podium) had called the program "socialistic" and one of their main committees, in its resolution, also denounced it as "socialism." I reminded them that conservative Republican Senator Taft was one of the principal Senators in support of the housing legislation and wouldn't like being called a "socialist." I told them about the utility repairman who had been hauled before his boss on a customer's charge that he had used a lot of loud profanity while half way up a post repairing a line with a co-worker. The man's defense was that the other lineman, working above him, had spilled some hot molten lead on the back of his neck, but that he had accepted it very calmly, looked up to his fellow workman, and simply remonstrated in a mild voice, saying, "Albert, do be careful." I thought Senator Taft would want me to say to their president, "Joe, do be careful." The audience rolled with laughter. They sensed a good fight. We were off to a good beginning.

I then went through the program, point by point, step by step, chapter and verse, the background of the housing problem, its bright booming future, and the reason for each and every part of the Veterans Emergency Housing Program. I was saturated with the subject from my weeks of research and meetings with many of the most knowledgeable people in the business. I commmunicated my conviction to the builders in a speech that lasted almost an hour. Then I asked for questions from the floor. These lasted for almost another hour. Mostly they sought information, facts, answers. At last they called an end to the question period. Drew Pearson (not renowned for compliments) reported, "Finally, when he finished, every builder in the huge dining room rose to his feet and cheered."

The next day I appeared before the executive committee of the association for a further "let the hair down" session. The following day, back in Washington, telegrams of support for the program were received from Chicago. The National Association of Home Builders had reversed its stand. They sent their wires not only to me but to the leaders of Congress. The *Houston Post* wrote: "Like Daniel leaving the lions' den, Wilson W. Wyatt left the convention of the National Association of Home Builders Thursday with a victory for the Government's housing program. In a complete reversal of its stand against the Housing Czar and his plan, the convention gave all but complete approval of the program and promised to 'go down the line' with Wyatt to build homes for veterans." The action by the homebuilders helped mightily and the emergency housing legislation was passed by the House on March 7. The House even went so far as to write in (it was not requested) the power of directive over every other branch of government, including every member of the Cabinet. Then came the Senate hearings. On March 26 I testified before Senator Wagner's committee from 10:00 to 1:00 and, after lunch, from 2:00 to 5:00. The Senate adopted the legislation on April 10, and conference committee members were appointed to harmonize the differences between the bills passed by the two houses. For one thing, the house bill did not include the subsidies for accelerating the production of building materials. Knowing from many admonitions that Congress did not like subsidies, I had named them—which they plainly were—Premium Payments for Production. These added payments to high-cost producers were to enable them to compete with the low-cost producers and thus add to the total supply of desperately needed materials. Had I called them building subsidies, I don't think Congress would have approved them. But the three words premium, payments, and production carried their own argument. Furthermore, by following Senator Barkley's advice I had plenty of room for compromise. The matter went back to the full House for instruction to its conferees. Premium Payments for Production became such a positive concept that, almost to my dismay, the House on May 9 instructed its conferees not only to approve them but to leave the amount unchanged at $400,000,000—an amount far in excess of the program's need. The power of semantics had joined with logic to overwhelm a philosophical objection to subsidies. (Ironically, when late in the year I had committed little more than $100,000,000, several congressmen made speeches criticizing the under-use of the subsidies.)

The bill was passed on May 13, and was signed into law by President Truman on the 22nd. This had been extremely rapid action, especially for legislation of such a sweeping and complex nature, but it still had consumed a considerable part of the year. Nevertheless, the constantly growing likelihood of its passage had made it possible to put things in readiness, and builders, laborers, and producers had been responding to the challenge of the goal.

The wartime L-1 limitation on building had been reinstated by presidential Executive Order despite loud cries from that section of the economy interested in commercial and industrial construction. The Civilian Production Administration was implementing the order with its nationwide staff. This had the effect of channeling huge quantities of materials to housing, materials that otherwise would have been

President Truman signing the Veterans Emergency Housing Act. *Left to right*: Congressman Wright Patman, Senator Robert F. Wagner, Administrator Wilson W. Wyatt, Administrator Raymond M. Foley, Congressman Brent Spence.

unavailable for the purpose. I had met with the barons of labor in their National Building Trades Council and received their cooperation in accelerating the training of thousands of new apprentices—a reversal in their attitude that came only when they were convinced that there would be such a great volume of housing construction that no jobs would be lost to carpenters, plumbers, electricians, bricklayers, and plasterers.

During the year strikes in steel and coal had slowed the economy, and more were threatened. I appealed to the Building and Construction Trades Department of the American Federation of Labor and, on June

20 it signed a public agreement "to do everything in its power to prevent any work stoppages."

The Congress of Industrial Organizations was cooperative throughout. It had no stake in the building trades but a great opportunity in factory-built and prefabricated housing. The one disappointment in the program was factory-built housing, and it really was the only part of the goal that was not achieved. In the first place, I should not have expected a new industry to become productive in the very first year. Early in the program, Eugene Meyer, formerly a governor of the Federal Reserve Board and then the owner and publisher of the *Washington Post*, a strong supporter, cautioned me on this and, in addition, warned me about the matter of public acceptance. He pointed out how long it had taken mankind to shift from tents to log cabins, and then from these to lumber and brick houses. He correctly foresaw that people might be slow to accept factory-built houses, many made from new building materials such as aluminum and steel. The risk was great. Only large companies could produce such houses and even those companies were unwilling, without government-guaranteed markets, to take the risk of public acceptance. With the promise of guaranteed markets (a part of the program) several major companies decided to enter the housing business in a big way. Among them were Consolidated Vultee, Douglas Aircraft, and Henry J. Kaiser. But with the ending of government controls after the Republican landslide of November, 1946, they understandably abandoned their plans.

My enthusiasm for factory-built housing was reinforced by the following paragraphs from the founding genius of General Motors, Alfred P. Sloan, in his book *Adventures of a White Collar Man*: "In General Motors Corporation we have recognized for many years the opportunity represented by housing. It could well be the greatest industrial opportunity since the development of the automobile began." Also: "Industry can, and I hope will, solve the housing problem but it will take large resources, great courage, and ability of the highest order to put the job across in a big way."

Since the discontinuance of government controls in late 1946 ended the dream of factory-built houses of new materials we had to content ourselves with the program's affirmative impact on the production of housing components, prefabs, trailers, and mobile homes.

I was overwhelmed by the enormous amount of time that had to be devoted to congressional hearings. They seemed almost continuous. There were three major pieces of housing legislation—the Veterans

Emergency Housing Act (introduced as the Patman Bill) which authorized most aspects of the emergency program, the Mead-Lanham Act (authorizing construction and use of temporary housing), and the long-range General Housing Act (known as the Wagner-Ellender-Taft Bill). And then there were the budget bills for the various government agencies over which I presided—the Office of the Housing Expediter (the emergency position), the National Housing Agency, and its three components, the Federal Home Loan Bank System, which is to the savings and loan associations what the Federal Reserve is to the banks, the Federal Housing Administration, which administers the FHA mortgage system for private housing, and the Federal Public Housing Authority which builds, finances, and manages public housing—five separate budgets. For good measure I had to appear also with reference to various support and cooperating agencies such as the Civilian Production Administration, the Office of Price Administration, the Veterans Administration, and others. Since authorization is by one bill and appropriation of funds by another, there was a double-up as to each. And it was quadrupled by the need for duplicate hearings in the Senate on each bill passed by the House. In addition, there were the usual confirmation hearings by the Senate, once as housing expediter and, separately, as administrator of the National Housing Agency. There were many weeks when it became very difficult, in view of the extensive Congressional hearings, to find enough remaining hours to direct the work I was there to administer, let alone to squeeze in necessary office appointments, correspondence, and the incessant telephone. But the legislation was essential to the program and had to have first priority.

The emergency part of the legislation—the Mead-Lanham and Patman Bills—were enacted by Congress in record time. The Wagner-Ellender-Taft General Housing Bill took longer. But in due course Congress approved it all and with remarkably little change.

Underpinning the entire housing program and these multiple legislative enactments was the philosophy that all Americans are entitled to decent housing and that the government is prepared to help make this possible. Housing, always a major segment of a prosperous economy, had become a major part of the Truman Fair Deal.

In tandem with the legislation we completed the necessary staffing and nationwide organization. To keep all of the various activities in harness, regular meetings were required: weekly sessions every Monday morning with the expediter's staff, monthly with the three housing commissioners, and periodically with the heads of the cooperating agencies—the CPA, the OPA, the VA, and Economic Stabilization. There were also regular sessions with the regional representatives of the various housing-related agencies. Outside of government there were important monthly sessions with various advisory committees— the veterans, labor, builders, architects, and the various public interest groups. All had to be synchronized into a total program of action. Of key importance, of course, were the sessions with the president. I met with President Truman at least two or three times a month, and more often when the occasion required. I never experienced any problem about seeing the president when I felt it was appropriate to report or consult. On one occasion I told him that his appointment secretary, Matt Connelly, had become a little difficult. He immediately responded, "Don't bother about an appointment. I'm here in my office every morning, early—long before Matt arrives. Just come by the White House around 7:30 or 8 any morning you need to see me." I accepted this invitation and had several sessions in the Oval Office at eight in the morning. He was always helpful and considerate.

Because of the economic problems in the immediate postwar period (VJ Day, with the Japanese surrender, had been just the previous August 14), a number of Cabinet meetings were devoted almost exclusively to the attendant problems and I was invited to attend and participate in all of these.

I prepared a formal monthly report of progress and held a regular press conference with the release of each. Historically, it had been the custom of the Bureau of Labor Statistics to give housing figures in terms of "starts"—the number of housing units started in each month. But in 1946, the first year after World War II, and the year of such enormous housing stress, the word "start" became a serious stumbling block in communication. What is a "start"? Is it a housing permit? Or the digging of the foundation? Or a builder's announcement? Or just what? Did every "start" become a house? How long would it take for a "start" to be completed as a house, something that could be occupied? I had learned from the builders—and tried almost in vain to convince the press—that there is almost no such thing as an uncompleted "start." At the April Gridiron Dinner of the Washington press one of the skits put me on the gridiron, depicting old veterans with long white beards doddering around on canes waiting for a "start" to be completed. They carried placards saying "Waiting for a Wyatt Start." All of this problem was aggravated by the inevitable stretchout of construction time caused by the irregular flow of building materials in this postwar changeover period. One night, in browsing through some British housing reports, I noticed that they used a typical English spellout, "houses put under construction," not the briefly efficient American "starts". I immediately instructed our office to change the phraseology to "houses put under construction." In a matter of a month's time the communication problem was cured. The persistent cynical interrogation at press conferences about "starts" ceased. With the graphic phrase "houses put under construction" semantics and clarity had again triumphed—just as with "Premium Payments for Production" and with the "Veterans Emergency Housing Program."

From my arrival in Washington, a threshold question had been whether to have a specific numerical goal or target or whether it was best just to try to get the maximum amount of housing under way. Before the program was announced the Producers Council estimated "the building of about 300,000 dwelling units during the year," 1946. The National Association of Real Estate Boards said "Prospects for production in 1946 do not exceed 400,000 units." The authoritative F.W. Dodge Organization, the bible of the construction agency, was even more negative. They said that the housing problem "probably represents the most widespread need of the country. . . . Total residential building in the entire United States, including all price ranges and all types (single-family houses plus housekeeping suites) is apt to approximate 325,000 units in 1946. . . . Present estimates should probably be discounted substantially in the event the ceilings on sale prices of new houses are imposed."

I became convinced that the need was so great that the country would support a program that stretched to meet it. I recalled that the architect Daniel Burnham, in his famous advice against "little plans" that President Truman had alluded to, went on to explain that "They have no magic to stir men's blood." I agreed with the president that the housing program was an extension of the war effort and that the same spirit that made an annual production of 50,000 planes possible during the war could produce housing for returning veterans now that the war was over, provided that spirit was again sufficiently challenged. Furthermore, the producers of materials, the builders of houses, and the labor to assemble the materials into houses—all needed to know the magnitude of the effort asked of them. All of this led me to the conclusion that, even with the obvious hazards of doing so, a specific goal should be established.

After days of wrestling with the problem I settled on the figure of 1,200,000 for 1946—almost four times the best estimate of F.W.

Dodge, and six times the average of the two previous years. No country had ever built that many housing units in a single year, not even at the height of the prosperity of the twenties, and we were launching from virtually a standing start. But the critical situation of 1946 had never existed before.

With a growing belief in the practicality of the program, the goal became in many ways self-fulfilling. Labor had been concerned about having enough work. They feared that new apprentices would threaten their jobs in the kind of housing economy they had become accustomed to. Once convinced there would be a housing boom, they relented and cooperated to expand the labor force. And well that they did, since by summer we started running into labor shortages. Producers became willing and eager to expand production once they saw that the goal was realistic. Builders reversed their attitude toward the program as they realized the opportunities of large-scale housing developments. Companies that had contributed heavily to war production now converted their facilities to participate in the housing effort. I recall spending almost an entire Sunday in Detroit with the enthusiastic Henry J. Kaiser (at his request) to discuss ways in which his enterprises could assist. His son, Edgar Kaiser, finally interrupted our session by saying, "Dad, when are we going to get to talk about aluminum and steel?" Mario Giannini came to Washington for a dinner session with me to ask how his Bank of America (the largest in the country) could assist with mortgage financing. The air of excitement carried over to the employees in the government housing agencies. Early in the program we lengthened our work week to include Saturdays. Even so, throughout the week, the lights were usually burning late into the night long after the other government offices had closed for the day. My fellow housing officials, from my general deputy, Joseph L. Rauh, on down, were devotedly loyal to the program and determined to see it succeed. They demonstrated an enthusiasm and conviction that is rare in government. They worked long hours uncomplainingly, convinced that they were not merely doing a job, but performing an important national service.

Nineteen forty-six was to become a watershed year in housing—so much so that nearly forty years later the *Los Angeles Times* (April 3, 1984) reported the soaring residential construction of the spring of 1984 under the headline "Biggest Rise Since 1946." I found great solace too in reading Prime Minister Harold MacMillan's statement that he regretted England's not setting a specific goal for its postwar housing effort. He said, in effect, that merely trying to do "the best they could" had failed to challenge British industry to do as much as it really could have done and as much as the country needed. And in late November 1946, while going down the receiving line at a Washington reception for Vyacheslav Molotov, the Soviet foreign commissar, I received commendation from a surprising source. When I was introduced to him, Molotov said through an interpreter that he wished Russia could have built as many houses that year as we had built in the United States.

As I had been president of the American Municipal Association (now the National League of Cities) when I was Mayor of Louisville, I knew that I could count on the effective cooperation of the mayors of the country. And I was not disappointed. They were urged to appoint local emergency housing committees to assist in modernizing building codes to permit the use of new materials, building low-cost housing, recruiting labor and training apprentices, breaking local bottlenecks, encouraging veterans' preference, and giving community expression to the entire program. By May 350 such committees were actively at work covering 90 percent of the urban population of the country—and by November, a total of 715 with a membership of some 8,000 volunteers. Some 150 established their own local goals for housing.

Premium payment programs accelerated the needed production in key industries of such basic materials as plywood, cast iron soil pipe, hardwood flooring, housing nails, brick, and gypsum board and laths. The full complement of some 200,000 temporary housing units was completed as authorized by the Mead-Lanham Act. (Years later I found all too many of these really not very attractive temporary units—especially on college campuses—still in active use as a continuing reminder of an old saying that "There is nothing so permanent as a temporary house.") As a minute sign of the pervasive extent of the housing program that year, it was part of my responsibility to order an increase in the sugar rations (wartime rationing was still in effect) for loggers in the northwest as a necessary inducement, to lure the needed hard-working manpower into the forests. We caused some 3,000 miles of new access roads to be built to open up theretofore inaccessible areas of government land for the increased production of essential lumber. In order to encourage more rental units (for many veterans could not afford to buy), I went to the Bureau of Internal Revenue (now the IRS) and asked the commissioner to authorize, as a tax incentive, the rapid amortization of investment in rental housing. He not only granted my request but made it effective at once. The building of apartments, until then almost at a standstill, blossomed immediately—even more than I had hoped—and this principle of accelerated depreciation has since been widely invoked to speed up many sections of our economy.

The power of directive over other govenment agencies and officials was one I was reluctant to use, but as I was cautioned early that (especially in the Washington arena) "power atrophies if unused," I looked for an appropriate first example. Good fortune soon brought me the answer. Shortly after Congress had conferred on me this unusual power it developed that the War Department was holding a large supply of nails as inventory for future use, but not actually needed that year. I met with Secretary Robert P. Patterson and asked him to release them for the veterans housing program. For understandable bureaucratic reasons he was reluctant to surrender them voluntarily but suggested that he had no objection to my issuing a directive to him and thereby removing from him the responsibility. I promptly did so. The precedent was set, and as the first directive had been issued to the secretary of war, the need for future use was greatly diminished. Cooperation increased enormously. Nevertheless, I was convinced from the outset that the power was wrong in principle and should not have been conferred (it is more accurate to say it was imposed), as it tended to relieve officials of their responsibility to exercise their best judgment in the execution of their own duties.

In order to bring about greater equity and support, we rewrote the FHA mortgage code to eliminate racially discriminatory provisions. In this work I placed great reliance on my racial adviser, Dr. Frank Horne, who described his niece, the celebrated singer and film star Lena Horne, as a "very sweet girl."

Since the housing post was the hot seat in government in 1946, there were unending requests for speeches over the country and unending social invitations in Washington, but the demands of the program required that acceptance be confined to those that were of real benefit to carrying the work forward. Speeches were, for the most part, to the national meetings of the builders, public interest housing groups, veterans, the Business Advisory Council, and producers of materials, with an occasional out-of-town speech before an organization such as the Detroit Economic Club. Most of my radio appearances were on programs originating in Washington, such as Meet the Press, American Forum of the Air, March of Time, and Town Meeting of the Air. I made one visit to the northwest because of the significance of plywood and the lumber industry and one to California to salute the excellent

THAT WOLF GETS BIGGER AND BADDER

Jim Berryman, *Washington Evening Star*

cooperation of Governor Earl Warren (later chief justice of the Supreme Court) and to address the American Legion.

Governor Warren's public-spirited participation in the housing program was in sharp contrast with that of Governor Tom Dewey of New York, who played a partisan political hand. On two occasions he answered official letters from me by public statements that I first saw in the *New York Times*. When I saw him later at a cocktail party before one of the Washington Gridiron dinners I joshed him by saying he had caused me to become a subscriber to the *New York Times* in order to obtain prompt responses to my letters. Showing it was not accident, he replied sharply, "I only did that to you once."

On one occasion, at the request of a then promising young congressman from Texas, Lyndon Johnson, and of the greatly admired and very significant leader of the House, Speaker Rayburn, I flew to Austin, Texas, for several speeches there and in Dallas, followed by a side visit to Louisiana to address the joint session of the legislature and the Louisiana Municipal Association. The day I spent in Austin impressed me with Lyndon Johnson's hard-driving political ambition. On several occasions I went to New York both for public meetings and for program-related activities such as inspection of the large housing development known as Stuyvesant Town, where the chairman of the Metropolitan Life Insurance Company (the developer) was my tour guide. Always on such trips I met with the local officials of the housing agency and the various local housing interests, including the mayor's emergency housing committee, veterans, and builders.

Traveling out of town, though kept to a minimum, was both time-consuming and personally expensive. In accordance with the then current "standard government regulations", I was "allowed $6 per diem in lieu of subsistence when away from (my) official station" on housing business. All too often, cordial local hosts would reserve for me a very commodious but expensive hotel suite, totally oblivious of the fact that the government would be paying only the first $6 of a very large bill. That meant every out-of-town trip was a personal out-of-pocket cost.

Family life was very limited. Most nights were at the office in meetings, or deluged with reports and essential reading matter late into the night. Rarely during the week would I arrive home in time to have dinner with my children, Mary Anne, Nancy, and Wilson, Jr. My two young daughters were in school at Whitehall, my son was of preschool age. Most Sundays were my "catch-up" time, an opportunity to recharge the battery with a welcome full night's sleep (most weekday nights I was lucky to average as much as five hours), a walk with Anne and the children, and then a review of the week's papers and magazines, correspondence, and reports, punctuated with a fair sprinkling of telephone calls. Anne, as usual, was a fantastic and understanding partner. She looked after all personal and family matters—our three youngsters, their school activities, their usual problems of childhood diseases, including surgery for adenoids and tonsils, our personal bills and banking, the running of the house, and our social life, including periodic official entertaining at home. At the same time, she was active in the Woman's National Democratic Club and had a large circle of friends. She was constantly an understanding and helpful partner in the successes and tribulations of my official responsibilities. In the first weeks in Washington I stayed at the Shoreham Hotel, but soon the press started exploiting this fact with articles about how the housing expediter could not find a house to live in. Typically, Anne flew to Washington and promptly rented an attractive house in the Spring

Valley section and moved the children up from Louisville. I recall one pleasant Sunday when we took the children to the tidal basin for an afternoon of paddle boating. On the 4th of July we went as a family to the Washington Monument to enjoy the fireworks. On another occasion Anne and I took our daughter Mary Anne to New York on her way to summer camp. The three of us rode the upper deck of a bus along Fifth Avenue, took a ride on the subway, shopped for a dress for her, initiated her to the Automat, and then took a horse-drawn carriage ride through Central Park. It was our daughter's first trip to New York. These vignettes stand out because they were so rare. Official life, in a preemptive public undertaking, eliminates all chance for anything even resembling normal family life. That, in my judgment, is clearly the greatest price exacted by public office. The financial cost is great but can be taken in stride. Nothing, however, can replace the lost years of relationship with one's young children.

As I hear and read, from time to time, about political interference and favoritism I recall with great pleasure my year in housing. Never once did I have any request for political favors of any kind. Bob Hannegan, who headed the Democratic National Committee at that time, was most cooperative—and asked nothing in return, such as special consideration for friendly contractors, or positions for political favorites. Normally one would have expected otherwise. Not only was that also true of the White House (which I would have expected) but it was true, as well, of the people on the Hill. Maybe it was due to the nature of the crisis. At all events, it was most satisfying.

Early in my tenure, on March 13, I was scheduled to make my first report on a national radio hookup over ABC on 197 stations (this was before television). On the same night I was invited to Bob Hannegan's house for a stag dinner with the cabinet and congressional leaders. All of us were told not only that President Truman would be present but the time he would arrive. Protocol required one's arrival before the president and one's departure after his. Unfortunately, I had to violate both. My speech was not out of the typewriter until too late for me to arrive on time, and I must admit to some nervousness over its being my first national radio performance about my new undertaking. I recall trying, and hoping, to arrive before Truman but as I neared the Hannegan residence, to my dismay I encountered Secret Service and police barriers—sure signs the president had already arrived. When Truman found I had to leave early for the radio station he bade me good luck and did nothing to soothe my nerves by telling me he would stop the party at the time of my speech and gather the entire group (and it was most of official Washington) around the radio to hear me. Throughout my reading of my speech I pictured that group with the president, gathered around the radio set—it seemed much more upsetting than the thought of any number who might be listening throughout the nation.

While most of the columnists, editorial writers, commentators, and cartoonists were very supportive throughout the year, there was one striking exception, Fulton Lewis, Jr. He launched a series of attacks, which he even labeled by number as they progressed. Meaning to equate youth with inexperience, he referred to me sarcastically as "the former baby mayor of Louisville." (I had just turned 40 when I was appointed to the housing job.) But he got more and more acerbic as he proceeded, and finally one night in November he charged what amounted to fraud (at least so I construed his broadcast) both by me and the Housing Agency. It so happened that on that very evening, Anne and I were having dinner with Walter Lippman and his wife at their home. Lippman had listened to Fulton Lewis, Jr., just before we arrived and was livid at the injustice of the broadcast. With a good deal of emotion, Lippman urged me to take Lewis to task; he said it had needed doing for a long time, but no one had been willing to challenge him. In those days, Lewis had a tremendous following and a nightly audience of millions over the Mutual network system. Lippman said I owed it to my children—that I owed it to the public, since Fulton Lewis, Jr. had become such an outrageous figure. I was convinced.

The next day I put in a call for the president of the Mutual Broadcasting System and for Fulton Lewis, Jr. I demanded an apology and a retraction. Mutual was very fair, and agreed. In response to my demand of Lewis that he not only apologize but turn over his program to me for my personal reply, he said, "Instead, in the good old American way, suppose you join me on the air and we'll have a debate." I said, "I will be glad to debate if, in the good old American way, you first turn over to me the same number of broadcasts (fourteen) you have taken against the program—and then we'll debate." He wanted time to think it over, but he did include in his next broadcast, "I regret that Mr. Wyatt felt there was any implication that he was personally involved in this matter. That was not intended and I am sure that was not the case." But he left the impression of guilt about people in my agency. Again I remonstrated. Lewis then included the following statement in his broadcast, "I certainly had no intention of questioning the integrity of any individual in the Housing Agency. Mutual and I regret that anybody feels there was any such implication." He asserted he was making these statements voluntarily, of his own accord—hardly an accurate statement. Finally he did, in fact, in response to my demand, release his national network to me for my reply on November 27. The reaction was overwhelmingly favorable. Typical was the wire from Bryn J. Hovde, of the New School for Social Research: "Bully for you. You made Fulton Lewis, Jr. apologize. Mutual too. That job has needed doing for a long time."

It was quite a triumph and was duly chronicled in one of the professional media journals, as there was a growing sector of the public who were resentful of Fulton Lewis, Jr., his arrogance, and his methods. But the circulation of the media journal was confidential compared with Fulton Lewis's audience. Subsequent events demonstrated to me the truth of the old saying, "Don't get into an argument with anyone who buys ink by the barrel"; I could add, or who broadcasts every night to millions. Obviously smarting from eating crow, Fulton Lewis, Jr., never lost an opportunity thereafter to pay me his most uncomplimentary respects. I remember a couple of years later when, back in private life, I went by the White House for a personal call on President Truman. That night in his most sarcastic nasal twang Fulton Lewis, Jr., implying by his tone all manner of evil, said, "And guess who was at the White House today!" I had certainly won an important battle—but about the war I was not so sure.

In the late summer or early fall of 1946 Paul Porter, the chief of the Office of Price Administration, strongly urged that my housing agency take over the bureaucracy which administered price controls. After all, he argued, the remaining controls were largely for the benefit of housing. About the same time Jack Small, the chief of the Civilian Production Administration, urged that I relieve his organization of the burden of the Limitation Order since it was for the purpose of channeling materials to housing and away from other construction. I resisted both offers. All three of us were engaged in the very reverse of empire building. Each of them wanted to cede territory and enlarge my domain, and I was just as anxious for them to continue to share the problem. Fortunately, the president sustained my position and they retained their agencies. In the atmosphere of waning controls, we each felt a little like Paul Porter when he was asked by a Senate committee at the end of a gruelling hearing if he could return after lunch for further questioning: he said yes, he could stay until 3:00, when he had an appointment with his dentist and added, "Oh, how I am looking forward to it!"

With every passing week and month in the fall of 1946, the American public, weary from the years of war, fretted over the inconvenience and red tape of general rationing, price controls, and all of the many other restrictions which pervaded the entire economy. On October 14, President Truman announced the beginning of a policy of general decontrol. This posed significant questions for the housing program, with its rent and sales ceilings, channeling of materials from commercial to residential construction, veterans' preference, premium payments, guaranteed markets for factory-built housing, and price controls on building materials. It was all an interrelated structure, and the removal of some parts weakened all the others. On Election Day in November, 1946, the voters expressed themselves in a landslide and the Republicans captured both Houses of Congress for the first time since 1928. On November 9 President Truman held a special cabinet meeting to consider what further action should be taken about the restrictions in the American economy. Prices on building materials were then decontrolled. With this action, priorities became useless. Premium payments had little function in the absence of price ceilings. The inevitable inflation would put most of the housing beyond the reach of the average veteran. Channeling and all the rest were of little avail except in the framework of the original program. When the government discontinued its guaranteed market program Consolidated-Vultee and Douglass Aircraft understandably discontinued the factory-built housing program on which they had embarked. On November 20 I made a lengthy report to the president to point out the impossibility of continuing the existing program in such a completely changed atmosphere. And yet I understood the president's problems. The *Kiplinger Letter* of November 30, 1946, correctly reported, "It's a race between Truman and the Republicans, for Truman knows that unless he slashes controls soon, the Republicans will beat him to it." I reminded the president that I had only planned on one year when I first came to Washington, and that with the total change that would be required in the program, I believed it was an appropriate time for me to resign and return to private life, as I had planned. He urged me to stay and was very gracious. I told him it would obviously be necessary to make major changes in the program in view of the general decontrol of the economy, that having urged emergency action by labor, builders, producers and public interest groups, it would be difficult, and perhaps unavailing, for me to return to these same groups and undertake to justify a totally different course. Consequently, I commended to him the British system of changing leaders with the change of program.

Accordingly, I resigned and held my last press conference on December 5. It was (except for presidential sessions), the largest press conference in Washington that year, in keeping with the hot seat nature of the housing post in 1946. I reported (with some pride, I must admit) on the last month of the program and its substantial fulfillment. Many producers of materials were operating at the highest point in their history. There was an all-time high number of apprentices in training. Housing was going at full tilt. I thanked the press, saying that I wanted to tell them how very grateful I was for their "very friendly understanding of a very difficult problem—the problem of housing. . . . You have shown a very sympathetic and friendly understanding of this problem throughout, and you have been very fair and very accurate, and I wanted to have this opportunity to tell you that before I left."

President Truman wrote me a very generous letter: "Your achievement has been outstanding, as I have today emphasized in a statement reviewing the year's activities. I desire here to reiterate my own appreciation of all that you have done. You have earned the thanks of the Nation and the special gratitude of the veterans whom you have served with such singleness of purpose and with such practical results."

The Veterans Emergency Housing Program had launched the greatest housing boom in the history of the country. The momentum was well under way. Homebuilding had been force-fed into a strong postwar beginning. Production of all building materials was proceeding at record levels. Many new building materials had been successfully introduced—plastics, wall panel boards, flooring made of waste products, core-type sandwich panels, lightweight concrete, and many metals. In November the Advisory Board of the Office of War Mobilization and Reconversion had issued an official statement saying:

An unprecedented acceleration in the American home building industry has brought the construction of dwelling units today up to the level of America's peak building years of the Middle Twenties. Furthermore, the number of homes started this year promises to be 100 percent greater than the number either government or the industry estimated could be undertaken without emergency action.

The housing shortage which has confronted the Nation since VJ-Day has been an emergency of grave proportions. In meeting this emergency, Mr. Wilson W. Wyatt, the Housing Expediter, has carried forward a program which has the approval of most Americans.

The final tally for the year 1946 showed 1,003,600 nonfarm housing units put under construction, admittedly not the full 1,200,000 of the original goal, but still more than had ever been done before in one year, either in this or in any other country, and far greater than the 325,000 that had been forecast by F.W. Dodge on the eve of the program. It was the first million unit housing year in history. Except for factory-built houses, all elements of the program had been substantially achieved. The one shortfall was, at least in part, the inevitable result of the unavoidable lifting of controls.

It had been a hectic year, an exciting year. There had been great battles and great cooperation. All sections of the economy had contributed to the huge result. The postwar housing program had been launched, and I was grateful for the loyalties, the friendships, the achievements, and the spirit the year had brought.

Opportunities don't always knock on the door at a convenient hour. One morning—midway of the program in the summer of 1946—Tom Clark, then the attorney general, told me that the night before he and the president had been discussing the vacancy that had just developed in the post of solicitor general of the United States. He said they had decided to offer it to me. With greatest regret, however, I concluded that my obligation to the housing program, in which I was so deeply immersed, was overriding. I expressed my deep appreciation to him and the president. That they had both agreed on me was a matter of enormous satisfaction; that preoccupation with a program of national emergency prevented my taking it was a matter of enormous disappointment. In the government the solicitor general is the lawyer's lawyer—and I would normally have given my eye teeth for the appointment, especially at the age of 40. But both Tom Clark and I— and, more important, the president, as well—agreed that the postwar housing program, and my complete personal involvement, took priority. It was an ironical turn of events. A post I did not seek prevented my accepting the only position in government I would have wanted.

Chapter 5

Talking Sense to the American People

After five years of intensive public life I returned to my profession and launched my new law firm in January of 1947. Except for the excitement of the 1948 convention and campaign my political participation was limited to that of an interested citizen. I was chairman of the Truman-Barkley victory dinner in Washington and took part in both civic affairs and the elections. But my primary concern was in the law.

Well in advance of the 1952 convention President Truman announced he would not be a candidate for reelection. This left the field wide open. Senator Estes Kefauver became an active candidate and travelled the country in quest of delegates. Senator Russell, another Southerner, was widely supported. Alben Barkley, as vice president, was an obvious possibility except for his age; he was seventy-four and would turn seventy-five before inauguration day. The country was in the postwar letdown. Patriotism and the urge for survival, which bound us all together throughout the prewar days and in the critical years of World War II, had now subsided, and people wanted to turn back to everyday living again. The inevitable release of wartime controls had turned the economy loose with all the resultant problems of inflation and the scrambling to make up for the years lost by the defense buildup and then the war itself. In the midst of all this came the Korean War. At first the president's actions were widely supported, but as time went by, as more men were called to service, as casualties mounted, and victory or at least the cessation of fighting seemed to be less and less likely, the American public became restive. The country was tired of war. Russia, our ally against Hitler, had become a contentious and threatening force. In this climate, Joe McCarthy, a Senator from Wisconsin, found the right milieu for his unfounded and demogogic charges of "communism in high places." Minor peccadilloes by some of the officials in Washington brought exaggerated but dramatic charges of corruption. The great successes of the Marshall Plan, the Point Four Program, and Truman's general foreign policy were less clearly perceived in this foggy atmosphere than they are now in the perspective of history.

"Time for a change," which had been the battle cry at the end of Roosevelt's second term, twelve years before, then again with the threat of a fourth term in 1944, and still louder in 1948 in the aftermath of World War II, was now embraced even by many thousands of Democrats. It was easy to wring applause from almost any audience with the shouting of "Korea, Communism, and Corruption."

General Dwight Eisenhower, who had led the forces of the free world to victory, was universally acclaimed. Even back in 1948 many Democratic leaders had tried to draft Eisenhower for the Democratic presidential nomination. I am convinced he could have won in 1952 on either ticket—all he had to do was decide which party he would join. He was not only the national hero, he spoke well, and he conveyed a calm reassurance. He removed the New Deal from debate by a sweeping acceptance of its principles, but he was at the same time a new face, the perfect answer to "It's time for a change." The General had returned from command of the NATO forces in Europe, doffed his uniform, and won the presidential nomination of the Republican Party. The Democratic Party was disheartened. The outcome of the election seemed beyond question. The people wanted Eisenhower, and he had agreed to serve.

An interesting coincidence occurred in January, 1952. I had been asked, along with a dozen other State Savings Bond Chairmen, to go to Europe for a week's tour of European capitals (Paris, Rome, Berlin, Bonn, and London) to observe and report on our country's progress in postwar defense and economic recovery. Just before my departure I had a telephone call from the Republican former governor of Wisconsin, La Follette. He had read that I would be meeting in Paris with General Dwight Eisenhower, then commanding general of the NATO forces. He acknowledged that his request was odd, coming from a Republican to a Democrat, but as we had known each other for several years, he asked me to deliver a message to Eisenhower: if he would resign his command and return to the United States as a civilian,

With General Eisenhower in Paris, Reno Odlin (Tacoma, Washington), Wilson W. Wyatt, and General A.M. Gruenther

La Follette would assure him the state of Wisconsin at the Republican convention that coming summer. I delivered the message the following week in Paris. And later, as fate would have it, it fell to my lot to manage the campaign for Eisenhower's opponent, Adlai Stevenson. I had first met Stevenson when I was mayor of Louisville and he was active in the writing of the charter for the United Nations at San Francisco. We had many friends, both personal and political, in common.

There was little zest in attending the Democratic convention in July, 1952. I wanted to see a Stevenson nomination but Adlai had declined to run and a nondescript campaign seemed likely, in a race that appeared already decided. Anne and I had been invited by Governor Munoz Marin of Puerto Rico to be his guests for the celebration of his commonwealth's new constitution. I was sorely tempted to finesse the convention completely, but finally decided I had a duty as a delegate-at-large from Kentucky and left for Chicago in a white linen suit, prepared to stay only for a couple of days and then fly to Louisville, pick up Anne, and go on to Puerto Rico. As things turned out, Stevenson was drafted, I became his personal campaign manager, and I hardly got home until mid-November. Such again is the surprising kaleidoscope of national presidential conventions.

In Louisville, just before the convention, Vice President Barkley had confided in a small group of us in a session at the Seelbach Hotel that he did not believe the convention would nominate him for the presidency and that he did not plan to seek it. Because of his advanced years, this was not a surprising conclusion. When he reached the convention, he encountered so much urging from various friends that he reluctantly permitted his name to be pushed forward as a candidate for the presidency. Although there was universal affection and even considerable support for him, his candidacy was effectively terminated by a group of his long-time adherents from the labor organizations, who made public their rather cruel statement that they thought he was "too old" and should not be nominated. This was a crushing blow to Barkley. He had really not intended initially to run for the presidency, had been urged to do so, acquiesced against his better judgment, and then suffered the disappointment of being publicly almost pushed from the race by his labor friends.

While all of this was going on, President Truman, as is now well known, had been undertaking without success to get Governor Stevenson to seek, or at least to say he would accept, the nomination.

Stevenson's address of welcome on the morning of the 21st of July, as the governor of Illinois, was a breath of fresh air. Not only was he a new figure on the political scene, but an articulate idealist who inspired. He gave new hope to an otherwise lifeless convention:

> This is not the time for superficial solutions and everlasting elocution, for frantic boast and foolish word. For words are not deeds and there are no cheap and painless solutions to war, hunger, ignorance, fear and imperialist communism. . . .
>
> Where we have erred, let there be no denial; where we have wronged the public trust, let there be no excuses. Self-criticism is the secret weapon of democracy, and candor and confession are good for the political soul. . . .

What counts now is not just what we are *against*, but what we are *for*. *Who* leads us is less important than *what* leads us—what convictions, what courage, what faith—win or lose. A man doesn't save a century or a civilization, but a militant party wedded to a principle, can.

I appealed to my fellow Kentucky delegates to join me in urging Barkley to go before the convention to nominate Stevenson and thus not only save face after the devastating statement of the labor leaders, but become the one responsible for Stevenson's nomination, which I thought increasingly probable. I also sent Barkley a note to that effect but apparently it was detoured by a nonconcurring staff person. Barkley later told me that he had never received it and that he probably would have done what I suggested.

From time to time during the convention I would leave the floor and call Louisville to ask Anne how things were developing about the Stevenson situation. She had the advantage of being able to watch all the important developments, both on and off the floor, on television—something that those of us who were participating in the convention did not enjoy. Communication among delegates is always difficult in such a large gathering—and in 1952 it was especially so, in the absence of our modern electronic marvels.

By the afternoon of the 24th, when the roll was called for nominations, delegates all over the convention were talking about drafting the undeclared Stevenson. No single announced candidate had a strong hold on the convention delegates, but you could sense a growing emotional surge for the one unannounced figure—Adlai Stevenson. As to the multitude of candidates seeking the nomination, there was a general feeling of what has been called "apathy, at a fever pitch." No one of them appeared a possible winner against the national hero, Dwight Eisenhower. But the inspiration and eloquence of Stevenson's address of welcome, the excitement of a brilliant new performer on the political stage, Stevenson's outstanding record as governor of Illinois, together with the fascinating fact that he was not seeking the nomination—all this was creating a mounting eagerness.

Senator Richard B. Russell, a highly respected Southerner, was placed in nomination by his fellow Georgian, Senator Walter F. George, the powerful chairman of the Senate Finance Committee. Senator Kefauver was nominated by his fellow Tennessean, Governor Gordon Browning, and his nomination was seconded by Mayor Hynes of Boston, James Roosevelt, and the governor of Alaska. Governor

Robert S. Kerr was placed in nomination by his fellow Oklahoman, Congressman (later majority leader) Carl Albert. Senator J. William Fulbright was nominated by a fellow Arkansan, followed by the speech of Franklin D. Roosevelt, Jr., nominating Averell Harriman. But a spontaneous and spirited ovation swept the convention floor when Governor Schricker of Indiana placed in nomination the name of Adlai Stevenson, who had even then not indicated a willingness to run. In due course others were placed in nomination, including Governor G. Mennen Williams of Michigan, Governor Dever of Massachusetts, Senator Hubert H. Humphrey of Minnesota (interestingly—in view of their later rivalry—by Eugene McCarthy, then a congressman), and Senator Alben Barkley. In all, twelve candidates had been nominated.

On the first ballot Kefauver reaped the reward of his active primary campaign. He led with 340 votes, a significant showing but still a long way from the magic 616 needed to nominate. But the surprise was the Stevenson vote—second, with 273. It was a remarkable total for a man who was steadfastly refusing to seek the nomination or even to say he would accept it. Close behind was Senator Russell with 268, followed by Harriman with 123½. Barkley trailed with 48½. Stevenson did not come to the convention floor for the balloting but instructed his alternate to cast his vote for Harriman.

As a great many delegates were bound by instructions through the second ballot, the real excitement would be the third ballot when most delegations would be free for the first time to vote their preference. On the second ballot (during which both Fulbright and Humphrey withdrew), Kefauver gained 22½ votes, Russell 26, but Stevenson 46½. The tally showed Kefauver 362½, Stevenson 324½ and Russell 294. Harriman lost 2½ and Governor Dever lost 4½. Excitement was mounting as the convention recessed two hours for dinner. A wave of Stevenson sentiment was sweeping the convention. During the recess Averell Harriman, at the request of President Truman, prepared a statement withdrawing his name and asking his supporters to vote "for my old friend, Governor Adlai Stevenson of Illinois." Immediately upon the convention being brought to order for the evening session, the chairman of the New York delegation read Harriman's statement to the cheering delegates. Governor Dever asked to make a statement. He announced that during the afternoon Governor Stevenson had told him that if nominated he would be willing to accept. Dever withdrew his candidacy and threw his support to Stevenson. The rapid move to Stevenson was on. The third ballot roll call continued. More and more

Conferring with Averell Harriman, 1952

delegates switched, and by the end of the ballot Stevenson had been given the unsought nomination with 617½ votes—just 1½ to spare. Kefauver had dropped to 275 and Russell to 261. Both of them immediately withdrew in favor of Stevenson who was then nominated by acclamation.

President Truman introduced Stevenson for his acceptance speech with these words: "He was nominated on a draft. This is the first time in my recollection that we have nominated a man for President on a real, honest-to-goodness draft." And it was indeed a draft, in that the man who had been nominated not only had not sought the nomination, but had studiously (to Truman's disappointment and almost chagrin) refused to take any step or make any statement to advance his candidacy. Stevenson genuinely wanted to run for reelection as governor of Illinois. He had carried the state by a landslide; he made an excellent record in office; he had a program that was incomplete and he wanted to finish it; he was assured of reelection; and, after all, as he often said, being governor of Illinois is not accepting a consolation prize. Also, one cannot help but assume that he preferred running on his own record to defending the record of another. But despite his sincere reluctance, he had now been nominated for the presidency, and he was determined to do his best.

Stevenson's acceptance address—even though it was at two in the morning—was a real masterpiece and so inspired the delegates that they left Chicago in the newfound belief that the election might be won:

When the tumult and the shouting die, when the bands are gone and lights are dimmed, there is the stark reality of responsibility in an hour of history haunted with those gaunt, grim spectres of strife, dissention and materialism at home; and ruthless, inscrutable and hostile power abroad. . . .

Let's face it. Let's talk sense to the American people. Let's tell them the truth, that there are no gains without pains, that this is the eve of great decisions, not easy decisions, like resistance when you are attacked, but a long, patient, costly struggle which alone can assure triumph over the great enemies of man—war and poverty and tyranny—and the assaults upon human dignity which are the most grievous consequences of each. . . .

The people are wise—wiser than the Republicans think; and the Democratic Party is the people's party, not the labor party, not the farmers' party, not the employers' party—it is the party of no one because it is the party of everyone.

That, I think, is our ancient mission. Where we have deserted it we have failed. With your help there will be no desertion now. Better we lose the election than mislead the people; better we lose than misgovern the people. . . .

And finally, my friends, in the staggering task that you have assigned me, He would counsel me to say that I shall always try "to do justly, to love mercy, and to walk humbly with my God."

On the last day of the convention, Senator John Sparkman of Alabama, who had been agreed upon, was nominated for vice president, and on the same day Stevenson asked me to serve as his personal campaign manager. So ended the usefulness of my white linen suit and my planned visit with Anne to Puerto Rico.

I will not undertake to recount the oft-told story of the 1952 campaign. It was an exciting adventure—three long months of twenty-hour days, but even forty-eight-hour days would have been insufficient for the task. Almost everything had to be improvised as there had been no preparation for a candidacy that had not been sought. There was no treasury, there were no position papers, there was no staff. Unlike other presidential campaigns, it all had to be created from scratch.

On arriving in Springfield to manage the campaign, my first chore was to establish quarters, obtain staff personnel, and install telephones, equipment, and supplies. Ed Day (later postmaster general under President Kennedy) took this burden off my hands and we were soon under way. Adlai's old friends Dutch Smith and Jane Dick agreed to organize the Volunteers for Stevenson as a national campaign umbrella under which independents, Republicans, and various groups of Democrats could comfortably gather in Adlai's support. After all, there were many Democrats and independents, especially in certain states, who felt uncomfortable with the professional regulars, and relished a fresher environmemt.

Correspondence was overwhelming from the outset. There was no time to recruit and train people for the important task of responding for Governor Stevenson, or for me, or for others, with due sensitivity to the one who wrote, the one responding, and the national issues, campaign developments, and personal relationships involved. From my Washington contacts and experience I knew that many administrative assistants to Senators not only possessed that skill and knowledge but were thoroughly experienced. Adlai wanted to answer every letter that came to him, expecially those from personal friends and from people in significant positions. But even these were arriving by the hundreds; it was a startling change to move from the state level to the

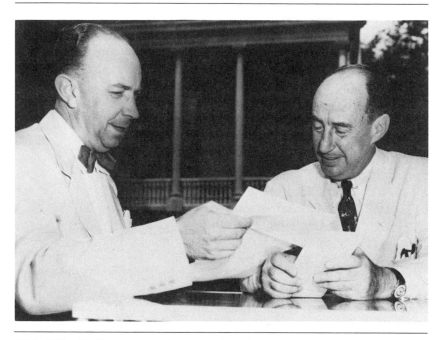

With Adlai E. Stevenson, planning the 1952 presidential campaign

national level. The multiplier was overwhelming. I prevailed on Senator Fulbright and a couple of other senators (whose administrative assistants were well known to me) to give these correspondence specialists a leave of absence and then coaxed them to Springfield for the duration. They set up, developed, and expanded the correspondence unit, which performed admirably and indispensably for the entire campaign. After they arrived my next problem was to get Adlai to surrender his treasured letters for our response, as they were accumulating to a depressing degree and, important as they were, Adlai's time was needed for matters still more important. With Bill Blair's deft assistance Stevenson finally commented one day that his correspondence was dwindling. Bill was diverting a large part of Adlai's inbound mail and leaving him only the most sensitive and personal. Several of us met periodically with the senatorial assistants to keep them briefed and to deal with specific matters, but to this day I marvel at the extraordinary success of the correspondence unit.

The following spring, when the campaign was over, the senatorial assistants gone, and Adlai had reverted to his normal habits, he wrote me, "I am still gasping for breath in this smothering avalanche of correspondence. Why didn't you tell me the campaign lasted until March?"

At the very beginning I developed a general strategy for the campaign and then held a long review session with Carl McGowan, Bill Blair, and Arthur Schlesinger before presenting it to Stevenson—the issues to be addressed, the outline of the geographical itinerary to cover the country, the method for utilizing the vice presidential candidate and other speakers, the blending of the volunteers and the regulars, and the use of the then new technique of television. This was quickly hammered out and approved.

Weekly itineraries were developed, first at headquarters and then by telephone or conference with state and local leaders. An interesting complication was that in 1952 a national or regional TV hookup could be originated in only a limited number of cities throughout the country and our itinerary had to be developed with concern for this electronic limitation. While local leaders were extremely cooperative, there were problems almost daily about special events to be included, factional divisons and rivalries to be coped with, the irrepressible and sharply articulated desires—from everywhere—for more speeches and campaign appearances than the limited weeks of the campaign could accomodate, and—since human beings were involved—the egos and ambitions of many (sometimes quite surprising) political prima donnas. No day was dull, no day was long enough.

Each weekend, within the general strategy of the campaign, I would discuss with Adlai the subject matter of the principal speeches for the next two or three weeks. Inevitably events and developments would dictate changes. At least once a week I would meet with the speechwriters at the Elks Club, which was the only suitable building available for this purpose in Springfield. It had a big central room with small offices off to the side. We would review the areas of subject matter that Governor Stevenson wanted to treat during the following week and, after discussing who would be best for each, I would make assignments among the group for working drafts on the different subjects. The quality of Stevenson's speeches caused superb writers to flock to Springfield to volunteer to assist in preparing working drafts. We almost never had fewer than four Pulitzer Prize winners in residence. It was probably as accomplished a group of writers as has ever participated in a presidential campaign. They were all devoted to Adlai Stevenson. When he would take a draft and use part of it, the writer was tremendously pleased. If he rejected it entirely they seemed to

Screening speeches with Arthur Schlesinger, Jr., and Carl McGowan

understand. If he merged a couple and then blended them into his own, they thought that too was fine. What was reflected in all of this was their profound respect for him and his ability. They felt that if he had just had the time he could have done better himself, and this made them willing and anxious to help. After our general session in what we called the bullpen (the central room) they would go into the adjoining offices to start working at their typewriters—or if the number were too large some would merely remain in the bullpen and start pounding away. It was very much like a city room in a large newspaper but instead of reporters at the typewriters we had many of the top-flight writers of America, working as though they were just reporters covering a police beat. But they did it with zest because of their conviction that Adlai Stevenson was a master of prose himself and that they were not writing his speeches but simply enabling him to extend himself in the preliminary drafting.

Early in the campaign I appointed a Campaign Committee, consisting of the principal party leaders in the country, and invited them to an all-day session with Stevenson at Springfield. A good part of every day was spent on the telephone or in personal conference with senators, governors, mayors, and other party stalwarts.

Not the least of our problems was money. Dwight Palmer and Beardsley Ruml accepted the difficult task of keeping the till sufficiently supplied to keep our staff paid, our candidate's speeches on the air, and our campaign planes flying. Although we ended the campaign with a substantial unpaid debt it was at least manageable, and Stevenson dutifully devoted himself to the various events that would see it paid before the time for the next campaign.

I suppose it would be a fair criticism of Stevenson that he spent an inordinate amount of time writing, rewriting, reworking, and even fiddling with his speeches. A speech was never really done until it was actually delivered, and usually the refinements continued up to the very minute of delivery. It was interesting to compare his approach to a speech with that of his kinsman, Alben Barkley, the "Veep." When Adlai came to Louisville he was to make an important foreign policy speech. He, Barkley, and I had dinner together at the Seelbach just before going to the hall. Adlai, as usual, was working hard on the last-minute alterations in his speech. He was changing a word here, punctuation there, starting a paragraph a little differently in another place, and was engaged in the usual, typical, constant fretting over his forthcoming speech.

On the other hand, the Veep, while sitting back, relaxed, with a drink of "bourbon and branch water", said casually, "Well now, Adlai. I wish you and Wilson would tell me what you'd like for me to talk about tonight." In less than an hour we were to leave for the rally. He had no written speech, no notes, not even a subject, and of course the length had to be precise since it was to be on television. But Barkley, even though up in years, by this time had mastered the electronic change (which he had not done earlier) and could hit precisely the time to quit. Barkley said he thought it might be good to talk about how the Republicans were accusing the Truman administration of imperfections about refrigerators and deep freezes while they had been guilty of the Teapot Dome and other more serious scandals and corruption.

Adlai continued to work on his speech; I think he was too preoccupied to focus on what Barkley was going to say. I suggested that I thought Barkley's proposal was too defensive and was dredging up ancient history. Why not talk about something more current?

Jim Berryman, *Washington Evening Star*

Agreeably he suggested a new subject. Adlai said he thought that was fine. I thought it was fine. Shortly we got in the car, went to the auditorium, and Barkley spoke on the new subject. What a contrast between these distant cousins!

In a minor but typical way I saw Adlai's modesty in the early days of the campaign when we leased an old red brick residence near the Governor's Mansion in Springfield as the presidential campaign headquarters. I told him I would see that a sign was erected to identify the building and he quickly cautioned, "But let it be a very small sign." He was offended by the thought of the usual headquarters sign all across the building in letters two feet tall. In compliance with his direction it was indeed a very small sign, and I have it among my treasured souvenirs of the 1952 campaign—it says simply, and with much dignity (in gold letters on black background), "Stevenson Campaign Headquarters." It measures 15 x 25 inches! But that's exactly the way he wanted it.

One aftermath of the Truman-Stevenson reluctant relationship was the nature of the participation by President Truman in the campaign. Governor Stevenson strongly felt that he would like to make an affirmative campaign on his own and not merely campaign in defense of the Truman record, even though he admired a great many things about President Truman. The Republicans were talking about the "mess in Washington" and "Korea, Communism, and Corruption." Governor Stevenson, obviously, wanted to establish some distance from all this. That was one of the reasons for the separate headquarters at the Illinois capital in Springfield. As a matter of fact, Stevenson wanted as few "give 'em hell" speeches by Truman as could politely be negotiated. At the outset of the campaign, with the good offices of Clayton Fritchey, a valued Truman assistant whom I invited to join me in the management of the campaign, I arranged for a session at the White House to develop campaign strategy. It had been generally agreed that we would undertake to limit the number of speeches, four as I recall, by President Truman. This was readily agreed to by President Truman. We flew back to Springfield very pleased that Truman had been so pleasantly cooperative. The very next day, however, President Truman announced that he would make these specific speeches we had agreed on, but he added that he would ride the train to these destinations and if, along the way, people wanted to gather and say hello to him, he would be glad to stop and speak to them. The result was a regular Truman triumphal whistle-stop with each of these four main speeches enlarged into a very great number of additional speeches. Truman had been very agreeable with Governor Stevenson and very canny in arranging to do exactly what he intended to do anyway.

I declined the offered position of chairman of the Democratic National Committee as this position is usually occupied by a professional politician (such as Hannegan or Farley or Flynn) and I did not see myself in such a role. Steve Mitchell, an old friend of Stevenson's from Chicago, was then agreed upon. Carl McGowan, Adlai's counsel—often referred to as the "keeper of the conscience"—was a pillar of strength to Stevenson, to the campaign, and to me as campaign manager, as was Bill Blair, Adlai's invaluable personal assistant. Arthur Schlesinger was the principal writer and George Ball was not only active with the Volunteers for Stevenson, along with Jane Dick and Dutch Smith, but invariably on hand to assist me at every time of crisis—and there were many of these. One concerned the Stevenson fund.

It developed that Nixon, Eisenhower's vice presidential candidate, had a political fund in California that came under great scrutiny and question as to its source, purpose, and propriety. It presented serious ethical problems. This became such a critical point in the campaign that some leading Republicans were demanding that Nixon should withdraw from the ticket. Finally Nixon booked national television time for his famous demagogic "Checkers" speech (in which he referred rather nauseously not only to his wife's "cloth coat" but to his little dog Checkers) and won Eisenhower's approval. To counter all this, charges were levelled against a very different fund contributed by Stevenson's friends to permit him, as governor, to add to the compensation of a few staff people who would not otherwise have been obtainable. As if in retaliation for the public embarrassment of the Nixon fund, enormous furor was fomented about "the Stevenson Fund" by the "one-party press," 92 percent of which was for Eisenhower. Although most of the working press were attracted idealistically to Stevenson, the owner-publishers who determined press and editorial policy had joined the Eisenhower bandwagon early, most of them even before the Democratic candidate was chosen. So pervasive was this furor that it became necessary to take steps to eliminate this issue from the campaign. George Ball and I recommended to Stevenson that he take the then unprecedented step of revealing his income tax returns for the previous ten years so as to prove there had been no impropriety. Adlai almost blanched at the idea; he treasured his own privacy and respected the privacy of others. But reluctantly he agreed, and the splash of his tax returns filled the press. It succeeded as a tactical ploy in wiping the Stevenson Fund issue from the campaign, but probably has been the cause of tax return revelation by candidates ever since—a loss of privacy which, regrettably, may cause many worthwhile people to be unwilling to seek elective office. Adlai referred to this event in his Gridiron speech after the election by saying he had "won the bosom-baring and public-stripping contest."

To those of us who knew him well Adlai was very warm and comfortable as a companion but to strangers I think he appeared a difficult person to know—a bit distant. He did not bare his soul to many people. He was very mannerly and courteous, very gentlemanly, and not in any way a gregarious back-slapper. People were attracted to him by his ideas, his sense of humor, his beautiful prose, his high principles, and his historical perspective. But many who worked for him devotedly had never met him and felt awed by him. Early in the campaign when my wife was visiting in Springfield she was startled to find that so few of the staff had ever met Stevenson, even among those occupying rather important positions. The word "staff" sounds almost secondary and yet it included major political leaders, journalists, successful businessmen, and other people of significant accomplishments.

Anne suggested a reception as a get-together for Adlai and the campaign staff. Adlai was immediately delighted, but significantly, the idea had not occurred to him. We arranged with the headquarters hotel and invited the entire group. At the last minute the hotel learned that we had some black staff members. This was 1952; amazingly, it turned out that the hotel had "overlooked" another commitment and the facilities were not available after all. Anne immediately called Buffie Ives (Adlai's sister and official hostess) and said, "Buffie, I have a little surprise for you. You're having 100 people as guests at the Governor's Mansion in about four hours." When Buffie asked "How will we do it?" Anne responded, "I'll come right over and somehow we'll work it out together." The arrangements were quickly perfected (thrown together would be more accurate) and the reception at the Governor's Mansion was much better than it would have been at the hotel. It did wonders for the morale of the group in Springfield. The moment Adlai was among them he was the charming and personable host. They had a wonderfully relaxed time together. They liked him and he liked them. From that moment forward they "knew" their candidate.

I recall vividly one of his earliest press conferences. We had been through a thorough preparation and skull practice to be sure that there would be no slips. His lead point—calculated to be the headline from the session—was carefully prepared in an affirmative statement, which he read at the outset.

Then he started fielding the questions from the national press. One of the first was whether he would follow Roosevelt's and Truman's example in sending an emissary to the Vatican. This was a very controversial question at that time. Since a decision was not required unless, and until, he should be elected—or in any event, not required at that early date in the campaign—the typical candidate position would have been to keep the matter under study and to confer with other appropriate persons. Adlai hesitated for a moment and then, to the unhappiness of his supporters, stated that he thought he would not do so. This was a departure from recent precedent and clearly was disappointing to the large Catholic segment of the Democratic party. By his reply, he completely scooped his planned lead point, which was then lost in the shuffle. He told me afterward that he just thought it best to put the matter clearly on the table from the outset and not build false hopes.

There was no question that his answer was politically hurtful—especially as he was a divorced man and divorce carried a political scar in those days, especially with Catholics. But the danger of loss of support was never a factor in his equation. His compulsion was to tell the whole truth, even beyond what was required of him at the moment. No one would have criticized him had he held to the lead that he had planned for the conference, and stated his Vatican decision on another occasion, more conducive to his election interest. But that was not in the Stevenson character. This is but one of the many instances that were to follow in the days of the campaign.

Another, soon to come, was on the tidelands oil question. This was a question of serious economic concern to states with huge blocs of electoral votes—among them, notably, Texas and California.

Governor Allan Shivers of Texas, in keeping with the custom of the late summer of 1952, announced that he would be making a pilgrimage to the Stevenson headquarters at Springfield to confer with Adlai Stevenson. Shivers was not thought to be fond of Stevenson or to have favored his candidacy. Additionally, his visit threatened to enlarge the off-shore oil issue and to dramatize it before the campaign could even get under way.

In the presence of a small group of intimate advisers, the two met and conferred about the campaign. Governor Shivers then stated his position on the off-shore oil issue and emphasized its importance not only to Texas but to California, Louisiana, and other states bordering the oceans. Seeing that he was not preaching to the converted, he even indicated that while he would prefer an outright commitment to his states' rights view, he could go home to Texas without embarrassment if Stevenson would merely announce that he would give the matter serious study. But Stevenson told the Texas governor very frankly that he disagreed with him on the issue and that it was best that he make a public statement of his opposition without equivocation or delay. One person present gave the final and (he hoped) telling remonstrance: "But Governor Stevenson, if you insist on doing that, you can't win." Coldly and resolutely, Stevenson replied: "I don't *have* to win." That ended the private conference and Stevenson went before the press to put the tidelands issue to rest.

As the campaign progressed there were many more such occasions, although few as dramatic or as costly. What earned him admiration often did not gather him support. But his candor, his honesty, and his lack of equivocation became evident to the entire country.

In mid-September I had a call from Governor Wetherby of Kentucky to ask what I could do to help get Barkley active in the campaign; he was badly needed in Kentucky and was, in effect, "sulking in his tent." I telephoned the Veep, whom I greatly admired and with whom I had a very warm relationship, that I would like to bring "the presidential campaign caravan" for a visit to his home, The Angles, at Paducah. He responded very warmly and was obviously quite pleased that he would have this nationally visible courtesy—especially in view of his embarrassment at the convention. I told him our only problem was whether or not the large planes we were using in the campaign could land at the Paducah airport in view of the length of the runways. He said he would check it out and call me back. In a very short time he called me that he had been to the airport, checked out the runways personally, and that he felt confident we would be able to land the planes. This was clear evidence of his happiness over the proposed visit. Actually, we had to change to smaller airplanes to use the Paducah airport, but we felt that it was well worth doing in order to be able to bring the Veep actively into not only the Kentucky but also the national campaign.

The Washington press corps was very pleased at the prospective trip, as they liked Barkley and looked forward to a homey visit to The Angles. I think they also looked forward to a good drink of bourbon and branch water at the Barkley party. The vice president, however, out of a sense of propriety (highly misjudged, according to the members of the press), decided that it would be inappropriate to serve intoxicating liquor to the party and therefore gave them soft drinks. He reserved the bourbon and branch water for Adlai and the handful of us who lunched with him in his dining room. Barry Bingham, Sr., quickly sensed the disappointment of the press and had a well-supplied press bar awaiting them in Louisville later in the afternoon.

Adlai's respect for the individual and for his audiences kept him from doing what becomes customary in most campaigns—giving almost a set speech in place after place after place. As his personal campaign manager, I found this a particular problem on the whistle-stop tours I had arranged for him. Knowing that the different political leaders who boarded the train at each stop were eager to meet the candidate and, if possible, spend a few minutes with him, I became distressed that my candidate was spending all of his time closeted in his compartment preparing a new speech for the next stop. I talked with him about it and he listened quietly, attentively, and in apparent agreement. I pointed out that at best the media could carry only two speeches a day, one in the morning and one in the evening. I felt I had convinced him that, after all, the principal purpose of his appearance at each whistle-stop was merely that people might see him in the flesh, hear his voice, and make a sort of incidental passing judgment about Stevenson, the man.

To assist him I asked Phil Stern, one of the excellent writers in the campaign, to prepare a list of what I captioned "whistle-stop vignettes". They consisted of a dozen brief paragraphs on different subjects, extracted from Adlai's speeches. I suggested that Adlai use one as the key point at each of his whistle-stops and pointed out that, after, all, these were not scheduled to be major policy speeches. He completely agreed that this was a reasonable approach and would give him time to meet more of the political figures as he crossed the country.

This happened one evening. The next day I watched with interest. And lo and behold, he had prepared a new speech for his first whistle-stop—and immediately after that, retreated to his compartment to prepare another one for the next! The carefully prepared "whistle-stop vignettes" lapsed into the forgotten. Adlai simply could not bring himself to be repetitious even though each audience was different.

Any presidential campaign is physically gruelling but this was true to the nth degree in 1952 as there had been no preparation in advance for a nomination that had not been sought. Added to this enormous difference was the fact that Stevenson worked on every speech as though history absolutely depended upon it. By contrast Eisenhower took his speechwriter's drafts in stride. One of the press corps who had travelled with both candidates and had observed the difference irreverently circulated a myth that Ike once told an aide, "Don't give me my speeches in advance—it ruins my spontaneity." At all events, I started receiving criticism that I was killing my candidate with an almost humanly impossible schedule of incessant meetings, speeches, and travel. Social friends of his, unaccustomed to the rigors of the campaign trail, were particulary insistent. Also they pointed out to me that one of the aides listed in Eisenhower's retinue was really a masseur and that he had been a great help in keeping Ike in the pink of condition. I said that I had tried to convince Adlai of the benefit of a daily rubdown but that he would have none of it.

By coincidence Senator Stuart Syminton dropped in my office one day and told me of the wonderful Puerto Rican "rubdown artist" who had been with him throughout his just finished successful primary in Missouri, and what it had meant to him in keeping fit. I told him of Adlai's unwillingness, but then an idea struck me. I said "Stu, Adlai is winding up this week in St. Louis. At the end of the day, how about your going by Adlai's room at the hotel, accompanied by your Puerto Rican friend, tell Adlai of your wonderfully healthy result and leave the masseur with our candidate for a rubdown. He can hardly resist such a courtesy, will become convinced, and we'll solve the problem for the rest of the campaign." Stu liked the idea.

That Saturday night I went, as usual, to the airport to welcome Stevenson back to Springfield and to spend a few minutes reviewing the week. Nothing was said about the Symington episode until I finally (dying with curiosity) asked if Stu had been very helpful to him in Missouri. Adlai almost exploded. He said that at the end of the day's circuit of speeches, just at dinner time, Stu came to his hotel room, told him some enthusiastic something about how he had practically won his senatorial nomination through the invaluable daily rubdowns, pushed the masseur into the room, and left. Adlai said the the Puerto Rican gave him a superb rubdown, but, he added, the result was absolutely awful—the worst experience he had endured in the whole campaign. Just a little later that evening he went on television for his major speech and he said he was so relaxed that he had to struggle to avoid a constant yawn—he said his eyelids were so heavy he could keep them open only by heroic effort. He added, "I tell you it was one of the worst—one of the most painful—experiences of my life. I don't know how I ever managed to struggle through the speech." That ended the effort to give him a masseur for a campaign aide. Long after the campaign had become a memory, I confessed to the plot with Stu Symington and Adlai's only comment was a laughing, "So now you tell me."

I recall an extremely difficult moment at the very end of the campaign. It was the night before he was scheduled for an intensive day of decisive campaigning in New York City, to conclude with a major

TV speech at night. His New York speeches were to start at seven in the morning and continue throughout the day. It was, in a sense, the most important day of the campaign.

At midnight at the New York headquarters at the Biltmore I had a telephone call from Adlai from the train on which he had been whistle-stopping across Pennsylvania. He said that, in a few moments, he must leave the campaign train and fly back to Illinois because of a riot at the Menard Prison; would I please arrange for Senator Fulbright and others on the train to substitute for him at the remaining whistle-stops and on the various occasions in New York City; and that he would try to return to New York in time for his evening television speech.

But I said, "You have a lieutenant governor who is supported by you to be your successor—and tomorrow is the most important day of the campaign. Why can't he take care of the Illinois prison problem? No one can substitute for you in New York City. These are key appearances." I knew he could count on his trusted young legal assistant Newton Minow, at the governor's Springfield office, to keep him fully advised. Calmly Adlai explained: Guards were being held as hostages at the prison; the plan was to storm the prison at daybreak; he had approved the plan but there was the risk that lives might be lost— and that was a risk he could not delegate.

Of course I agreed. And after giving him a few minutes to slip unnoticed from the train, I communicated to Bill Fulbright the startling news that he was taking Stevenson's place in giving a speech at seven o'clock the following morning.

Adlai returned to Illinois; the entry to the prison was successfully accomplished the following morning; the guards were rescued without loss of life and order was restored. He missed all of his speaking engagements at the various New York rallies throughtout the day. As his campaign manager, I spent all of that eventful October 31 explaining—mostly to irate and unwilling listeners—why Adlai Stevenson had had to make a last minute cancellation of his most important day of campaigning.

His return from Menard was one of anxiety and frustration. His special charter flight to New York was delayed by fog, then rerouted to Philadelphia for refueling, and finally caught in a stack-up over the LaGuardia Airport. An hour before his major television speech in the evening it was still nip-and-tuck as to whether he could land in New York, get through crowded traffic (even with police sirens blaring), and make it to the television theatre in time for his scheduled hookup.

Frantically the New York sponsors decided they couldn't risk it any longer and insisted that I should prepare at once to substitute for Stevenson. Hastily I put a speech together, finishing the last lines as my taxicab pulled up to the auditorium. I went backstage. Adolf Berle, who was to introduce Stevenson, quickly revamped his script to introduce me. All of us were breathless from the last-minute frenzy of traffic, telephones, and change of plans.

Like an old-fashioned melodrama, just as Berle and I were walking on stage, a scant minute before the New York hookup was to begin, the rear door of the auditorium burst open, and in rushed Governor Stevenson! The ovation was tumultuous. I told Adlai that he had just ruined the best speech I ever "almost made".

It had been a nerve-wracking and disappointing day in the campaign, but there was never a moment's hesitation in Stevenson's mind about what he should do; the Menard responsibility, with its attendant risk of life, was one he could not delegate.

After New York the campaign concluded with a nostalgic whistle-stop by train to Chicago. A major stop on the way was at Notre Dame, where Adlai delivered a magnificent speech. While Adlai was at the college I remained on the train to carry forward my managerial duties by telephone. I received a call from Senator Wayne Morse of Oregon, then a Republican. He told me he was convinced Adlai should be elected and was thinking about coming out publicly for him that night—even considering announcing a change of party affiliation to Democratic. Just at that moment Adlai reentered the train flush with the success of his speech at the college. I gave him Wayne's message and turned the phone over to him to express his appreciation. His response was interesting. After Senator Morse told Adlai again of his proffered support Adlai hesitated and then said that while he appreciated what Wayne was about to do, he must caution him to consider the step most prayerfully as it could be hurtful to Wayne with his own party—and then added that with a switch in party allegiance there was even some question as to how much he could bring with him. Adlai counselled that a change of party often leaves a person unwanted in either the one he leaves or the one he joins. I could not help but admire the candor and the integrity of the advice.

Many counseled Adlai against overuse of his sense of humor but Adlai continued with it and his audiences loved it. Again he was following that famous advice of Polonius, "To thine own self be true." Humor was a part of Adlai, and he brought it into every speech. It

On the campaign trail in 1952

helped mightily to keep his speeches and his counsel from becoming stuffy or ponderous. He always inspired—but with a twinkle that made his wisdom human and digestible. His humor showed constantly, even in his famous concession statement on the night of the 1952 election.

It was a night I shall never forget. The one-sided returns poured in. The Eisenhower precincts—especially those with voting machines—came all too early. They were almost consistently of landslide proportions. Before seven o'clock John Bailey (a skilled pro, later National Committee chairman) telephoned me from the normally Democratic state of Connecticut, "We've been murdered." One bright spot was Philadelphia. We were carrying it handily. My home state of Kentucky predicted a hundred thousand Stevenson margin, but that margin kept fading until at the end we won by a scant 700 votes. The TV cameras were set up in the ballroom at the St. Nicholas Hotel, but the various political leaders who had come to Springfield for election night and who normally would have appeared (very happily, I might add) before the cameras throughout the evening could hardly be pried away from the Governor's Mansion, so gloomy were the returns. The result was that Vic Sholis (who was assisting me in the campaign) and I had to respond to a disproportionately large number of the interviews. I kept remonstrating, "But look at Philadelphia." New York conceded to Ike before the California voting had been concluded. State after state conceded. Finally, toward midnight, I telephoned Adlai on our private line from the presidential campaign headquarters to the Governor's Mansion a few blocks away. I said simply, "Adlai, I think the time has probably come for a statement." Just as simply he answered, "So do I. Suppose you come by for me."

We drove together to the television room at the hotel, which was jam-packed with reporters and enthusiastic adherents. On the way he showed me the statement he had dictated a little while earlier. And as we neared the hotel he said, "I thought I would tell a little story."

"But," I asked, "is this really a night for humor?"

Then he told me he had in mind the now famous Lincoln anecdote and I heartily agreed. And the one statement everyone still recalls from his concession to President Eisenhower was that story: "Someone asked me, as I came in, down on the street, how I felt and I was reminded of a story that a fellow townsman of ours used to tell—Abraham Lincoln. They asked him how he felt once after an unsuccessful election. He said he felt like a little boy who stubbed his toe in the dark. He said that he was too old to cry, but it hurt too much to laugh."

I frequently glance at his inscription on a photograph on my office wall—one he sent to me shortly after the election in 1952, the election in which there was so much discussion about his reluctance to be a candidate. This inscription showed his modest habit of jesting at his own expense. Stevenson had endorsed it to me as "A cruel taskmaster and dear friend whose heart is always high, from his reluctant dragon."

Although Stevenson lost the election by an electoral landslide (89 to 442), he won more votes than any other defeated candidate in history. Elmo Roper, one of the two leading pollsters of the day, told me that as against his poll taken immediately after the adjournment of the two conventions, the final tally on election day showed that Stevenson, by his high-level campaign, had changed more votes than ever before in any other presidential election—that he had narrowed the gap between himself and Eisenhower by some ten million votes.

On the morning after the election I had to go before the press for a concluding press conference. I did not relish the prospect. There was little in the outcome to buoy my spirits. At my last conference before the election I tried to shy away from predicting the outcome in any particular state and explained that if asked about a doubtful state I would not want to admit the doubt and therefore would prefer to avoid predictions about any individual state. Soon a reporter ingeniously asked, "What about Kentucky—you surely don't mind answering about your home state." At that I slipped into error and said confidently we would carry Kentucky (which in fact we did, though barely). Soon another politically wise reporter asked about Illinois and justified it by saying it was Stevenson's home state. I claimed it too. Then came Alabama, Sparkman's home state. Of course I claimed it. And on one pretext or another, they continued with New York, California, and a few others. As campaign manager I claimed them all. It was like sin— once you start, how do you stop? Finally the *New York Times* reporter Bill Lawrence smiled in a friendly way, and said, "Mr. Chairman, I have just been adding up the electoral votes of your predictions. I don't know whether you realize it or not, but you've just predicted a landslide."

At the conference on "the morning after" I told that same group of reporters that I could anticipate their first question—you could almost read it on every one of their expectant faces. So my statement was, "At our last conference I predicted a landslide. I was right—we've just had one. But I was wrong about which candidate would win. Still, that's one out of two, and you've got to admit 500 is not a bad batting average?" They laughed and forgave me. I concluded the conference with the very truthful statement, "There were no compromises, there were no commitments, and we have no regrets."

On Friday night after the election Anne and I were having a threesome farewell dinner with Adlai at the Governor's Mansion before closing the books on the campaign and returning to Louisville and the law firm. We were unwinding after months of exhausting tension. I told Adlai that the time had now arrived for his long desired trip around the world—something he had often talked about. Furthermore, I suggested that it was the best thing he could do for the country as well, as he would then not be "in Eisenhower's hair" during the launching of the new presidency. Inevitably the press would be asking him for comments on the various measures instituted by the new president and it would be best for everyone if he were simply unavailable. He concurred in the reasoning but protested that he had agreed with Random House to produce a book and the time required for the writing would definitely foreclose the trip. I responded that the book need not stand in the way. "But," he continued, "I've agreed to do it, and I must—and that will take time. No, it's not possible." "But you've already written your book," I persisted. I think he felt I did not understand. I explained that all he need do was to review the speeches he had made during the campaign, select the ones he preferred to publish, write a preface—and lo! his book would be done! Then off to Europe, and the rest of the world. A happy gleam came into his whole countenance as he exclaimed, "And dancing girls, too?"

He later talked to Random House and found them delighted with the proposal. The book of speeches was a great success and in due course Adlai embarked on his foreign travel, which became almost a triumphal tour, so enthusiastic was his reception everywhere. In addition, but adding a great deal of work to the tour, he produced enroute a series of articles for *Look* magazine. He invited me to accompany him for at least part of the journey but my ever present taskmaster, the law practice, made acceptance of the invitation impossible.

Adlai was also troubled about his future. He was being urged to write a column for syndication, to return to his law firm, to become a commentator, to lecture, to write more books, to become affiliated with the *Encyclopaedia Brittanica*, and to undertake a wide variety of other pursuits. I strongly advised that he return to the practice of law. His response was interesting, "Oh, not all those indentures again!" I knew that had been the sort of meticulous work he had done back in his law firm days before he was elected Governor of Illinois, and certainly it was not very challenging to such a mind as Stevenson's. But I countered that his practice would now be of a totally different nature— for a relatively few large clients, and mostly of a broad advisory nature and no doubt involving foreign travel as well. To underscore my proposal, I told him I was authorized by one of my clients to offer him an annual retainer of $50,000 for general advisory services and that George Ball had a similar offer for him of $25,000 a year from another client. And obviously there would be others to follow. Such a course would leave him completely free to participate in public affairs, to speak out whenever he felt the need to do so, to write, to travel and to attend the various affairs that would be held to defray the party debt. The course was so appealing that after due consideration he adopted it. And obviously inherent in this entire concept was the unexpressed thought that it was probably the best possible way to continue his own preparation and availability for the nomination four years later.

Chapter 6

The Conscience
of American Politics

Even though Stevenson had not triumphed in the Electoral College he
had won an enduring place in the hearts and the admiration of
Americans. Anne and I joined Adlai and Carl McGowan and his wife
for a restful vacation at an Arizona ranch. On the second day we took
a horseback ride across the border to the little Mexican town of
Nogales, where a large crowd immediately gathered to greet Stevenson, who quipped in surprise, "Oh, I ran in the wrong country." It was
typical of the acclaim with which he was greeted on his later tour
around the world—a tour that professional commitments prevented me
from joining.

The four years between the 1952 and the 1956 elections passed
quickly. To make up for the time spent in the 1952 campaign I
concentrated on the legal practice and the continued growth of my
Louisville law firm. Periodically I would go to Libertyville, Chicago,
and Washington to counsel with Stevenson about his plans, his participation in public events, and position papers being developed on
domestic and foreign policy. Often these sessions included people who
had been active in the 1952 campaign. Of particular importance was a
group chaired by Tom Finletter (later ambassador to NATO under
President Kennedy). It came to be known as the Finletter Group. It
undertook to develop Democratic positions on a wide range of issues
and many outstanding authorities cooperated in the authorship of
learned white papers that were to serve as background for the next
presidential campaign. Adlai had an active interest in this effort and
met with the varying members of this group as often as his crowded

schedule permitted. He maintained an active speaking schedule in response to the flood of invitations from around the country. Everybody wanted him for their special events, and he felt a sense of obligation both because of all they had done in his behalf and because many occasions were for the purpose of raising funds to pay off the party's 1952 debt. Federal financing had not been enacted at that time.

Although Stevenson became more optimistic during the actual progress of the 1956 campaign I, personally, do not believe that he felt before the campaign, or even in its early days, that it had much likelihood of succeeding. His willingness to run that year and his seeking the nomination came, in my opinion, largely from a sense of public duty and responsibility, as the leader of his party.

An incident that occurred in 1955 typifies, I think, Adlai's approach to public life in general and to his 1956 decision to make the race. Following a vacation together in Jamaica, Adlai, Anne, and I flew to Puerto Rico, where we were guests of Governor Munoz Marin in his historic residence, La Fortaleza. One night while we were philosophizing together as we sat on the battlements sipping a refreshing drink, Munoz told us of an incident that had impressed him, as it did us. He said that at the end of a long day of traversing the Puerto Rican countryside in the course of a campaign he climbed up a steep hill to talk with some back country supporters who had gathered to hear him. He saw a log nearby and sat down to catch his breath and rest a moment. When saluted happily by one of those waiting to hear him he confessed, "I am tired." But his devoted adherent quickly replied, "But you can't be tired—you are our leader." Munoz had been reminded that when you lead much is expected, much is required, and much must be delivered. Munoz was a great leader of the Puerto Rican people and had he had a larger base I was always persuaded he could have been one of the world's significant people.

Sharply engraved in my memory is the conversation I had with Adlai as we were returning from that vacation. He turned to me, as the plane was coming down at Miami, and said, "Do you think I should run in 1956?" I answered with an emphatic "Yes." He then asked a question I would have given my eye teeth not to have heard, "Do you think I'll win?" And, hesitantly but clearly I said, "No, I don't think so." He then asked, "Then why do you think that I should run?"

I explained that I thought the nomination for the high office of president, in his hands, would be next in importance to being elected president; that Wendell Willkie, who had lost to Roosevelt, had demonstrated the significance inherent in the position of leadership that is conferred by nomination and the campaign. I reminded him that without Wendell Willkie we might not have had the destroyer deal with England, an important step in winning World War II, and that there were other very critical moves on which Roosevelt needed and received Willkie's support in unifying the nation at times of crisis. If Adlai were the leader of his party, the nominee of his party, and the spokesman of his party he could have a statesmanlike effect on the country. I thought he had a duty to seek and accept the nomination; and that the leadership he would give, even though defeated, would be invaluable to his party and to the nation. It was a conversation I would have liked to avoid, but my relationship with Adlai was such that I thought I could not be less than frank.

The first year in which Democratic presidential primaries were really significant was 1956. Four years before there had been the New Hampshire primary and several others, but they did not represent enough delegate votes to be in any sense determinative. Nor had they become significant in the public consciousness. On the other hand, Senator Kefauver's success in 1952 in assiduously pursuing the primary trail (he might even be called the father of the modern primary movement) brought serious consideration to the primaries as a means of obtaining the nomination. Additional states had enacted presidential primary laws. No one who seriously sought the presidential nomination in 1956 could afford not to enter them and compete for the first ballot votes that these primaries would determine. The primaries had become a very real factor in presidential selection. Once Stevenson decided to run it became imperative for him to go the primary route in order to be a contender at the convention. The 1952 draft was a political miracle— it would not happen again. This meant a full year of politics in pursuing the campaign trail from state to state, and I could not remove myself from my law firm and the private practice for such an extended period. In our Libertyville sessions at Stevenson's home we therefore decided to employ a full-time campaign manager and selected Jim Finnegan, an excellent pro who was then Governor David Lawrence's secretary of state in Pennsylvania. I agreed to be available from time to time throughout the year as personal adviser to Stevenson and, once the nomination was obtained, to spend full-time in the fall as general coordinator of the campaign divisions.

Stevenson viewed the presidential primaries with considerable distaste. It was like going from wholesale to retail. Not only was it expensive in money and exhausting in time and energy, but invariably a host of truly local issues made their way into the process (fruitflies in Florida, for example) and personalized campaigning at the factory gate and in the supermarket became essential in seeking the election of individual delegates committed to the cause. Stevenson regarded the participation in presidential primaries, state after state, as a vulgarization of the presidential election process; he felt it reduced the high office of president to the level of campaigning for county sheriff. He greatly preferred to deal with national issues in major addresses. On the other hand, Kefauver, wearing his coonskin cap, gloried in the handshaking campaign and was very good at it. He had made progress in this way in 1952 and declared he would make a full go at the primaries, now more numerous, in 1956. He had received extensive publicity from his chairmanship of a congressional committee that had investigated organized crime and had held hearings throughout the country. His opposition, if ignored, could be most formidable.

The first significant primary was in Minnesota. With the enthusiastic backing of Governor Orville Freeman, Senator Hubert Humphrey, and their formidable Farmer Labor Party organization, a Stevenson victory seemed likely. Adlai campaigned vigorously, but so did Kefauver. When primary day arrived Kefauver, to the astonishment of most, emerged with 56 percent of the vote. It gave him 26 of Minnesota's 30 delegates. Since Minnesota permits crossovers, the defeat was explained by Finnegan as the result of Republicans moving into the Democratic primary to upset Stevenson. But, whatever the reason, there was consternation—it was clearly a setback of major proportions.

The most significant primary was to be in California. The jolt of a second defeat, especially in such a populous state with its great group of delegates, had to be avoided. Adlai called on me to go to California to join Jim Finnegan in organizing his forces. This was to be a major battleground. I spent some ten days in California working behind the scenes with Pat Brown and the other California leaders. The news on that June election night was almost sensational. Stevenson had overwhelmed Kefauver with 62 percent of the vote, a plurality of almost half a million. The California victory set the stage for the coming convention.

I recall very poignantly one incident that was very revealing as to Stevenson's revulsion against seeking the high office of president by this state-by-state, handshaking, person-to-person, detailed type of

With Arthur Kling and Estes Kefauver in Louisville

campaigning—campaigning for which Estes Kefauver was by disposition ideally suited. Estes would walk down a street almost robotically shaking hands with everyone he met, indefatigably, and with apparent pleasure—and he would do it day after day after day. He was far better at this kind of campaigning than at delivering major addresses on complex issues of foreign policy, although he was both intelligent and well educated.

At Adlai's request I met him one day at the Los Angeles Airport in the midst of this frenzied dawn-to-midnight campaigning. On the way from the plane into the airport barbershop, tense and saturated with fatigue, he said to me, "Wilson, if I had known these primaries were going to be like this, I wouldn't have done it if Western Civilization had depended on it!" But Western Civilization did stand, Adlai did go ahead, he did win California, and things improved.

In due course the primaries had been fairly conclusive. Stevenson had won most of them, and when we reached the convention it seemed to observers a foregone conclusion that Stevenson would again be nominated to lead the party. It fell to my lot to put things in shape at the convention for his nomination. This involved selecting people to make the nominating and seconding speeches, and the structuring of the strategy both to win the nomination and to put on the best national show before the television cameras.

Each convention is governed by its own rules, although usually the procedure of past conventions is duplicated in those that follow. I checked carefully the rules of the two preceding conventions, to be certain that my strategy would not be thrown off the track by any procedural quirk. Under the practice, the states were called alphabetically when the time for nominations arrived, and each state had the right to place someone in nomination, to pass, or to yield to another state. At the conclusion of each nominating speech, the seconding speeches were then heard for the candidate who had just been nominated. Then the roll call proceeded to the next state for the next nomination, which in turn was followed by seconding speeches. There is valuable momentum in showing as much support as possible and as early as possible in the process, as there are always many more votes still to be won. As a result of many conferences, I had planned for various states to pass and to yield in order that the leaders we had selected would appear in a prearranged order for the nomination and the seconding speeches.

I had arranged for Alabama to pass and for Alaska, the next on the roll call, to yield to Washington, when Senator Henry Jackson would nominate the other Washington senator, Warren Magnuson, who would then withdraw and say that if he were a delegate he would suggest that all the delegates "cast their ballots for the next president of the United States, Adlai E. Stevenson."

The next state, Arizona, was to yield to Massachusetts and Senator John F. Kennedy was then to nominate Adlai Stevenson. Kennedy was selected for a number of reasons. Stevenson liked him; he was articulate and intelligent; he was young and attractive; his state (Massachusetts) was Stevenson territory. Under the rules and prior practice, I had then arranged for seconding speeches to be made by Governor Luther H. Hodges of North Carolina, Senator Herbert H. Lehman of New York, Governor George Leader of Pennsylvania, Congressman William L. Dawson of Illinois, and finally, by Congresswoman Edith Green of Oregon, each with a time limit of two minutes. In this way, before the name of any other candidate could even be mentioned, let alone nominated, I would have had Stevenson placed in nomination and would have demonstrated delegate strength for Stevenson in

Alabama, Alaska, Arizona, Massachusetts, Washington, North Carolina, New York, Pennsylvania, Illinois, and Oregon.

To be doubly sure that there would be no change from the procedure of the prior convention, I caught Sam Rayburn (the convention chairman) at a dinner party the night before the nominations were to be made, reviewed the situation with him briefly, and received his full concurrence in the procedure I had arranged. Although Mr. Sam was the potent, long-time Speaker of the House of Representatives, he said at the end of the conversation that while he was sure there would be no problem, it might be well to check—just as a matter of courtesy—with the parliamentarian, the crusty Congressman Clarence Cannon of Missouri. But unfortunately, Mr. Cannon was not to be located anywhere, either that evening or the next morning. It was simply impossible to track him down. I was not really apprehensive, however, as he had also been the parliamentarian at the two previous conventions and I was merely following the procedure he had sanctioned before.

When I finally found him, it was just before the convention was to open, as he and Speaker Rayburn, together with the minister and others, were mounting the platform. I outlined the procedure to Mr. Cannon hastily and received from him a very curt disapproval. He said he was going to rule that each state when called should nominate whomever it chose and also make seconding speeches for anyone it chose, thereby mixing the nominating and seconding speeches for the various candidates, and that he would proceed down the list alphabetically without any yielding or passing. I remonstrated that if we changed to the method he was then suggesting, it would upset the entire nominating procedure and the whole thing would be a mess. He was adamant. I then pointed out to him that the procedure I had arranged was in accordance with the procedure of the two prior conventions where he was also the parliamentarian. He stuck to his guns and said in effect, "We were wrong before." With that he marched through the curtain and out onto the stage.

I made my last quick appeal to Mr. Sam and urged him to try to get the parliamentarian to change his mind even though he would have to do it during the opening prayer. Without a change from what Parliamentarian Cannon then had in mind, all of my arrangements would have gone awry. Other nominations would have preceded the Stevenson nomination; states would be making seconding speeches before nominating speeches had been made, and what seemed like a beautifully flowing strategy and a unified, dramatic presentation would be ripped asunder. Although, even in those days, there were telephones interconnecting the various state delegations on the convention floor, they were a very imperfect communication system, frequently unmanned at the receiving end, and the conversations were often all but inaudible. Consequently, it would have been virtually impossible to communicate with the various states on the floor and to rearrange the procedure that I had evolved in personal conferences with quite a number of state leaders during the preceding day.

I waited anxiously for the end of the opening prayer. The backstage curtain parted and out walked my good friend Hale Boggs, congressman from Louisiana, a strong and very effective protégé of Sam Rayburn. With a very quiet, pleasant smile, and in his mellifluous southern accent, he said, "Mr. Sam persuaded him—everything is all right again." I offered up a thankful prayer of my own.

The nomination procedure moved forward like clockwork, just as planned, and I felt very relaxed. Hale asked me to sit with him in the Speaker's box and when we were seated, in the privacy of a two-some, he said, "Do you know who would like to be vice president?" I replied that I knew several who wanted very much to be vice president, and then told him of the puzzling conversation I had with Speaker Rayburn as we sat backstage waiting for Clarence Cannon to arrive and for the convention to be convened. I had said, "Mr. Speaker, what do you think about the vice presidency?" He said, "By the way, I have been trying to get Adlai Stevenson and he hasn't answered my call," and he seemed right upset about it, almost a little truculent. Sam Rayburn normally had such a pleasant disposition that I hastened to assure him, "Well, Adlai probably didn't get your message, but I'll see that he calls you right away."

Knowing that Adlai would be interested in Rayburn's views, I then asked, "What do you think about Jack Kennedy?" I remember vividly his reply, "A mere boy!"

Then I said, "Well, what do you think about Estes Kefauver?" "Well," he said, "nobody in the Senate has any regard for him. If he were nominated he wouldn't be able to get another senator to second his nomination." I was surprised to hear the Speaker dismiss out of hand the two most likely candidates, the very ones most delegates were considering. I then proceeded to ask him what he thought about Hubert Humphrey and about Albert Gore, the next two most widely discussed candidates. He was equally adamant that they wouldn't do either. At that point Cannon had arrived and they parted the curtain and went out on stage to open the convention.

"What did all that mean?" I asked of Hale, whom I had known for years. He was very close to the Speaker—almost like a son. Hale bowled me over with his reply, "Sam Rayburn would like to be vice president." I said, "Hale, I can't believe it. Why, he's about the same age as Barkley and we both know the problems that Barkley's age caused at the last convention when both of them were four years younger." Hale then told me something that I had not in the least suspected. He said that Mr. Sam and Alben Barkley had come to the Congress at the same time under Woodrow Wilson and moved along together under the Roosevelt leadership; Barkley had gone to the Senate and become the majority leader; Sam Rayburn had become the Speaker of the House; and that, in a general way, the two of them had progressed in parallel lines of ascending leadership. But there was one big difference: Barkley had become vice president; and it was as simple as that—Sam Rayburn would also like to become vice president. It had merely been difficult for him to say so directly to me.

But Hale was positive. "I'm telling you, I know that Sam Rayburn wants to be vice president." I was sure that he was giving me the message straight from Sam Rayburn. I then understood why Sam Rayburn had felt that Kennedy was a "mere boy," why Estes Kefauver was not worthy to be seconded by another senator, and why neither of the other two front-runners would do.

I mentioned the Hale Boggs conversation, of course, to Adlai Stevenson later that day, and while he had great admiration for Sam Rayburn he did not feel that a Rayburn vice presidency was in the cards.

Many important things at national conventions are decided and executed on the spur of the moment. It must have been ten o'clock on the night before the nomination was to be made, that the final decision was reached to ask Jack Kennedy to place Adlai in nomination. I telephoned Jack Kennedy and asked him to be ready to nominate Stevenson the next day. The response was an immediate and excited acceptance. I rather imagine—although this is merely personal speculation—that Kennedy also felt that the invitation for him to make the nomination was probably a forerunner to consideration for the vice presidency.

After the Stevenson nomination procedure was completed, the clerk continued the roll call for other nominations. Arkansas passed.

Next California announced, "California, which in June by over one million votes proved that Adlai Stevenson will be the next president of the United States in November, passes." Then the Canal Zone joined suit with the statement, "The candidate of the Canal Zone has already been nominated, Adlai Stevenson, and we therefore pass." As Kefauver had clearly lost the primaries to Stevenson, he was not placed in nomination. He was then basing his hopes on the vice presidency. Delaware passed to Texas and John B. Connally nominated Lyndon Johnson for President. Then Idaho yielded to Oklahoma and Averell Harriman was placed in nomination. Interestingly, former President Truman was then recognized to say that he was supporting Harriman. Kentucky nominated Happy Chandler—who had succeeded in having the Kentucky delegation committed to him as Kentucky's "favorite son" despite the spirited opposition of Earle Clements in bitter county battles across the state. Massachusetts nominated John McCormack, Virginia Governor Battle, Missouri Stuart Symington, and South Carolina Governor Timmerman. Speaker McCormack released his Massachusetts delegation and the roll call started.

The balloting contained no surprises for us—all went as we had planned and the tally on the first ballot, with only 687 necessary to nominate, gave Stevenson a comfortable majority of 905-1/2 votes. Next was Harriman with 210 and third was Lyndon Johnson with 80. Chandler trailed with 36-1/2 of which 30 were from Kentucky under the unit rule. His effort for the presidency had garnered 6-1/2 votes from the rest of the country. Stevenson was declared the nominee, and the motion to make it unanimous was adopted. Once again Stevenson was to lead the party.

Following the nomination a group of us, including George Ball, Jim Finnegan, Bill Blair, and Tom Finletter, were asked to get together to help advise what should be done about the vice presidency. One view was that Stevenson should avoid the "anointing" of an individual by the usual back room selection. Another was that there should be a completely open convention. There were two reasons for this course: it was a good thing to do in and of itself, as a matter of principle, and an open convention was also good practical politics as a means of avoiding the alienation of supporters of the several vice presidential candidates, all of whom had strong constituencies.

At one point in the conference it was urged that Stevenson should ask for the convention to be declared open for limited selection as between Kefauver and Kennedy; another amended this proposal to suggest that the convention be declared open for decision as among four individuals, adding Humphrey and Gore. I felt strongly, however, and so urged, that if the convention were to be declared open on the vice presidential nomination—and it seemed to me there was good sense in doing so—it should be completely open, and that as much harm would be done by a limited opening as by an "anointing" of one individual. But Tom Finletter, with support from others, thought that for Stevenson to open the convention completely might appear to be an act of indecision, as though he were unable to make up his mind just what person he would like to serve as vice president with him. This possibility was discussed against the background of what was thought to be Stevenson's reputation for indecisiveness. I stated, however, that I thought the decision could be so worded as to make it clear that it was a point of principle and a point of determined leadership. Consequently, the general decision was reached that the convention would be declared completely open, but that I should undertake a suggested Stevenson statement in language that would demonstrate leadership rather than indecisiveness. I prepared such a statement; the group agreed, and when I reviewed it with Stevenson he also agreed. After some preliminaries, the action paragraph was as follows: "In these circumstances I have concluded to depart from the precedents of the past. I have decided that the selection of the Vice Presidential nominee should be made through the free process of this Convention so that the Democratic Party's candidate for this office may join me before the nation not as one man's selection but as the one chosen by our Party even as I have been chosen." The next day I was delighted to see the emphasis placed by the *New York Times* on the words of decisiveness and to read the comment from several editorial writers that this represented a very positive act of leadership on the part of Stevenson.

Opening the convention for the vice presidency was not as easy as it seemed it might be. Following the Stevenson nomination, Adlai sent word to Sam Rayburn at the night session that he was on the way to the Stockyards Convention Hall to make a statement to the convention, asking that it be declared open for nomination the following day for vice president. When Mr. Rayburn got the word, just minutes before Stevenson arrived at the hall, he was thoroughly displeased and tried to gavel the convention into adjournment before Stevenson could reach the platform. Although Rayburn was thoroughly experienced in wielding the gavel, the word of the open convention had reached enough people on the floor so that the clamor and shouting drowned out the adjournment gavelling and the convention was still in session when Stevenson arrived on the platform.

Adlai made his statement to a wildly cheering convention, which then adjourned until noon the following day. Campaigning for delegate support in behalf of the various candidates went on frantically throughout the night. Kennedy, I think, was disappointed that he had not been tapped; so was Hubert Humphrey. Kefauver was delighted that he was having his chance, as he knew he did not stand high in Adlai's personal estimation and, therefore, probably would not have been "anointed."

Immediately following the adjournment of the convention, near midnight, in accordance with good Democratic tradition, most of the leaders of the party came by the Stevenson suite at the Blackstone Hotel to congratulate the party nominee and to negotiate and argue with each other about the vice presidency. I recall all too well greeting Mr. Sam and his young lieutenant, Lyndon Johnson, at the door as they entered, and in an awkward attempt to be polite, I said, "Mr. Sam, what do you think of developments?" He replied—in very explicit Texan vernacular, "It's hit the fan!" Mentally, I recalled my conversation with Hale Boggs. Rayburn knew his nomination as vice president could only come about through the customary process of "anointment" and that there would be no possible chance for it to occur in an open convention.

On the next day when the roll was called at noon for nominations for vice president, both Tennessee senators, Gore and Kefauver, were nominated, as well as Kennedy, Humphrey, Mayor Robert F. Wagner of New York, and Governors Collins and Hodges. Most of the delegates had been up almost the entire night soliciting votes and being solicited. They were too tense and excited, however, to realize how tired they really were. On the first ballot the five leading contenders scored as follows: Kefauver 483½, Kennedy 304, Gore 178, Wagner 162½, Humphrey 134½.

On this first ballot, still acting under the Chandler-imposed unit rule, Kentucky announced "the independent and unpredictable delegation from Kentucky, with a sincere expression of appreciation, votes 30 votes for Pitt Tyson Maner of Alabama." Maner had seconded Chandler's nomination for the presidency.

Then came the exciting roll call for the second ballot. At the conclusion of the initial calling of the roll and before the passed states were re-called the score stood: Kefauver 479½, Kennedy 559; and on this ballot Kentucky cast its 30 votes (again under the unit rule) for Senator Albert Gore. The clerk then called the roll of states that had passed. The excitement intensified. The ballot at this point was Kefauver 552½ and Kennedy 617½. Bedlam broke loose on the floor. Kentucky then came into the act and announced, "The delegation from Kentucky, which has consistently been with the minority all through the convention, enthusiastically joins the majority and changes its vote to John Kennedy." This brought Kennedy to 647½, only 39 short of a majority. But fate was to elude both Chandler and Kennedy. Senator Gore withdrew in favor of Kefauver, switching 32 votes. Oklahoma transfered 28 to Kefauver. Minnesota added 16½ votes it had previously cast for Humphrey. Then Missouri and Michigan changed to Kefauver. But South Carolina gave its 20 votes to Kennedy, Florida split its vote between the two contenders, Illinois cast 54½ of its votes for Kennedy. It was like a seesaw. Finally, in a breathless finish, Kefauver crossed the magic 687 vote mark and the second ballot result was announced: Kefauver 755½, Kennedy 589. Senator Kennedy quickly arose and made a brief but generous speech which he concluded by asking that the nomination of Kefauver be unanimous.

While the vice presidential nominating speeches were being made and while the vote-taking was in process, Stevenson was closeted quietly in his office writing his acceptance speech. Arthur Schlesinger, George Ball, Tom Finletter, and I were in various offices nearby with one eye on the television set while at the same time reviewing various passages of the acceptance speech and then returning them to Stevenson with suggestions. Finally, when the last vote was tabulated and Kefauver had achieved his exciting victory over Kennedy, I opened the door into Stevenson's office, walked in, closed the door and said, "Adlai, your running mate has been selected. It's Estes Kefauver." In disdain and disappointment, and with an unaccustomed expletive, he said, "That man cost us over a million dollars in the primaries!"

In truth, he had no real admiration for Kefauver and was unhappy that the convention had not chosen Kennedy or Humphrey, with either of whom he would have been vastly pleased. I think he thought Kefauver lacked intellectual depth and was something of a superficial showman. Also, he disliked Kefauver's style of campaigning for the presidency—certainly the coonskin cap had not elevated him in Stevenson's estimation. And—just possibly—he may have resented the fact that such a person had not only forced him into all of those primaries but had made some rather successful inroads at the beginning. I prepared a brief statement for Adlai to make to welcome his vice president to the ticket and experienced some trouble in keeping Adlai from downgrading the statement to the point where it would become publicly evident that he was unhappy about the choice. I would insert a good adjective and he would eliminate it. He would insert a negative one, and I would eliminate it. But finally an acceptable middle-ground kind of statement was issued. It was not as negative as he wanted it to be nor as affirmative as I wanted it to be, but it was moderately acceptable, and I would say no better than that.

I am afraid Estes Kefauver thought it was no better than that either, because when he came to Libertyville after the convention, and after first taking a very deliberate vacation, he entered Stevenson's home with head very erect, almost statue-like, looked calmly round the entrance hall, and rather deliberately went over and shook hands with a couple of secretaries and one or two of the staff people, then shook hands with me, then with one or two others and then, for the first time, acknowledged Adlai's presence and walked over and shook hands with him. He seemed very distant, willing to answer when spoken to but not very eager about it all. The relationship got better as the campaign went on, but it started out as close to an arctic freeze as anything I have seen.

Even though Kefauver got the nomination for vice president, Kennedy came out with colors flying. He had made a terrific race in the convention and had become a major figure in the party. His gracious acceptance of defeat and his active support of the ticket throughout the campaign earned him many enthusiastic and admiring adherents for the next convention.

Stevenson had worked hard for the first-ballot nomination and was the clear leader of the party. He was now ready to launch his second campaign against Eisenhower. Before the campaign began I was asked to join Tom Finletter and George Ball at Tom's house in New York for two days of brainstorming. Our purpose was to try to come up with the theme of the 1956 campaign—words to epitomize Adlai's philosophy and program, similar to what the New Deal had meant to Roosevelt and the Fair Deal to Truman. It was an interesting session as all three of us had worked closely with Adlai, both in the 1952 campaign and in the four years that followed, including the sessions of the Finletter group. Tom would write, and George would write, and I would write. Then we would meet together and exchange ideas. We would discard, throw away, and start again. Toward the end of the second day Adlai Stevenson joined us along with Bill Blair and Willard Wirtz (later secretary of labor under President Kennedy). Jointly we discussed the results of our sessions and each of us had certain suggestions to make.

My suggestion was "The New American Revolution," but with the caution that the word "Revolution" should probably be eliminated and some appropriate re-phrasing devised. The words seemed to me to connote the things that Stevenson had advocated and would expound in his speeches. In due course, after much discussion, Adlai agreed with the suggestion and followed the old adage, "When in doubt, cut." He shortened it to the simple phrase "The New America," which became the refrain in all of his major speeches in the 1956 campaign. And four years later, in 1960, it became Kennedy's "New Frontier." (It is interesting that President Reagan employed the phrase "A Second American Revolution" as descriptive of his objectives in his state of the union address at the outset of his second term.)

The volunteer organization again became an important part of the campaign and Adlai was fortunate in getting his old friend Barry Bingham, Sr., of Louisville to head it, with Jane Dick of Illinois as cochairman. It fell to my lot as coordinator of campaign divisions to launch various other special groups including scientists, conservationists, businessmen, and others. Henry H. Fowler (later secretary of the treasury) responded to my request to join me in bringing the Business for Stevenson group into activity. Even though Hubert Humphrey was quite disappointed that Stevenson had not asked him to run as his vice president (he told me that conversations with Stevenson had left him with the impression he would be asked), he was most helpful and cooperative throughout. I had known Hubert well for years. I first met him in Washington in the early forties while waiting in line at a White House reception. An eager, enthusiastic young man left his place in the line, ran up to me, and introduced himself, saying he had lost his first race for mayor of Minneapolis and that Bob Hannegan, the National Committee chairman, had suggested he talk to me as another young mayor about how I had won my race in Louisville. Our friendship continued in his later successful races, our work together in the ADA, his vice presidency under Johnson, and his run for the presidency against Nixon. He had a quick intelligence, human sensitivity, and political courage.

At one point during the 1956 campaign we were recording brief television programs on various policy issues and had asked Humphrey as a leader from the agricultural state of Minnesota to appear with Stevenson on farm policy. We were at the time out west. Adlai, Hubert, and I rode together out to the farm that had been selected as the proper backdrop for the program. Adlai usually professed to be more ignorant of any subject than he really was. It was part of his modesty and self-effacement, as well as a means of getting more information from the other person. On the way out to the location Adlai was saying, "Well, now, Hubert, let's see—we're going to talk about farm affairs." He brought up two or three aspects and then asked, "How do you propose we should do this?" Hubert immediately responded (he was never at a loss for words), "Well, Adlai, why don't we do this?" He then suggested that he and Adlai could each make certain comments. And Adlai said, "That sounds fine. Now on this next aspect (and he would mention another, such as price support, parity, or marketing of perishables), what's your suggestion?" And Hubert just as quickly had another proposal, not only quick of statement but sound in fact and principle. Not too many minutes later we got out of the car and walked over to the barn lot where the cameras were set up, and the conversation started. It proceeded exactly along the line that Hubert had suggested—the statement, the questions, the comments, the principles. It was a beautiful demonstration of quick and sensitive perception, vast knowledge, and excellent articulation. It was obvious that the two worked well together and it was easy to see why Adlai liked Hubert and felt so much at home with him.

Stevenson was reluctant to speak on a subject when he did not feel that he had the answer. I tried to convince him (sometimes with success, sometimes not) that in a campaign I did not believe the American people really expected a candidate to have all the answers, and in fact should be wary of one who said he did; that sometimes the best he could possibly do was to demonstrate that he knew the problem existed, that he had an understanding of the problem, and that he would devote his attention to the effort to achieve a solution.

Typically when Adlai gathered a group of experts on a particular issue he would meet with them at the outset, raise the question, and remain for the first part of the discussion. At the end of what often would be a very lengthy session he would receive either a verbal or a written report on the conclusions and choices. There is never a reason for a presidential candidate to be ill-informed, as the best experts in the land are almost invariably willing—in fact, honored—to respond (and as volunteers) to a request from one who may become the president of the United States.

One outstanding example of the benefit of Stevenson's 1956 race was his advocacy of an end to atomic bomb testing. Many told him that the issue was too complex to be understood in the frenzy of a campaign and that it would make him seem weak in his candidacy against a great general. "Can you imagine," some asked him, "Mayor Daley's Chicago precinct workers walking up and down the streets wearing sandwich boards imprinted in big type with 'Down with Strontium 90'?" So completely did Adlai believe in the issue, however, that he went forward with it and, while he did not win the election, the signing of the Test Ban Treaty by President Kennedy in 1963 can well be said to be the result of what Stevenson had launched in 1956. And so it was, also, with the issue of the draft. He was the first to propose the end of the draft and reliance on a volunteer army. Politically in 1956, it was a weak issue, but he believed it was important policy. And much later it became the law of the land. Again and again he was before his time, but the country was his heir.

Stevenson's reputation for indecision was due to his very careful and judicious nature. He always looked at both sides of every question to weigh the merits, pro and con. (When you do this it is surprising how little in life is either definitely black or definitely white.) In this respect Truman and Stevenson were very different people—Truman tended to see every problem in its simplest, most essential form, without all the refinements and gradations. And when he made a decision he did not look back.

I symphathized with Stevenson's concern on matters of policy and principle—but when this judicious approach carried over to procedural situations I once told him he should apply the "Oh Hell Doctrine" more often. I told him a story I heard in Washington at a cocktail reception of the American Law Institute, when a respected and learned senior judge of the United States Court of Appeals was commiserating with a new appointee to the bench, who was complaining about the many difficult cases which were awaiting his decision. He told the young judge that in some cases he would be greatly troubled, would first be convinced that the appellant was right, then that the appellee was right, then that there was genuine doubt as to which was right and that finally he would just have to throw up his hands in despair and say "Oh, hell, I'll decide it this way"—and he would find over the years that the "Oh Hell Doctrine" would be one of the most important doctrines in the law. But Adlai never accepted that doctrine.

Ever mindful of his sense of history, Adlai asked me to remain after a staff meeting late in the campaign. After the others had gone he looked at me, smiled, and said, "You know the one thing for which we are unprepared—is victory." He then recalled the fact that there was no precedent for the transition from the Republican to the Democratic party under the new and very different circumstances brought about by the Twentieth Amendment, which requires that the president take office on January 20, rather than on March 4, and which, even more significantly, provides for the Congress to take office on the 3rd of January—seventeen days before the inauguration.

Before the ratification of the amendment in 1933 (it became effective in October of that year) Congress did not come into session until months after the president's inauguration unless, as was frequently the case, the president himself called the Congress into a special session. A newly elected president, therefore, was able to wait until after his inauguration to make the final decisions as to his cabinet and to evolve and state his policies, since Congress did not convene until the president was ready for them to act.

Since the Twentieth Amendment, however, Congress waits impatiently from January 3 to January 20 for the new president to be inaugurated, to announce his cabinet, and to send his legislative program to the Hill, with the result that it is now imperative for a new president to be prepared to act at once, from the moment he takes the oath of office—and, in many statements and appointments, even from the very night of election day. All of this Governor Stevenson realized.

He asked me to research the problem and prepare for him by election day a full, confidential memorandum of all of the steps to be taken, from the moment the outcome of the president's election should be announced on election night through to the day of inauguration. He wanted to know all that should be done about the transition—what statements he should make, where he should set up his office in the interim, how he should handle appointments, when the first appointments should be made, which should be appointed first, how to arrange the transition with the outgoing administration, what to do about specific items of pending legislation, names that I would know he would want to consider for various posts in the new administration, and all of the other steps incident to the transition. This involved, as he knew it would, a complex consideration of timing, of personalities, of officials to be appointed, of legislation to be addressed, and of policies to be announced. The remainder of the campaign found me mainly at the Library of Congress deep in research. It was an engrossing undertaking. Although I dictated my document on the transition to my personal secretary at the campaign headquarters, most of my compatriots thought I was merely working on speeches. On election morning in Illinois, I delivered to Adlai the detailed volume, which I had entitled, "The Transition." When I handed it to him we both joshed about being a little superstitious over counting the chickens before they hatched and agreed that it should not be read until the election results were known.

The events of election night made that volume unnecessary. But once again Stevenson had been before his time. Four years later, in early August of 1960, the Brookings Institution telephoned me to request a copy of the volume, "The Transition," for their use as they formulated their report for what became the Eisenhower-Kennedy transition in January, 1961. Again, Stevenson helped prepare the way.

On the morning after the 1956 defeat those of us who had been active in the campaign gathered with Adlai for a group picture. It is a graphic demonstration of the saying that there is nothing so temporary as victory or defeat. Four years later everyone in the picture (except Finnegan, who had died) held some significant post: Adlai was ambassador to the United Nations, Newton Minow was chairman of the Federal Communications Commission, Clayton Fritchey was a syndicated columnist, Tom Finletter was ambassador to NATO, Bill Wirtz was secretary of labor, Matt McCloskey was ambassador to Ireland. Bill Blair was ambassador to the Philippines, Arthur Schlesinger was at the White House as assistant to President Kennedy, George Ball was under secretary of state, and I served as presidential envoy for the oil negotiations with Indonesia.

In the late spring of 1960 Senator Mike Monroney of Oklahoma was spearheading an effort to have Stevenson nominated a third time for the presidency. I told Adlai that I thought he could be nominated and that this time I thought he could win; but only if he were willing to seek it, and to call various friendly party leaders like Dave Lawrence, the influential governor of Pennsylvania, Jack Arvey of Illinois, respected national columnists, and other loyal friends to tell them of his willingness to run and ask for their support. Otherwise they would, one by one, yield to the persistent entreaties of the active candidates and become committed before the convention. In view of his unique situation, I felt that if he would do this affirmatively he could probably finesse the primaries he so detested and still obtain the nomination for a third time.

The morning after: Newton L. Minow, Clayton Fritchey, Thomas K. Finletter, Willard Wirtz, Matthew McCloskey, Adlai E. Stevenson, Wilson W. Wyatt, James A. Finnegan, William McCormick Blair, Arthur E. Schlesinger, George W. Ball

This, however, he was not willing to do. It was against his nature to seek the presidency. He always felt it was an office that should seek the man. He had not sought it in 1952. He entered the primaries in 1956 with great reluctance and although he carried them through successfully, he did so with considerable revulsion. Having been nominated twice, he felt that if he were to become president, the office must seek him and that it would be unbecoming for him, in the tradition of William Jennings Bryan, to ask others to support him for a third nomination. The result was that he kept himself active throughout the country as a significant public figure but would not make any overt move of any kind in the direction of seeking the nomination.

On the other hand, he was also unwilling to remove himself from the race or to support Jack Kennedy, who was organizing effectively for the nomination against the equally active campaign of Lyndon Johnson. On the 3rd of June, I received a telephone call from Jack Kennedy asking me to try to encourage Stevenson to support him. He was very polite and low key. He said, "Wilson, it would be wonderful if Adlai would support me and I thought I would call you and tell you how much I would appreciate it. You might make some comment to him." Stevenson's unwillingness to do so could be explained by the assumption—but it is only an assumption—that he harbored a private hope that the party might again turn to him as in 1952 in a draft nomination. After all, there were many people around the country who were advocating Stevenson for president again. Dr. Louis H. Bean, a leading political analyst and a favorite forecaster of the Democrats at the time, said publicly that his analysis showed Stevenson would defeat Nixon 54 to 46. Many were circulating petitions for Stevenson. But political leaders like David Lawrence of Pennsylvania felt a responsibility to their followers to put them behind an active candidate, and this Stevenson would not become.

On Monday, July 11, the first day of the Democratic convention in Los Angeles, a telegram was sent from Mrs. Roosevelt, Governor Lehman, Senator Monroney, Tom Finletter, and Senator John Carroll to every delegate urging Stevenson's nomination and saying "over 1,000,000 Americans have signed petitions to draft Stevenson."

Pursuant to my campaign pledge for abolishing the unit rule, our Kentucky delegation went to the convention for the first time in memory with each delegate free to act, although most of them were influenced by Earle Clements to support his close friend Lyndon Johnson. Had the unit rule, so customary in the past, been in effect, the entire delegation would have been bound to support Johnson and all of us would have been silenced from any other participation. A few were for Kennedy. John Breckinridge and I were for Stevenson—if he would run. Bert Combs was the chairman and I was the vice chairman of the delegation.

On Tuesday night, the eve of the presidential nominations, Senator Mike Monroney, George Ball, and several others reached a last-minute decision to launch the Stevenson candidacy and came to me to assist them. I felt it was forlorn, but was willing to help. I suggested that among the several people (including Hubert Humphrey) they had in mind for making the nomination, Gene McCarthy would be by all odds the best, as he was sensitive to Stevenson's political philosophy, a fluent orator and, like Kennedy, an Irish Catholic, (an important consideration since Kennedy was the leading contender). The decision was made and Senator McCarthy quickly agreed.

Mrs. Roosevelt was in attendance at the convention, but as a spectator, as she had not been elected a delegate or even an alternate from New York. She was anxious to see Stevenson nominated and thought he would make a great president. She was eager to do anything she could to help bring the nomination about. Unfortunately, however, since she was neither a delegate nor an alternate, she had no right, under the convention's rules, to seek the platform, to speak, or to make a nominating or even a seconding speech.

Reluctantly, I agreed to the importuning from my good friends George Ball and Senator Monroney to make the last seconding speech for Stevenson (two others were to be made by Governor Lehman and the lieutenant governor of California) with the understanding that I would then try to get recognition for Mrs. Roosevelt to speak in Stevenson's behalf. This was a very "iffy" undertaking. I conferred with Governor Leroy Collins of Florida, the chairman of the convention. In his very gentlemanly way he was understanding of my problem, but said there was no way in the world that Mrs. Roosevelt could be recognized, unless one of two things occurred: either she must become a delegate or alternate from New York by substitution and agreement in the New York delegation or I must obtain unanimous consent of the convention. We tried the first method but the Kennedy control of the New York delegation was absolute. No one was willing to give way for Mrs. Roosevelt, since the purpose was all too readily apparent.

This left as the only alternate course getting unanimous consent of the convention. Normally it is almost impossible to get a Democratic National Convention to agree to anything—absolutely anything—with unanimity. The Kennedy nomination seemed to be on a very fast course, and the Kennedy supporters in the convention were very enthusiastic, very loyal, and very efficiently organized. Interestingly, a great many of them were Stevenson supporters from 1956 and 1952.

When Stevenson first appeared on the convention floor with his Illinois delegation, he received an enthusiastic standing ovation both from delegates on the floor and from a huge crowd of Stevenson supporters in the gallery, who were loud and constant in voicing their Stevenson preference. This caused many to believe the convention might well nominate Stevenson. Certainly the Kennedy people would never have agreed to risking an Eleanor Roosevelt speech in his behalf. They felt nervously confident of a first ballot nomination, provided they could keep tight control. But many delegates were bound to Kennedy only for the first ballot and might well return to their first love, Stevenson, if the convention went to a second ballot.

I talked to Mrs. Roosevelt and she readily agreed to try my plan: at the end of my brief seconding speech, I would ask for unanimous consent of the convention for her to address the arena, and she would be immediately at hand, on the platform, to rise and respond. Her response would be a strong speech for Stevenson's nomination. There was obviously great risk in the plan as the request for unanimous consent could easily be shouted down—furthermore, all it would take would be a single objection. To try and fail would be a demonstration of weakness. The only chance to carry it forward would be split-second timing.

When Kentucky was reached on the roll call for nominations, as vice chairman of the delegation and unshackled from the traditional unit rule, I asked that Senator Eugene McCarthy from Minnesota be recognized to nominate Adlai Stevenson. He whipped the multitude in the Sports Arena into a frenzy (with the gallery adding mounting decibels) when he challenged: "If you are confident and believe in democracy, why don't you let this go to a second ballot when every delegate will be free to make a decision?" There was a roar of approval, and even cheers from the Texas delegation, which hoped that, on a second ballot, they might be able to get for Johnson the votes of some of the delegates who had been committed by the presidential primaries to a first-ballot support of Kennedy. McCarthy continued: "Do you have confidence in the people of the convention to make that choice? . . . Do not reject this man who made us all proud to be called Democrats. . . . Do not leave this prophet without honor in his own party—I submit to you Adlai Stevenson of Illinois."

Utter pandemonium broke loose. The *Los Angeles Examiner* carried boxcar headlines in letters two and a half inches tall: STEVENSON GETS BIGGEST OVATION. The *Examiner* said, "There were mighty demonstrations for all (Kennedy, Johnson, Symington and Stevenson), but by any standard the absolute roaring insanity turned loose by the placing of Stevenson's name in nomination topped them all and climaxed the nominating procedure."

After Chairman Leroy Collins finally brought the convention back to order, Governor Lehman, Lieutenant Governor Anderson, and I proceeded with our two-minute seconding speeches. Mrs. Roosevelt had agreed that she would be close by and able to mount the platform at the right moment. As the nominating procedure went forward, however, I saw Mrs. Roosevelt was still seated in the balcony. In due course, she left her seat and started making her way slowly—and it was like a royal procession, as people continually stopped to shake her hand and talk admiringly to her, and she continually stopped to give a polite acknowledgment to their greeting. She made it down to the first floor and then started walking toward the platform. By the time I was introduced to speak, she had still not reached the platform. I feared that if she were not immediately on hand where I could almost push her to the podium at the very instant that I asked for unanimous consent, there would be no chance to make the plan work. I concluded my speech:

"To achieve greatly, we must dare greatly—with a leader of courage and conviction. To surmount the obstacles on our way, we must rise to our fullest stature—with a leader of dignity and stature. To choose the way, we must turn to the greatest foresight—with a leader of vision and wisdom.

This is a time for greatness. This is a time for the very best that we have. This is a time for a leader all the world can trust. This is the time for Adlai E. Stevenson."

As I was beginning these words I was watching Mrs. Roosevelt intently. Finally, at long last, she neared the platform. As I finished my last sentence, she mounted the platform and was only a couple of feet away. I then turned to the chairman and said virtually in a single breath without pause—"I now ask for unanimous consent of the convention to hear the First Lady of the World, Mrs. Franklin Delano Roosevelt." I pulled Mrs. Roosevelt by the arm to the front of the podium and she waved and started speaking to a hushed auditorium. There was not a moment in between—not even a second. The plan succeeded—at least insofar as getting Mrs. Roosevelt to speak.

I well remember seeing Bobby Kennedy's face in the audience as he sat, crouched on the floor, near the front of the convention hall and I am sure that for a long time he did not forgive me. His face was tense as he watched Mrs. Roosevelt speak and saw the enthusiastic reaction of the convention. I am sure the Kennedy forces were convinced they had to win on the first ballot. On a second ballot many of their primary-committed delegates would be released from their commitment—and still more on a third ballot. But the Kennedy homework had

DEMOCRATIC NATIONAL CON
1960

A great lady speaks for Stevenson, Los Angeles, 1960

been well done, their organization was superb, and all of their votes remained firm.

With 761 necessary to nominate, Wyoming, at the very end of the roll call, cast its 15 votes that put Kennedy over the top. The final tally was 806 for Kennedy to Johnson's 409, Symington's 86, and Stevenson's 79½. It had all been very dramatic; there had even been some moments of hope; but the battle was over. On the next day, Johnson, in response to Kennedy's invitation, agreed to the vice presidency and was nominated by acclamation. Johnson told a group of us who met with him at the Governor's Mansion in Tennessee soon after the convention that although some of his closest advisers had urged him to reject the vice presidential nomination, he recalled that his fellow Texan John Nance Garner, and such American heroes as Franklin Delano Roosevelt and Thomas Jefferson, had run for the post, so who was he to turn it aside?

I agree with the widely held theory that had Stevenson been willing to renounce the possibility of a nomination earlier and to announce his support for Kennedy, he would probably have become secretary of state in the Kennedy cabinet. Instead, he became ambassador to the United Nations, and while this position is significant it had neither the challenge nor the potential of the post of secretary of state.

I felt so dismayed by all the thoughts of what might have been that I did not see Adlai on Thursday, the day following the Kennedy nomination. But on Friday I went to see him. Just before he was to leave his hotel suite and go to the convention to introduce Kennedy for his acceptance speech, I walked into his room. His sensitivity was such that he was obviously recalling the advice of several months before, when I told him that I thought there was no chance for him to be nominated unless he was willing to seek and organize the support of national leaders at an early stage. He looked up at me, smiled wanly and said, "Wilson, you were right"—just as though responding to the advice of the previous spring. That was the only discussion we ever had about the 1960 convention flurry. It had been an exciting moment, but it was over.

Many historians of the American political scene agree that Adlai Stevenson became the conscience of American politics. But why?

I first met the American historian, James MacGregor Burns (author of *The Lion and the Fox*, *Kennedy*, and *The Power to Lead*), soon after the second Stevenson presidential race in 1956. I had been told of his great admiration for Stevenson and had looked forward to our lunching together at Williams College. Almost instantly after our introduction he said, "Let's talk about Adlai Stevenson. The defeat in 1956 I understand, but 1952 I am not prepared to concede." And that was the rapture with which Stevenson was generally regarded. For many reasons the 1956 run did not have the verve and the inspiration of 1952—but even in the second campaign he lit fires that were to burn brightly into later years.

Many attribute the Stevenson acclaim to the beauty and clarity of his speeches, the poetry of his prose. In truth he was a poet—and political poets are a rare species. That group does not include Reagan, or Ford, or Nixon, or Johnson, or Eisenhower, or even Truman, even though Republicans and Democrats alike now pay tribute to that embattled warrior as one of our great presidents. There was poetry, however, in some of our presidents—in Kennedy, who came after Stevenson, and in Franklin Roosevelt, Woodrow Wilson, and Abraham Lincoln who went before.

Rare was the person who listened without admiration and pleasure as he heard Stevenson speak. And his speeches read as well as they listen. They are beautiful. His political concepts were sublimated in the charm of expression in a way that has rarely been achieved in American politics.

The charge was often made that he talked over the heads of the people, but I have yet to hear anyone complain that he did not understand what was said. It was a popular myth, repeated by people about *other* people. It was, I believe, merely an obscure way of saying that Stevenson certainly did not talk like other political figures. And he certainly did not.

The grace of his language enabled him to speak bitter truths without sounding bitter, to give candid criticism without seeming to criticize or quibble, and to call a spade a spade without becoming too earthy. His speeches will be textbook examples of written charm long after the issues he discussed have become moot.

The poetry of his welcoming address at the Stockyards in Chicago so captivated and enchanted the assembled delegates that it became almost impossible for him to avoid the nomination he had not sought. And his acceptance speech a few days later so revived and inspired a weary convention that a November victory suddenly seemed possible.

There is no question that his mellifluous phrases and his poetic prose contributed to the understanding of his ideas, the acceptance of his reasoning, the inspiration for a better land, and the willingness, even the desire, of people everywhere to hear more from this political philosopher. He was a sort of political Walt Whitman or Carl Sandburg singing his song of America. And while a majority of Americans did not vote for him, all Americans listened happily to his song. Many a Republican said he wished he could have voted for Stevenson *in addition* to Eisenhower—there were thousands of Eisenhower Stevensonians.

But it was much more than eloquence that caused Stevenson to become the conscience of American politics. Just as it was with Wilson, and with Lincoln. His sense of integrity—integrity in all things—was pervasive, universal. He was not given to the normal compromises that are made even by very honest leaders. Often when it would have been (to most people at least) completely honorable to postpone to a more appropriate time the announcement of a particular position, or to be silent, he would nevertheless enunciate his stand and do it without ambiguity—in order to be certain that his postponement or silence did not in any way mislead. Admittedly this did not always advance his candidacy; often it hurt his own cause. His was an almost rigid and unbending integrity. He had a deeply ingrained sense of dedication to the public interest. You might say it was in the blood by inheritance from his Kentucky-born grandfather, the first Adlai E. Stevenson, who was Cleveland's vice president, and by political inheritance from Lincoln and Wilson. His conviction that he had work to finish as the governor of Illinois was one of the reasons for his disinclination to run in 1952. But once nominated he did all in his power to win—provided he could win while flying his own flag.

Stevenson abhorred demagoguery in all of its forms. Korea was a major issue in the 1952 election. From the outset Stevenson was convinced that, if elected, he should go to Korea immediately thereafter in order to help by his presence in bringing the conflict to an end. But despite the fact that this had been his plan for a long time he was unwilling to say so in the campaign for fear it would seem like an act of demagoguery. Also, his sense of dedication to the public interest kept him from making the comment as he feared that it might in some way weaken the hand of President Truman meantime, or interfere with the conduct of foreign policy during the campaign. But in view of all this his reaction was one of keen disappointment in Eisenhower when toward the end of the campaign Eisenhower made the dramatic announcement, "I shall personally go to Korea."

I think it was evident to everyone that Adlai Stevenson undertook to give serious answers to the difficult and complex questions of the day and to state the hard truths even when they seemed unpleasant. He did indeed "talk sense to the American people." That phrase, in fact, summarized his approach to the entire campaign. He had respect for the individual. He brushed off simplistic responses. When there were no simple answers to complex questions he said so, and said so very frankly. He even shied away from three-point or five-point or ten-point programs for fear the very categorization of points would indicate that the answer was clearer and simpler than he, in fact, thought.

Adlai was not only a person of conviction but a leader who had the courage to state his conviction, and to say it directly to an audience where his conviction, though at times completely contrary to theirs, was in his opinion important in their consideration. He made a point of saying the same thing in all parts of the country. When he had serious statements about civil rights, and minorities, and voting rights, it was important to him that he speak these truths in the South—and not just in the North, or the West or the East. So his civil rights speeches were delivered in Richmond and Atlanta. Just as he had done with the tidelands oil issue in speaking on it clearly in Louisiana and in Texas, so also he lectured a labor audience in Detroit's Cadillac Square on Labor Day, and the American Legion at their national convention on the true meaning of real patriotism.

Not only did he have the courage to speak out directly, but at times he even leaned over backwards to make sure that he did not mislead. I shall never forget his sense of deep disappointment that General Eisenhower had failed to defend his mentor and superior, General George Marshall, when he had been in the presence of Senator Joe McCarthy (a cruel critic of Marshall) in Wisconsin. On the contrary, Adlai had the courage to give challenge to Joe McCarthy long before McCarthyism was unveiled to the general public as the fraud that it was, long before McCarthyism became a word of anathema in our political lexicon.

Stevenson was a very modest man. His concern as to whether he was the one qualified to run for the office of president was one of the reasons for his reluctance in 1952. His modesty also contributed to his reputation for indecision, an appearance that arose from his modest concern as to the rightness of his own opinion.

He became a hero in defeat. He had indeed become the Conscience of American Politics. It was clear that Adlai Stevenson had brought a measure of greatness to the twentieth century. He had, in truth, elevated and inspired through his part in the political dialogue. His was the eloquent voice of conscience as he gave expression to the aspirations of man. His was the integrity that raised the moral tone of our country. His was the wit and charm and wisdom that caused him to be called the most civilized American since Benjamin Franklin. His was the idealism that Woodrow Wilson would have smiled upon with warm and admiring approval. His was the buoyant hope that spoke with clear vision of the "revolution of rising expectations."

His was the faith that would admit of no defeat in the upward struggle of mankind toward the dawn of a better world and toward the time when our swords might be turned into plowshares and man might be at peace. His was the quality that has inspired youth to turn, with dedication, to the honorable calling of public service.

This was the time for Adlai Stevenson. Not in the formal toga of the office of the presidency, but in a more enduring toga of the spirit, in giving leadership to the aspirations of free men everywhere.

Chapter 7

Kentucky's Quiet Revolution

"Land of Tomorrow" may well be the poetic meaning of the Indian word from which Kentucky derives its name, but it does little to connote the immediacy, the persistence, the emotion, and the utter unendingness of its political bent. We ascribe the quality of our horses and our bourbon to mundane specifics like limestone and water, but to what can we ascribe our innate, perennial, and preemptive fascination with the art of politics? Perhaps it has its origin in the independent spirit of the early Kentucky pioneer, or in the sometime description of our land as "the dark and bloody ground," intertwined somehow with Toynbee's theory of challenge and response. Or, it may be sheer chance that the chromosomes of history wove themselves together in such a distinct chain. But distinct it is—pervasive and infinite. No one initiated to politics in Kentucky will find himself a stranger to politics in any other state or any other country—ours embraces it all, the complete spectrum. In Kentucky, politics is a vocation for some, but at least an avocation for almost everyone. The moment a governor is elected the next campaign begins. It is often noted that, unlike any other state, we have an election every year, but that is an understatement—we are exposed to some aspect of future elections on almost as regular a routine as the rising and setting of the sun.

And so it was—in fact, a little more so—as Happy Chandler's second term as governor was reaching the midway point in the winter of 1957-58. From the day of Happy's election it was certain that his lieutenant governor, Harry Lee Waterfield, would be the candidate for succession in the Chandler faction. Since the early 1930s Kentucky had been divided politically (at least in the Democratic party, which is dominant in state politics) into two warring factions—the Chandler faction and the Rhea-Clements faction. There seemed no in-between. It was very natural, then, considering it was Kentucky, that serious concern was being given to the governor's election of November 1959 a good two years in advance. Many names were being advanced. Bert Combs had carried the Clements banner against Chandler in 1955 but had lost to Happy in the primary. In many ways he seemed the natural opponent for Waterfield in 1959, in view of the name recognition gained from his million-dollar anti-Chandler campaign of 1955, but many believed that he would not run. Many other names were propelled into the discussion—the faction leader Earle Clements, Keen Johnson, John Y. Brown, Sr., Adron Doran, Guthrie F. Crowe, Smith Broadbent, Foster Ockerman, Joe Leary, Rumsey Taylor, Jo Ferguson, Bert VanArsdale, and others.

An article in the *Sun Democrat* of Paducah put forward my name. The anti-Chandler faction was actively seeking candidates but there was no heir apparent. Dick Moloney, a state senator from Lexington, and some of his allies over the state had been urging me to give the race serious consideration. Dick was very persuasive with me as he had established a reputation for his canny and sagacious political judgment. The fact that the idea of my candidacy originated out in the state rather than in Louisville greatly increased my interest. Dick's suggestion found ready acceptance by the Louisville political powers of Lennie McLaughlin, Johnny Crimmins, and McKay Reed, as well as the local elected Democratic officeholders. In the course of considering the race I had a long, friendly meeting with Bert Combs and ended the session in the belief that he was not going to make the race again. At Dick's urging I started sounding out county seats. I went to Bardstown, Munfordville, and Bowling Green; then in Western Kentucky to Murray, Benton, Russellville, and Hopkinsville; and then swung back toward Louisville through Smithland, Morganfield, Clay, and Elizabethtown. I counselled again with Senator Moloney and the Louisville leaders as well as with my long-time friend Barry Bingham. Then I made another swing through Taylor, Green, and Adair counties and to Carrollton to talk with Lyter Donaldson. I confered with dozens of Democratic leaders by telephone. Finally, I made my decision and, on April 9, I announced for governor.

In the hope that I might become a nonfaction candidate, I stated in my announcement "I have no grudge to settle, no score to even, no enemies to punish." But even before my announcement Happy opened up with a typical Chandler barrage, "Just wait 'til I tell the country boys that Ole Wilson wears ankle blankets." Clements and some of the other anti-Chandler leaders continued to urge Combs to enter the race on the ground that he carried the anti-Chandler trademark of the prior campaign. The situation was becoming murky. Before the month was over, and completely contrary to my expectation, Combs announced he would make his second try for the nomination and that Clements again would support him, a statement Clements soon confirmed. Though we then became competitors, our mutual friendliness was indicated by his statement and mine in response to reporters when he announced. Combs stated, "I would say Wilson's a very outstanding citizen of Kentucky and he is my personal friend", and that he was not running "against Wyatt." I said about Combs, "I have great respect for him. . . . He is an awfully nice fellow."

Typical of the press and political comment across the state was a headline in the *Greenup News*, "Anti-Chandler Leaders Are Confused As Wyatt, Combs Enter Gubernatorial Primary." One by one the others named as potential candidates dropped out, and it settled down to a three-man race.

Had I known Bert was going to make the race again, I probably would not have entered in the first place. Had he known he was going to do so when I talked with him he probably would have told me. But events had moved rapidly and by now many people all over the state had become committed. It was too late for either of us to turn back. Lawrence Wetherby and Keen Johnson, both former governors, were supporting me; Earle Clements, another former governor, was the active maestro behind Combs. His supporters and mine were political friends. Fred Tucker, an innovative and indefatigable partisan of mine, organized the Young Kentuckians for Wyatt and we started winning polls on the various college campuses. Then Combs won a poll in Owensboro, and so it went. Both of us were making the rounds of Kentucky. As I was the newcomer to state politics, I felt a greater need to visit every one of Kentucky's 120 counties, not once but twice, and several populous counties many times. In one way, Happy was most helpful to me—though quite unintentionally. His constant ridicule of me as a "city dude" from Louisville who would have no interest in the rest of Kentucky put a special burden on me. He was rollicking his crowds with the charge that I wore spats in the city while ankle blankets were only for horses in the country, and then he would wave in the air a pair of fur-lined spats and say something like "wait 'til we get Ole Ankle Blankets out on the plowed ground." I was never privileged to see this show but Happy has always been a great showman and I am sure I would have been laughing too if I had been in the crowd.

So how do you answer such a ridiculous charge? It would sound mighty prim just to make the plain, matter-of-fact statement that I really didn't wear spats. Such a denial in a serious race for governor would merely have accentuated the ridiculous. So what to do? Happy was making a regular statewide chautauqua show out of his "ankle blankets" antics. It had to be dealt with. I reached the conclusion that there was only one solution—to go to every single city and town and crossroads in the state in an intensive, personal campaign and to shake hands with every voter I could possibly meet, from sunup to sundown, and later still as long as people were stirring. I found that Happy had really prepared the way for me. After hearing him repeatedly, most of the people rather assumed I would not be coming "out onto plowed ground" but would campaign only through mass media from Louisville. Consequently, as I walked up and down the main streets of Kentucky, and in the stores, the banks, the supermarkets, and the stockyards of the state, introducing myself, shaking hands, and asking each one for his support, I encountered literally thousands of people who one by one would respond, "Well, if it isn't ole Ankle Blankets. I didn't think you'd come to see us." The surprise of the visit gave me a double dividend. Many would even take a yank at my trouser leg and exclaim, "Why you don't wear ankle blankets after all!"

I grew very comfortable with the ankle blankets nickname. It had become almost a warm and friendly salutation. Long after the campaign was over Harry Davis, a close friend of Happy's, presented me with the fur-lined ankle blankets Happy had waved from the hustings and I retain them to this day as a treasured memento of the many, many weeks of 1958 when I made a personal tour of all of Kentucky and met, individually—if only for a handshake and a word of greeting—over 250,000 fellow Kentuckians. I know the figure is accurate because I started numbering my campaign cards early in the campaign and by the time the campaign was over I had crossed the quarter-million mark. Typically, the campaign day would begin in the dark before breakfast with a visit to a plant gate to greet the incoming shift, would continue with street campaigning, a speech or two or three along the way, an afternoon shift at another factory, and visits to the nearest supermarkets.

A memento of the 1959 campaign

Kentuckians are very kind to candidates who come to see them. The campaign gave me an opportunity I'd never had before, to go all over the state—literally all over. I remember one of the hardest— physically hardest—days in the primary when under the guidance of my friends Jim Stephenson, John Paul Runyon, and their loyal cohorts in Pike County, that huge area in the eastern Kentucky mountains, I campaigned "up Pond Creek" where the houses stretch for miles and are too far separated for a candidate on foot. The fatigue at the end of the day was not from walking or from handshaking but from getting in and out of the car as I moved from house to house, stretched unendingly along the meanders of Pond Creek. But it gave me a real affection for the people of Pond Creek and a sense of the great size of Pike County. From childhood I had always been intrigued by the eastern and western tips of Kentucky as I would ponder the Kentucky map. So one day in Pike County I went to the extreme eastern corner, where Kentucky joins Virginia and West Virginia. There I met Ira Blankenship, the proprietor of the store at the end of the road. His precinct did marvelously! No candidate for governor had ever been there before. And later, in Western Kentucky, I visited Madrid Bend, that tip of Kentucky created by the 1811-12 earthquake of the Madrid Fault, and separated from the rest of the state by the contortion of the Mississippi River. As an alternative to twice crossing the Mississippi and traversing a portion of Missouri, we had to drive down into Tennessee and then back into Kentucky's Madrid Bend to meet Alfred Stepp, the operator of a fine farm in the Bend. And that precinct did equally well!

It was—all of it—much more interesting than a trip to Europe. People were so friendly and so hospitable. Almost every day I would issue, particularly for the local media, a statement of some position on state government. One of my earliest was that economic development would be a prime purpose if I were elected, that we needed to provide attractive employment to offset the "brain drain" since "Kentucky is losing many of our fine young people to other states." These daily statements dealt with education, the abolition of the traditional unit rule for Kentucky's delegation to presidential conventions (a rule that bound every delegate to the candidate favored by the majority), agriculture, research, highways, tourism, the park system, voting machines, health and hospitals, taxation—the entire gamut of state government. I would meet the editor of the local paper, speak over the local radio stations, confer with the local county and city officials, and greet all of the employees of the banks and stores along the way. It was a complete reversal of my whole way of life as I was, in fact, a corporation lawyer from Louisville, rather reserved, and not accustomed to shaking hands with every person I met and asking him or her for support. But it was actually fun from the very first day, much (very frankly) to my own surprise. Had Happy not called me "ole Ankle Blankets" and a "city slicker" I probably would never have done it and I would have missed one of the greatest experiences of my life.

Early in the campaign my wife Anne joined me one day in driving to Mt. Olivet, the county seat of Kentucky's smallest county, Robertson. As I started around the town square from store to store I suggested she might like to do the same thing and we could meet midway. She

said "Oh, I couldn't do that—it would be so embarrassing." Nevertheless, when I walked into a store about an hour later the owner
smiled, took one of my campaign cards down from his cash register and
said, "Are you the one that lady was asking me to vote for? Your wife
beat you here." Sure enough, Anne had worked up her courage and
launched forth. She took an active part in many aspects of the campaign
and often was invited to meet with the various women's organizations
over the state. She was by no means a stranger to politics as she had
been a very active partner when I was mayor of Louisville and had
participated in the Washington swirl when I served under Truman in
the housing post. The *Kentucky Irish-American,* well known for its
political perspicacity, wrote in midsummer 1958, "Everyone agreed
Wyatt's smartest move had been taking along Mrs. Wyatt." And John
Ed Pearce in a *Courier-Journal* piece wrote, "In his wife, Anne Wyatt,
he has the perfect politician's wife—attractive, intelligent, tireless and,
as Caesar's wife must always be, above reproach."

By July Ed Paxton's column in the *Sun Democrat* carried the
headline "Primary Will Be a Horse Race." This typified a growing
body of opinion. The following week some 350 party leaders from all
over the state gathered for a luncheon at the Kentucky Hotel in open
support of my candidacy. Included were many of Earle Clements' old
allies—Golladay LaMotte, Rumsey Taylor, Ben Adams, Tyler Mun-
ford, Roscoe Murray, B.T. Moynihan, Thaxter Sims, and, of course,
Dick Moloney who had so early engaged my interest. Dr. Robert
Martin had become Combs' campaign chairman and J. David Francis
of Bowling Green had become mine. Dick Moloney was my state
organization chairman, Ed Farris my executive secretary and Mack
Sisk my publicity director. Things were well under way. By October
9 I had completed at least one visit to each of Kentucky's 120 counties
and on the 23rd I passed out my 125,000th campaign card in Owensboro.

There was no statewide race in the November election of 1958, but
the Democratic congressional candidates swept Kentucky. In fact,
Frank Burke upset the Republicans by recapturing the Jefferson County
seat in Congress from the three-termer John Robsion, making it
Democratic, seven out of eight, in the Kentucky representation in
Washington. My state organization was announced in November and
my headquarters opened at the Kentucky Hotel in Louisville in early
December. Until then my work had been almost entirely out in the
state. Street campaigning in Louisville was then rather unusual in a

governor's race but I decided that if it was good practice generally it should be good in Louisville as well, I started visiting not only the factories but the downtown stores and banks and the many Louisville supermarkets.

One thing was increasingly evident: regardless of how much progress I thought I was making, or how much progress Combs thought he was making, both of us were continually asked this question: "Why don't the two of you join forces, one run for governor, the other for lieutenant governor—either one for either place, but don't lose by dividing your strength." Some preferred Combs for governor, others preferred me, but everyone seemed to be getting more and more worried about losing to the Chandler forces in a three-man race. The Paducah paper wrote, "If the Democratic primary remains a three-man race the chances of either Combs or Wyatt winding up in the Executive Mansion are slim."

On one occasion Bert and I met in Cincinnati to discuss the race. We agreed on practically everything except who should run for governor. Various polls were taken. I won some, Bert won some. It was proposed that a statewide poll be taken and that both of us agree to abide by the result. I countered that since I was the newcomer to the state political picture, two polls should be taken, one then and the other ninety days later to determine the trend. This was unacceptable. I then called on Chandler to call a special session to enact a run-off primary, the very process by which he had first become governor. Happy saw no wisdom in the suggestion this time.

Then a poll was taken which showed Waterfield winning over both of us in a divided race, but with Combs and me having a comfortable lead over the Chandler opposition if our forces were somehow joined. We were running out of time. I think nearly everyone conceded that I would have a commanding majority in the Third District (Louisville and Jefferson County) and that Combs would carry Eastern Kentucky, but what about the rest of the state? As Bert was making his second statewide campaign for the Democratic nomination, each time as the Clements anti-Chandler man, it was quite possible that he may have had more support than I did in early 1959, but I was banking on winning, not in January, but in May, and I felt it was both possible and likely.

When Paul Jordan, for the Associated Press, put ten questions to Combs and me, in separate interviews for a lead article about the possibility of merging our forces, both of us agreed that our adherents would support whichever won the primary. Against this background I reached a difficult decision—that the time had come for me to compel a merger. It was clear one could not be negotiated. On the 19th of January I initiated a telephone call to Earle Clements in Washington and told him I thought he should meet me in Louisville that night. Without asking any questions he said he would catch the next plane.

All sessions with Earle are lengthy; this one was especially so. We met just before midnight at the Standiford Airport Motel, and our conversations continued until eight the next morning. Obviously, I would have preferred to be the nominee but I felt it was equally clear that the Paducah *Sun Democrat* was right and that neither Combs nor I would be the nominee if the three-man race were permitted to continue. Oh, there was the lingering hope that somehow the next four months might make me the winner, but logic dictated that merger would produce an almost certain victory and that continued division would result in the great, the almost overwhelming likelihood of a Chandler-Waterfield victory. There was one way to compel a merger— make an offer that could not be refused: I would be willing to run for lieutenant governor jointly with Combs if the principles on which I had been campaigning would be fully embraced by Combs. Because of Clements' posture in the Combs campaign of 1955 and again in 1959 and as the leader of the anti-Chandler faction, I felt he would have the authority to speak for Combs. I was convinced that, to be completely effective, the merger should be virtually instantaneous and not weakened or perhaps frittered away by rumors and delay. It should be announced as a fait accompli. I felt a strong obligation to the people who had so loyally supported me at considerable political risk to themselves. A further consideration was that our campaign should be run as a completely fused team—that the Combs campaign chairman and my campaign chairman should become the equal cochairmen of the merged effort, and that the same policy should be immediately effected in every county. I further stipulated that no punitive measures would be taken against leaders who had supported me, but that they would receive equal treatment as supporters of the joint team. In turn, I agreed to campaign just as actively for the team as I had been campaigning for myself, and as evidence of the fact that it was a real merger of our total effort I agreed that I would work full-time in Frankfort as lieutenant governor, and not limit myself to the one constitutional duty of presiding over the Senate. We decided this could best be accomplished in a fruitful way by my handling the various phases of the work of

Wilson Wyatt and Bert Combs with former governors Keen Johnson, Earle C. Clements, and Lawrence W. Wetherby

economic development on which I had placed such great emphasis in my campaign. Thus, I would become a working partner in the administration. It was further evidence of the unusual nature of the merger that I would serve as Democratic national committeeman for Kentucky, a post customarily held by the governor.

We also agreed to try to work out a full ticket so that we might run as a complete team. For example, I stipulated that John Breckinridge, a great Kentucky name and a person of unquestioned integrity, should be our candidate for attorney general.

After returning home for a three-hour nap I made various telephone calls to explain to my cohorts the decision I had made and the announcement I was about to make. A second meeting was held in the afternoon, this one with Bert Combs, Earle Clements, Bob Martin, Dave Francis, Dick Moloney and me—from 4:30 until 10:00 p.m. We prepared our statement and made the public announcement. It was a political bombshell. Typical of the banner headlines across the front pages of Kentucky's newspapers on the following day was that of the *Glasgow Daily Times*: "Combs and Wyatt Team Up in Governor's Race." On the other hand, the Chandler paper in Versailles reported the merger in a somewhat quieter fashion and captioned their article, "Courier-Journal Candidate Withdraws." The *Louisville Times* featured the merger with an eight-column streamer. On its front page it stated, "Wyatt agreed to run with Combs 'to bring unity to the Democratic Party,' Combs agreed to accept in its entirety the platform and program on which Wyatt has been campaigning since last April 9." The article continued, "The new alliance ends the impasse which has divided the anti-Chandler bloc for nearly a year. The development casts the primary in an entirely new perspective. Heretofore Waterfield has been the favorite to win the primary election on May 26. However, a public opinion poll taken in December—and which was one factor in Wyatt's decision today—showed that between them Combs and Wyatt had a clear majority of all the decided votes."

Combs made a very generous statement. "I find it hard to express the pride, gratitude and deep satisfaction that I feel in accepting Mr. Wyatt's magnaminous offer to join forces with me. Never in the political history of Kentucky has there been a more unselfish action, and I know that the people of Kentucky share my sincere gratitude to this outstanding Kentuckian who has put aside personal ambition in the interest of the welfare of this State. . . . It is a pleasure to join with him in the statement of principles which he has enunciated."

As part of the announcement of merger I emphasized that "far more important than position or pride are the principles which caused me to enter this race in the first place. These principles must triumph if Kentucky is to go forward. In the interest of complete harmony among anti-Chandler Democrats, I have therefore offered to combine forces with Bert Combs on the basis of these principles and to run with him as a team. I have expressed my willingness to be a candidate for Lt. Governor. My agreement to run with Judge Combs was conditioned upon acceptance of the program which I have proposed for Kentucky throughout the campaign. This program has been enthusiastically endorsed by Judge Combs and will constitute the guidelines and principles of our joint effort. I want to express my appreciation to my many friends and co-workers who have been supporting me. I know they will understand this decision and I urge them to join with me."

We announced that we were completely agreed on our program:

• Major new economic development program to bring new businesses to Kentucky and to expand existing businesses

• Complete civil service program for state employees

• Elimination of the historic practice of the 2 percent assessment on employees for political campaigns

• Home rule for local government

• Major election reforms (voting machines in every county, a registration and purgation law, and a modern, absentee voter law)

• Elimination of "sleepers" (nonproductive workers) from the state payroll

• Abolition of the unit rule for Kentucky delegations to national conventions so as to free delegates to support any presidential candidate

• Independence of the judiciary

• Independence of the General Assembly

• Tourism promotion

• Use of regional compacts with neighboring states for interstate cooperation

• Close cooperation with the Kentucky Congressional delegation

• Abolition of various wasteful practices then in effect in state government (advisory highway commissioners and the Court of Claims)

• Increased salaries for public school teachers, expanded Foundation Program, and building of major college facilities

• Roads to be built when needed and where needed and four years out of four, not merely announced in the last year for political purposes

• Expanded agricultural programs for new sources of income, research and new markets

Five of the Democratic congressmen immediately expressed themselves as elated with the Combs-Wyatt merger. State Senator Cassius M. Clay, John Breckinridge, and several others who had been seeking the lieutenant governor's post announced their support of the Combs-Wyatt merger and withdrew from the race. The *Sun Democrat* carried an editorial captioned "Service Above Self." The Hopkinsville New Era gave their story the headline "Great Step for Kentucky." The AFL-CIO's Committee on Political Education (COPE) gave the merger labor's endorsement.

From that day the bandwagon was rolling. All of the separate county organizations were merged as a Combs-Wyatt team. The local

The Wyatts, with Wilson Wyatt, Jr. and daughters Nancy K. and Mary Anne, on the campaign trail

Combs chairmen and the local Wyatt chairmen became the Combs-Wyatt cochairmen. The entire campaign was reorganized and run as a joint team effort.

Finally, the four remaining candidates for lieutenant governor—John Y. Brown, Sr., J.B. Wells, Violet Kilgore, and Ben J. Butler—tried unsuccessfully to agree on a single candidate to oppose me, but the attempt was unsuccessful and they all continued in the race.

May 26, Primary Day, was a day of triumph. Again, there were eight-column headlines, this time heralding the "Combs-Wyatt Landslide."

The outcome of the primary was convincing proof of the need for the merger. Under the *Courier-Journal* banner headline: "Combs Wins on Jefferson Margin; Race Stand-off Elsewhere in State," the Hugh Morris story stated "Bert T. Combs captured the Democratic nomination for Governor on the strength of the vote in Louisville and Jefferson County. Outside Jefferson County the race against Harry Lee Waterfield was a virtual stand-off." Under the *Louisville Times* heading "Combs Sweeps in on Big City Vote; It's a Landslide Victory for Wyatt," the Richard Harwood story stated "Louisville's Wilson Wyatt, Combs' running mate since the merger of their candidacies for Governor in January, has won the Lt. Governor nomination in a landslide. The liberal former Mayor and federal Housing Administrator has swept every district in Kentucky and lost only five of the 120 counties and seems headed for the biggest plurality ever given a Democratic primary candidate." The final tally in my home county of Jefferson gave Combs a majority of 29,139 and me, as a hometown boy, a majority of 46,698. The final tally in the state as a whole gave Combs a majority of 33,001 and me a plurality over my four opponents of 191,000. Of course, I had benefited from the division of my opposition among four candidates, just as Waterfield would doubtless have benefited had there been no merger.

Those supporters of mine who had been disappointed by my concession in the merger were soothed by comments like that in the *Courier-Journal* editorial, "Ankle Blankets Did Right Well . . . He has won the nomination for the office of Lt. Governor by the largest margin ever given a candidate by Kentucky voters."

Chandler continued his opposition after the primary. He called Combs "a dunce" and the "biggest liar in politics" and lambasted me as "the worst Mayor Louisville ever had" and as the first chairman of the Americans for Democratic Action.

Combs and I spent the summer months getting our program in readiness for what we confidently expected would be a November victory. Nevertheless, we campaigned just as actively in the fall as if it were a close election, for we believed a major victory would increase the chances of moving our program into reality. During the lull of August, Combs and I made learning trips to North Carolina, Wisconsin, and Pennsylvania to meet with the governors of those states and examine some of the very forward-looking programs that showed promise for adapation to Kentucky. We also met, for example, with civil service experts to evaluate the kind of program we hoped to institute in Kentucky government after the election.

At last came election day, the day for which we had spent two years in solid campaigning and preparation. It had been without a doubt the longest and certainly among the most spirited campaigns in the history of Kentucky politics. The outcome was everything we could have hoped for, and then some. Combs won the governorship over John Robsion by a majority of 180,093—the highest ever given any governor; and I received an all-time record majority of 191,746 over my opponent Pleas Mobley. The landslide proportions of the victory put us well on the way toward enactment of our program.

In view of Happy's two years of spirited opposition to both Combs and me and our vigorous campaign against the continuance of the practices of the Chandler administration (practices that were in the main the very antithesis of our announced program), Happy's statement about our landslide victory was nothing less than intriguing: "It looks like an overwhelming approval of what we have given the people." Modestly he accepted our victory as a great tribute to his administration.

December 8—the day of our inauguration—was a day of celebration but also a day of dedication to the task of fulfillment of our extensive campaign program for "a better Kentucky." In recognition of the unusual nature of our relationship, the new lieutenant governor, contrary to tradition, was scheduled to speak as well as the new governor. Happy Chandler, as the outgoing governor, was of course seated on the platform. I started my public remarks by turning toward him and saying, "Happy, this is a report from Ankle Blankets on the condition of the plowed ground." He took the ribbing as a compliment and joined the roar of the crowd. I stated what I believed to be our mission: "We stand here today because our party has triumphed, but we go from here not as partisans. It is our purpose to work for all Kentuckians, not just some Kentuckians. . . . We stand here today because of a great victory—but it was a victory of principles, not of people."

Those December days were filled to the brim in preparation for the legislative session scheduled for January. We spent several days in the pre-General Assembly meetings at Kentucky Dam Village and worked with a most cooperative legislature. In addition, in order to attempt a limited constitutional convention, Bert called a special session, which started December 22 and adjourned on the 30th. I had a reunion with my friend Adlai Stevenson, who was visiting the Andersons in Louisville for the Christmas holidays, attended candlelight services at the Second Presbyterian Church with my wife and children on Christmas Eve, and enjoyed a family Christmas Day at my Louisville home, joined by my ninety-year-old mother. Anne and I arrived at the Old

Inauguration day, 1959, in Frankfort

Governor's Mansion (the Frankfort residence of the lieutenant governor) late on the night of the 28th and prepared for my first economic development dinner with thirty guests on the following night.

In addition to our well laid plans, Bert and I were benefited by a remarkable turn of fate on election day—the approval of the veterans bonus amendment to the Kentucky Constitution. In previous sessions the legislature had yielded to pressure to propose a bonus for the veterans of World War II. The drafters of the proposal had undertaken to meet the pressure by requiring an amendment to the constitution (something in itself very difficult to achieve) and by invoking as the means of payment the enactment of a sales tax—a tax that over the years had been anathema to all Kentucky politicians. They had put together a virtual monstrosity—in fact, it had been designed for defeat. It provided pensions for the veterans of World War II, and, in addition, the veterans of World War I, the Spanish-American War, and the Korean Conflict. It would be paid ($500 maximum for service outside the United States and $300 maximum for service inside the United States) not only to living veterans, but, if deceased, then to their widows or heirs or next of kin. The amount would be raised by a thirty-year bond issue. It was widely believed that the people of Kentucky would never approve such an amendment—in fact, that was almost certainly the belief of most of the very legislators who enacted it in the first place. But nothing should surprise anyone about the political kaleidoscope in Kentucky.

As election day approached, the perception spread that Kentuckians might in fact be about to approve the amendment, and when the ballots were counted it was adopted by a majority of 38,039. Overwhelmingly defeated in Jefferson County and a standoff in Central and Western Kentucky, it received heavy support in the mountains of Eastern Kentucky. What at first looked like disaster opened the door to some intriguing possibilities. The people had spoken. By their vote the Legislature was now required to enact the sales tax law—something legislators would never have dreamed of doing on their own responsibility. If a sales tax must be enacted to pay the bonus, why not make the tax a little larger and cure some of Kentucky's long-standing ills? The experts determined that a 3 percent sales tax would amortize the bond issue and, in addition, provide very substantial funds for education—both extensive new buildings and substantial increases in teachers' salaries. Considering the good that could be accomplished, it seemed in the public interest to follow this course rather than enact say, a 1 percent sales tax limited to the bonus bonds alone. What had not been planned or intended by anyone opened up great new advancement for Kentucky, especially in the field of education.

It fell to my lot to fashion regulations under the sales tax so as to leave Kentucky completely competitive in our economic development. We checked out the competitive situation in twelve nearby states (Ohio, North Carolina, West Virginia, Tennessee, Georgia, Indiana, Pennsylvania, Alabama, Mississippi, Arkansas, Louisiana, and Illinois) so as to be sure that the enactment of the tax would not impair our opportunities for expansion of existing businesses and the opening of new businesses. The work was so constant—every night as well as seven days a week, because of the severe limitation of time—that Ellis

Merrifield, a valued assistant in my office with a good sense of humor, finally exclaimed one evening near midnight, "Did we win or did we lose?"

Sears-Roebuck very generously loaned us the services of their national tax expert. His counsel was invaluable. Sears obviously did not want a sales tax, but since it was inevitable they hoped we would enact a sound law rather than a makeshift one. We also counseled with every pertinent group and industry. By telephone as well as from an examination of public documents, we checked out the applicable provisions of all of our competition. We carved out liberal exemptions to encourage new and expanded industry. In the end the law as so devised was enacted with the high compliment from the Sears expert that in his judgment it was "one of the best sales tax bills ever presented to a legislature." It was another example of what can be accomplished by the cooperation of the public and the private sectors. We had many occasions in the future to test the soundness of the exemptions created, and invariably we found they had made Kentucky completely competitive in our economic expansion.

The spirit of the merger was carried out in the appointments that were made by Governor Combs. His chairman, Dr. Robert Martin, became commissioner of finance; my chairman, Dave Francis, the chairman of the Public Service Commission; Frank Goad, one of my chief lieutenants, became chairman of the Workmen's Compensation Board; Ned Breathitt, from the Combs side, who became director of personnel, was always considerate of my recommendations.

The legislature also responded favorably to the repeal I had advocated of the income surtax, which had been enacted under Chandler. This repeal effected a 36 percent reduction in the personal income tax and removed some 140,000 low-income earners from the tax rolls. This step also made Kentucky much more attractive to new industry.

Bert and I worked quite well together. I told him from the day of the merger that there would be but one governor, but we agreed that I would be a working partner. I doubt if, before or since, there has ever been such an effective working relationship between the two top officials of the commonwealth. It was a product of the special circumstances that gave rise to the merger in the first place, and it worked out well for the entire four years because of the constant effort by each of us to make it work and the respect each had for the other and his position. The post of lieutenant governor (like that of vice president in Washington) is often rather dull and empty—presiding over the Senate when in session and filling minor ceremonial functions on occasion. With Combs and me it became a full-time undertaking on substantive issues. On any matter that directly affected economic development, Bert would say to me, in effect, "This is your bailiwick." This included the fashioning of the sales tax and the all-important regulations under it, the personal income tax reduction, the forestry program, methods of financing new and expanded enterprise, research (both industrial and agricultural), oil and gas regulation, geological mapping, the state's industrial advertising program, planning and zoning, the Commerce Department, and varying degrees of consultation about other programs that had a bearing on Kentucky's economic climate. This meant participation in certain phases of such programs as education, highways, parks, health, airports, and safety.

Bert and I were committed to such a sweeping program that there was more than enough for each of us to do. When the legislature adjourned it had enacted our entire program. In due course, there were special sessions to redistrict the state, to save the miners' hospitals in the mountains, and to increase the salaries of our judiciary. The General Assembly created the Kentucky Economic Development Commission and the chairman's post became my overriding responsibility and the means of my carrying forward most of my work. I had not only the effective assistance of my personal staff (Bob Bell, Ellis Merrifield, Fred Tucker, Bill Biven, and Helen Price) but of the entire Commerce Department under the direction of Bruce Kennedy, Jim Nutter, and Mack Sisk. None of my cohorts counted the hours—they were all dedicated to the success of the program and performed with a real sense of urgency.

We launched a ten-year program for the total geological mapping of the state. We funded the Kentucky Industrial Finance Authority and created the Business Development Corporation, which was privately financed by the banks, utilities, and other corporations interested in furthering new business. These two additions to available financing—both new to Kentucky—made the commonwealth fully competitive in available loans for business. The Commerce Department provided planning and zoning experts for our towns and cities and encouraged the creation of local industrial parks and authorities all over the state. Vocational training was greatly expanded. An Agricultural Research Center was built at the University of Kentucky. Spindletop Research Center was launched as an independent research organization with an appropriation of $3,000,000, and I became its first chairman. This was an exciting venture with a strong board, including Phil Sporn, the head of American Electric Power, and Harold H. Helm, the chief of New York's Chemical Bank, in addition to the chief executives of significant Kentucky corporations—again, the partnership of the public and private sectors. It made great strides and numbered among its early clients the Reynolds Metals Company, Sears-Roebuck, CBS, The Jockey Club, Time, Inc., Westinghouse Air Brake, NASA, the Air Force, General Electric, IBM, and the Atomic Energy Commission.

In our national advertising we emphasized Kentucky's central location (within 500 miles of 68 percent of the country's population), our extensive water resources (with more miles of navigable stream than any other state in the nation), our energy resources (the largest producer of bituminous coal, as well as a substantial producer of gas and oil), our productive labor pool, our excellent business climate, and our agricultural resources (not only first in burley tobacco but significant in livestock and various crops). We dispatched an industrial development team (combining representatives of both private corporations and the Commerce Department) to New York and other major cities in search of new plants for Kentucky.

As chairman of the Economic Development Commission I undertook to involve the local leadership of the various counties so as to make it a grassroots movement. Much of what we needed could be accomplished only by them.

The Old Governor's Mansion, which had been renovated by my predecessor, Harry Lee Waterfield, served a very useful purpose in all of this. We (Anne and I divided our time between our home in Louisville and the Old Mansion in Frankfort) entertained local development groups from all over the state, usually at luncheons. Dinners were held for various groups like the boards of the Economic Development Commission and the Spindletop Research Center. We entertained legislators and their wives at breakfast every week during the various sessions of the General Assembly, and periodically held receptions and coffees for state-related activities. We entertained an average of around four thousand people at meals each year in the historic building, which had been the home of Kentucky's governors until the new mansion was built during the McCreary administration around 1912. As a matter of fact, I found it necessary to supplement the state allowance from my personal funds. To avoid some of the controversies that plagued former administrations, we did not have troopers stationed at the building or use any of the prison trusties. Instead, there were three service people on the state payroll. This called for a great deal more supervision and participation from Anne, but she has always enjoyed people and it made for much more personal entertaining.

Anne was so active in the newly launched Arts and Crafts Program and other state affairs (not to mention in arranging all of the Economic Development functions at the Old Mansion, and looking after the Wyatt family) that we frequently found ourselves crossing paths out in the state. On one occasion her pilot in a private plane told her that the plane in sight off the wingtip was flying her husband, in the opposite direction. Over the microphone she greeted me that she was glad to say hello to me over Paradise (we were then over the TVA's Paradise Steam Plant in Western Kentucky). I replied that I'd just come from a forestry meeting in Eastern Kentucky at Kingdom Come and had visited Hell-for-Sartin for the first time, on the way to Kentucky Dam Village.

Bert launched an enormous new highway program with bonds supported by tolls to supplement the expanding Interstate System. Kentucky moved rapidly from a bypass state to an excellent transportation system. We built eighteen new airports and improved another twenty-five. Kentucky increased its expenditures for education by 62 percent. That year Kentucky became No. 1 in the nation in the extent of increase in our education budget. The merit system was enacted for state employees—a major departure from the old political ways. Voting machines were authorized for every precinct and phased in over the four-year period. Kentucky enacted its first gas and oil conservation law, so workable that Tennessee duplicated it. Our budget for forestry was doubled. Kentucky took the lead in launching the Appalachian Regional Commission. Five new community colleges were built. To meet their rapidly enlarging enrollments, the University of Kentucky and the state colleges carried forward the largest building program in their history. An educational television network (KET) was organized—the first in the nation to serve an entire state. Political assessments were ended. Home rule was increased; state government reorganized; Medicaid was launched as one of several new health and welfare programs; the Kentucky Commission on Human Rights was created; an arts and crafts program was begun with 31 production and sales centers; and the state library program was modernized and expanded.

The lieutenant governor and his staff: Fred Tucker, Helen Price, Lucille Estridge, Mack Sisk, Ellis Merrifield, Robert Bell

Although we were successful in obtaining an equitable reapportionment of the state's legislative districts in a special session, we ran into a stone wall in our effort to modernize the state's antiquated constitution.

New factories were springing up all over the state. Best of all, our existing employers were expanding. Month by month, my office walls became almost solid with symbolic shovels from ground breakings as new plants were built. Early in the program we employed Ford, Bacon and Davis to give us a report on the potential of the Ohio River Valley as a center for the aluminum industry. We made wide use of this report and were finally rewarded with success when the Harvey Aluminum Company built a $50,000,000 plant at Lewisport, just east of Owensboro.

The yeast of change was at work everywhere throughout the Commonwealth. Kentucky had become first in the nation in many fields:

• Personal income in Kentucky (in many ways the final test) was up 8 percent in 1961—two and a half times the national average and greater than the increase in any of the other forty-nine states.

• First among all the states in percentage increase in teacher salaries

• First in burley tobacco production

• First in the production of bituminous coal

• First in its arts and crafts program (and a Kentucky Guild Train for good measure)

• First in the expansion of its state park system

• First in the country in modernizing its rivers and streams

• First (and then the only) state to offer all five of the accepted government and private financing plans for new and expanded industry

• First state to win the Keep America Beautiful Award

• First to be given control and licensing of atomic materials for peacetime uses from the Atomic Energy Commission.

In January, 1962, at a ceremony in Washington, I had the great pleasure of receiving for Kentucky the plaque awarded our state by the Society of Industrial Realtors for having the second-best industrial development program in the nation. (Governor Ed Muskie's Maine was first that year.) The following year in New Orleans Kentucky was adjudged first in a three-way tie with New York and Florida, and in 1964 Kentucky received the award as a clear first-place winner for the year 1963.

All over Kentucky you could sense the growing pride of accomplishment. Our extraordinarily sweeping program had been labeled by John Ed Pearce in his *Harper's Magazine* piece as "Kentucky's Quiet Revolution." Public life makes heavy demands on family life and requires effort and dedication beyond most activities in private business—not to mention the serious financial cost it entails—but where else can there be such fulfillment? I can honestly say that I would rather have been lieutenant governor in the exciting period of the Combs-Wyatt administration than governor in many of the less eventful times in our Kentucky history.

Throughout the Combs-Wyatt administration it was widely assumed that I would run for governor, and I was urged on all sides to do so. It would have interested me very much had I served as lieutenant governor in the usual way, with very limited activities. But the Combs-Wyatt team was different from any before or since. It was actually a merger of two gubernatorial candidates with each contributing to the political forces that led to the landslide victory and each having participation in the development and administration of the program in office. We had put our entire program into effect. I really had no desire to spend four more years in the work at the state capitol— it was time either to move on to a different public position or to return to the also absorbing interests of private life and the building of my law firm. Under these circumstances I chose to look to the Senate. It certainly would not be an easy race. Thruston Morton, the incumbent, had served as assistant secretary of state, had defeated Earle Clements for his seat in the Senate, and had served as chairman of the Republican National Committee as well as chairman of the Republican Senatorial Campaign Committee. He would be certain to have the influential and monetary backing of his national party, which would regard his reelection to the Senate as important to their national scene.

Kentucky is normally Democratic in state elections, but has real ambivalence in national elections. At that time we had two Republican Senators, Thruston Morton, and John Sherman Cooper. In fact, Cooper had become virtually a Kentucky tradition. Eisenhower had carried Kentucky by 95,739 in 1956, and even Nixon had carried the state over Kennedy by 80,752 in 1960. In 1961 the Republicans had carried Louisville and Jefferson County (my home base) by electing William Cowger as Mayor and Marlow Cook as County Judge. I remember Adlai Stevenson's comment when I first told him I was going to make the race. He said, "But won't it be mighty difficult to defeat the former chairman of the Republican National Committee?"

In a very pointed way I was shown the tendency for Kentucky to be more Republican and more conservative in national politics than in state elections. Robert T. Caldwell, a distinguished lawyer from Ashland, was a very warm friend and supporter. As a significant board member of Associated Industries of Kentucky he had been most helpful to me in my state race. He came to me one day and urged that I should run for the succeeding governorship rather than the United States Senate and supported his argument with a very strong statement: a personal canvass of the entire board of directors of his organization showed that almost every single member would support me for governor, whereas almost all of the same people would support Morton for reelection to the Senate. But all aspects of the Combs-Wyatt program had been fully launched and I felt I had done probably all that I could in that area. Certainly it was not worth four more years just for a better title.

After the adjournment of our second biennial legislature in the spring of 1962 I announced for the Senate. I quickly found that it was much harder to raise campaign funds and develop an organization for a Senate race, where there is but little patronage, than for the election of a state administration that directly affects the lives and well-being of so many individuals and businesses in every one of Kentucky's 120 counties. This was doubly so since all too many, I found, were already preparing for the governor's race the following year. Happy Chandler was openly a candidate for a third term. Since Clements and Combs had become estranged, it soon developed that Clements would support his long-time political enemy Chandler rather than a candidate supported by Combs. Clements' antipathy to Combs carried over to me as well. Early in the preparation for the Senate race I visited Clements at his apartment in Washington and asked him for his support. He came quickly to the point and asked how I stood with Combs and with the *Courier-Journal*. I told him that, as he well knew, my relationship with both was entirely friendly. He responded sharply, "Then how can you expect me to support you?"

Immediately after my announcement Harry King Lowman, the Speaker of the House, entered the Democratic primary to oppose me, with the active support of both Clements and Chandler. Lowman launched a very negative campaign but it made no progress and soon, because of ill health, he withdrew from the race.

At an early date I asked Bert not to launch the campaign for the 1963 gubernatorial primary until after the 1962 Senate election; after all, the governor's primary would not take place until May, 1963, a full year after the Senate primary. I was convinced that the simultaneous running of both races in 1962 would alienate the Chandler wing of the party from my candidacy and could easily spell a Morton victory. Bert listened, but I could see that he was determined to defeat Chandler for governor and felt that an early start would help his candidate. One morning in May—before the Senate primary—Bert called me with the news that he had just announced his support for Edward T. (Ned) Breathitt against Happy Chandler in the gubernatorial primary to be

With John F. Kennedy in Louisville

held the following year. My response was, "Bert, that will cost me 50,000 votes."

I was certainly not opposed to Breathitt. But it was clear to me that if our adminstration was actively opposing Chandler in the gubernatorial primary I could not expect the support of a united party in the Senate race. I felt the Combs announcement had made the Senate race a hostage to the next year's governor's race. And events proved that conviction to be all too true.

Both Morton and I had easy victories in our primaries. Then preparations started for the fall campaign. I had two excellent state chairmen, State Senator Shelby Kinkead of Lexington and Mrs. Phyllis Wood of Williamsburg. At an early date they canvassed all former

Democratic governors and senators and on August 28 Senator Kinkead announced that all of them had agreed to campaign for me—except Chandler and Clements.

President Kennedy made his first announcement for Medicare in the fall of 1962 and it became, from the outset, an inflammatory issue, especially in the opposition of the doctors. As I completely supported the Kennedy programs, I felt the full brunt of the opposition to this new and not generally understood program of medical care for the elderly. One day it was reported that the doctors in just one Lexington office building had contributed $123,000 to the Morton campaign on the ground that the Kennedy program amounted to socialized medicine.

In September the complication of running the next year's governor's race simultaneously with that year's Senate race was intensified when the United Mine Workers, in a single announcement, endorsed Wyatt for the Senate in 1962 and Breathitt for Governor in 1963. It was symbolic of the Chandler problem. It was a constant reminder that any Democrat who wanted Chandler to win in 1963 should oppose me in 1962.

President Eisenhower came to Kentucky to support Thruston Morton in speeches at London and Louisville and both President Kennedy and President Truman came to speak for me—Kennedy at Covington and Louisville, and Truman at Louisville and in Western Kentucky. Kentucky had become a significant national battleground and many of the Washington press corps visited the Kentucky hustings. Until well along in October the race was rated either a toss-up or as favorable to me.

In late October Thruston Morton in a major speech to the large Louisville Rotary Club charged that "the policy makers for the *Courier-Journal* and the *Louisville Times* assembled some of their reporters in a room in the Pendennis Club in Louisville. The purpose of the meetings," he continued, "was to formulate policy with respect to the Senatorial contest which is now in progress. The reporters were told of the intention of these newspapers to endorse the Democratic candidate." He continued "I do not know to what extent the reporters were told that issues should be slanted and news reports pointed in the direction of the Democratic candidate. It was made clear to them, however, that their reporting of the campaign—day by day—was against a background of editorial endorsement of the Democratic candidate." And to make sure that his innuendo was clear, he continued, "Everyone abhors the thought that news must be reported in such manner as will reflect favorably upon one candidate for public office, and unfavorably upon another."

But no such meeting had ever been held and no such instructions had ever been given.

Barry Bingham, Sr., immediately denounced the entire charge and said, "Senator Morton's statement is an utter and complete fabrication. No such meeting has ever been held at the Pendennis Club or at any other place at any time." The *Lexington Herald* in a lead editorial stated, "The irresponsibility that has characterized many of the statements of Republican senatorial candidate Thruston B. Morton appears to have reached its zenith with his utterly unfounded charge that two Louisville newspapers recently assembled some of their reporters 'to formulate policy' with respect to the senatorial campaign and directed the reporters to 'slant the news'."

Some of my friends in Breathitt's home county, meaning only to intensify the local majority for me, ran a full-page advertisement in the county paper saying "a vote for Wilson Wyatt for United States Senator is an endorsement for Edward T. 'Ned' Breathitt for Governor in May." But what was helpful in Christian County was hurtful in Chandler territory (like Woodford, which went 2 to 1 for Morton). A hundred thousand reprints were made and the *Courier-Journal* reported that "Chandler followers circulated handbill reproductions of the ad to many parts of Kentucky." A spokesman in Chandler headquarters commented, "I can't say for sure that our people are doing this to pass along a message but I am in favor of them getting the message. They ought to know how these two men (Wyatt and Breathitt) are connected."

Throughout the campaign a great deal of the Morton effort went into an attack on the Americans for Democratic Action. They painted it as a very sinister organization—virtually Communistic. The attack was not only politically damaging to my campaign but personally hurtful to my family. They said nothing, of course, of the true nature of the programs that had actually been supported by the ADA—the Marshall Plan, which saved Europe from Communism, or Truman's Point Four Program for the strengthening of free enterprise and freedom in the nations newly emerging after World War II, or the many acts of legislation for equal rights, decent housing, social security, collective bargaining, and health care—all programs that Eisenhower himself had adopted back in 1952. Nor, of course, did they recognize that the launchers of ADA had been such outstanding Americans as

Averell Harriman, Hubert Humphrey, Eleanor Roosevelt, and Herbert Lehman. But the ADA was largely unknown in Kentucky and my activity with it had been fifteen years earlier, as the first national chairman. It was easy to take the relatively unknown and convert it, by innuendo, into the mysterious and the unsavory. It did not matter that from the outset the ADA had been aggressively anti-Communist. In one of Morton's TV question-and-answer programs—and this was typical of his approach in various local appearances—he was asked about ADA and then specifically if he thought I was a Communist. His reply, as if more in sorrow than in anger, was, "I'd rather not comment on that."

It was not an easy issue to meet. We circulated information about the ADA and its true nature, but it is difficult to make fact as fleet of foot as fancy and falsehood. Some of my advisers strongly urged me to make a personal counterattack, and cited things they felt should be said about Morton himself. But I declined. If that is what it took to win, then winning would not be worth the price.

At the very end of the campaign the Morton forces orchestrated a simultaneous speaking in every one of Kentucky's 120 counties and distributed brochures painting my ADA association and all of its supposed evil as the biggest issue of the campaign.

Despite the smear campaign from the opposition the race was still being called a draw. An experienced Washington political writer even wrote a national piece predicting my election. But two more events added to my problems. One was the occurrence of the Cuban crisis on the eve of the election and the face-off between Kennedy and Khrushchev with the world balanced uneasily on the edge of possible nuclear war. That gave added significance to the false charges about the ADA and increased the normal tendency not to upset the status quo by ousting the one who is "in." A sitting senator always has the edge, all other things being equal, over the one who seeks to unseat him. This tendency is increased by the occurrence of a major crisis. The other event was a heavy last-minute avalanche of Republican money from outside Kentucky—a powerful weapon in a close race.

On election night the returns were unusually early. Often theretofore the Kentucky count had taken even days to tabulate. But I had been responsible for the voting machine reform and this—the first election since the installation of the modern machines—gave us the result all too early in the evening: Morton carried the state by a 52-48 margin. At 10:00 P.M. I conceded and wished Thruston well. There were many recriminations afterward—Chandler and Combs publicly blamed each other. But what is done is done, and I issued the statement, "I have no one to blame, no fingers to point, and no alibis to give."

After returning to the United States from President Kennedy's mission to Sukarno to solve the oil crisis in the Orient, I sent a letter in September, 1963, to some five hundred Kentuckians who had been active in my Senate campaign to urge them to work for Breathitt and the entire Democratic ticket in the November election. Ned, when elected, asked me to continue as chairman of the Kentucky Economic Development Commission during his administration, but I felt the time had come to resume the full-time practice of my profession. And a few years later, when we were both back in private life, Thruston Morton and I served harmoniously at the request of the Chamber of Commerce as cochairmen of a citizens committee to devise a plan for the possible merger of Louisville and Jefferson County.

Had I been elected to the Senate I am sure I would have enjoyed it, and I believe I could have been of service, but after all I was the head of a major law firm and when my term as lieutenant governor ended the following year I was quickly swallowed up in the challenges of my clients and in a wide variety of public activities.

Chapter 8

Oil Crisis in the Orient

On a Friday evening in 1963 (it was the 17th of May) I was having a pleasant time talking with Barry Bingham at a Newcomen Society dinner in downtown Louisville when I was handed a message that I was wanted for an urgent telephone call. It was the acting secretary of state, George W. Ball. He told me President Kennedy wanted me to come to Washington the following morning for an immediate mission. As George was an old friend, I asked him to tell me the nature of the matter. He said they would explain it to me in Washington Saturday morning but, in brief, it involved my undertaking a mission to President Sukarno of Indonesia. Nothing I had read about Sukarno caused me to be exhilarated at the prospect, but of course I agreed to come to Washington as it was a presidential request.

When I returned to the dinner table and confided in Barry the nature of the call, we agreed that unless a very real national duty was involved, the mission should be avoided. Sukarno had a dubious reputation and was widely regarded as an irresponsible playboy, even though he was the beloved leader of the new Indonesian nation.

On returning home I discussed it with Anne and polished up my scant knowledge of Indonesia and Sukarno. A little over a decade before, Indonesia, under Sukarno, had emerged as a new nation after several years of armed rebellion, which resulted in throwing off the yoke of three and a half centuries of Dutch colonialism. I recalled Indonesia from my school days as the rich "Dutch East Indies."

On Saturday morning at the White House and at the State Department I learned that President Kennedy, in consultation with Acting Secretary George Ball (the secretary, Dean Rusk, was out of the country at the time) and Under Secretary Averell Harriman, had

At the Oval Office, May 1963

determined to send a presidential emissary to President Sukarno in an
effort to avoid a disaster in our relations with Indonesia. The American
oil companies were on a collision course with Sukarno's government;
they confided that they were ordering their tankers to bypass Djakarta
after June 15. The Indonesian government had issued a decree (Regulation 18) that unless agreement was reached before that date the oil
companies either would have to make a decision to pull out or to
operate under whatever conditions Indonesia might impose, and there
was no indication as to what those conditions might be. This brought
to an abrupt climax the stalemate that had existed for two and a half
years. There was no prospect of agreement. All attempts through
normal channels and by our ambassador had failed. The oil companies,
in disgust and desperation, had brought the situation to the attention of

the State Department, since it had now become not merely a matter of corporate business but a matter of really portentous national concern.

Only the previous month Liu Shao-chi, the chairman of the National Defense Council of Communist China, had visited Sukarno in Djakarta and it was widely expected that if the properties of the American oil companies were expropriated, Indonesia would fall into the Communist bloc. It was our stake in that part of the world. Next to the loss of China, the loss of Indonesia would be the greatest suffered by the West. Indonesia, as a country, lived on kerosene, with only a ten- to fifteen-day inventory, but was completely dependent on the West both to produce and refine her oil. Next to rubber, oil exports produced the largest amount of Indonesia's foreign exchange. An expulsion of the American oil companies would throw Indonesia into chaos in a matter of days.

The only other time the American government had intervened in an oil crisis was in 1951, when Averell Harriman, in the latter part of the Truman Administration, had gone to Iran to carry on those difficult, tedious negotiations with the ailing Premier Mohamed Mossadegh— negotiations that produced a truce in the threatened takeover of the properties of the Anglo-Iranian Oil Co.

In a few days, Sukarno would be leaving Djakarta for Tokyo and, after a week there, would move on to Vienna, Rome, and other cities in Europe before returning to Indonesia. In other words, the June 15 deadline would pass while he was travelling around the world with his retinue on what some called his "pogo stick" junket.

Under these foreboding circumstances, I agreed to undertake the complex mission, fully mindful of the prevailing despair. I stipulated, and the State Department agreed, that I would serve without compensation. The oil company executives were particularly pessimistic as to whether the Indonesians could be counted upon to act responsibly. Sukarno paid little attention to serious economics, and yet without his personal commitment the word of his ministers and agents vacillated like the March wind. More than two years of serious negotiations by the oil companies had resulted only in the hopeless provisions of Regulation 18. The companies had reached the point of utter frustration. Clearly we were on a collision course.

I returned to Louisville that Saturday evening in order to put my affairs in readiness as best I could for a departure of completely undetermined length. As lieutenant governor of Kentucky and chairman of the Economic Development Commission, I had a calendar completely booked with conferences, groundbreaking of new plants, and other official duties. In addition, the political climate (as is all too usual in Kentucky) was electric with the approaching gubernatorial primary between Happy Chandler and Ned Breathitt.

My problem was compounded by the fact that the president and the State Department were convinced that the Communists would "blow the ship out of the water" if my mission as presidential emissary in the oil crisis in the Orient were to become publicly known before I could launch the sessions with Sukarno. The Communist party was very strong and very militant in Indonesia, in fact in 1963 the Indonesian Communist party was the largest outside Russia and China, and Indonesia was then their number one target in the world. If the Communists could bring Indonesia into their orbit it would be their biggest prize since China. Sukarno seemed favorable to the West, but he was steering a careful and somewhat tenuous course. Furthermore, both Russia and China could be counted on for trouble if they had any advance inkling of American intervention in the Indonesian oil situation. There was serious concern in some quarters for the safety of the American oil employees in Indonesia. In addition, any advance publicity would appear as pressure on Sukarno and would bring rebuff and defeat to the mission.

The result was that I was not permitted to tell anyone what I was about to do, or where I was about to go. Even my travel orders called for me to go to "Tokyo, Japan, and such other places in the Far East, Middle East, and Europe as may be necessary, and return to Louisville, Kentucky, upon completion of mission."

All of this put my wife in a most difficult and embarrassing position. She substituted for me when she could, hosted an economic development luncheon at the Old Governor's Mansion, appeared at the Pine Mountain Festival, and gave vague answers to inquiries as to my whereabouts. It was not easy.

In Washington, Averell Harriman similarly was having to be very noncommittal in responding to the press, which was daily becoming more aware that something was astir in the Indonesian oil drama. Every day and every evening, oil company executives and their lawyers were seen entering and leaving the Foggy Bottom headquarters of the State Department. Unexplained conferences were being held for long hours by Ball and Harriman. McGeorge Bundy and Mike Forrestal were involved from the White House—and, of course, the president himself.

In the goldfish bowl of Washington all this was noted by the eager

With George W. Ball at the State Department

eyes of the press. Questions were being asked but only vague and ambiguous answers were being given. Cables were being sent to and from Djakarta, Tokyo, and Washington in the attempt to put together the pieces that might bring about the mission.

I returned to Washington on Wednesday and spent every waking hour in an accelerated crash course of briefing. There were endless documents to be read and analyzed about the precarious economic situation of Indonesia, its foreign exchange problems, and its sky-rocketing inflation. Our ambassador, Howard P. Jones, later told me that our embassy in Djakarta was at that time the most expensive of our outposts anywhere in the world (not even excepting the large embassies in London and Paris) since we met our obligations there in legal exchange at fantastically exploding prices while much of the Indonesian economy was functioning at black market rates.

Walter Levy entered the conferences at an early stage. He was and is one of the half dozen acknowledged experts (many say the best) in the world oil situation. He had been the oil adviser to Harriman twelve years before in the Iranian oil crisis. He was an independent consultant, accepted by everyone as both remarkably knowledgeable and completely objective. On different occasions, he had represented most of the major oil companies of the world, and many of the oil-producing countries, as well. He was prevailed upon to be a part of the mission as my oil consultant. This was exceedingly important since oil is a world commodity and no arrangement can be made with one country or in one situation without reckoning with the consequences everywhere else. This fact also made it necessary for me to gain such information as time would permit about the prevailing rates, customs, and practices in the world oil picture. There was no time for all this to be fully mastered, nor was there the need, since Walter Levy would be with me. But a general understanding was essential in order to lead the mission and negotiate personally with Sukarno and his ministers.

It was arranged that I should leave for Tokyo the end of the week. That meant four days—Wednesday, Thursday, Friday, and Saturday—for preparation for a negotiation which would involve literally billions of dollars as well as our national posture in the Orient.

It was clear from the conference with the oil company representatives that little, if any, optimism surrounded the mission. They were convinced that every logical approach had been made, that every common-sense effort had proven fruitless. They were willing to join this last-ditch effort, but more as a patriotic accommodation than because they entertained any hope of success. And they must have felt (though they didn't so indicate) that not a lot could be expected to come from a Kentucky lieutenant governor without knowledge of, or experience in, the complexities of the world of oil. After all, these senior executives had spent their entire careers in this field, with every oil-producing country in the world, and thirty months of persistent effort, assisted and counseled by our ambassador, had resulted only in the impossible conditions of Regulation 18, which in their opinion amounted to expropriation, and then a likely Communist takeover.

The State Department and the White House gave me an excellent accelerated course in the complexities of pending congressional legislation, as well as in the political situation in Indonesia and the personnel of Sukarno's court. Our people saturated me with the facts and figures of the Agency for International Development program for Indonesia, the International Monetary Fund arrangements, the Food and Agriculture Program, the Clay Report, and the Hickenlooper Amendment. Both of the latter dealt specifically with the question of fair treatment and expropriation and their effect on the continuation of our assistance programs.

Toward the end of these preparatory sessions George Ball, still the acting secretary of state, drafted Abram Chayes, the legal adviser of the State Department, to accompany me as my counsel. As the general counsel of the entire department, he was skilled in all the legal areas pertinent to the negotiations as well as department procedures and protocol. In his earlier days a law clerk to Supreme Court Justice Frankfurter, he was later (and is now again) a professor of law at Harvard. He has a brilliant mind and a storehouse of knowledge. I commented, "There is nothing so luxurious for a lawyer as to have his own lawyer—and I am blessed with an extra good one."

And so the mission of four was constituted: I was to lead the delegation as Presidential Emissary, flanked by Walter Levy as my oil adviser, and Abe Chayes as my counsel, the three of us to be joined in Tokyo by Ambassador Jones.

The State Department cabled Jones in Djakarta to advise President Sukarno that President Kennedy would like to send his personal representative to Tokyo to meet with him. Sukarno—who greatly admired Kennedy—readily agreed, but expressed the hope it could occur at a later stage in his itinerary, preferably in Rome. We knew, however, that Rome would be too late. My travel orders contemplated that I would have preliminary sessions with Sukarno in Tokyo and, if these were successful in opening the way, that I would proceed to Djakarta where I would request the senior executives of the oil companies to join me for detailed sessions with the Indonesian ministers. Then, if desirable or necessary, I was to meet again with Sukarno (wherever he might then be) in an effort to conclude an acceptable arrangement. All of this might entail travel to any number of places throughout the world because of Sukarno's projected itinerary.

During those four days in Washington the oil companies presented the question of the safety of their American employees in Indonesia. There were some who were convinced that these employees should be evacuated at once, as their lives might be placed in serious jeopardy by the militant Indonesian Communists the moment the oil negotiations became public. Harriman decided, however, that they should remain at their posts, as their sudden departure might easily prevent the very success we all sought. He commented that he sympathized deeply with their predicament and hoped for their safety, but that their risk was not unlike that of soldiers who must endure hazards for the sake of the country's interests.

We then addressed the serious question of what might be done to engage favorable consideration by Sukarno, the man. The original concept by the president, George Ball, and Averell Harriman was excellent: underline the strategic importance of the undertaking by sending a Presidential Emissary. Since this is done only under very special circumstances and since, in terms of protocol, the position of Presidential Emissary outranks that of ambassador, Kennedy would be sending a strong message.

The next question was what present should be sent Sukarno, a friendly token. A book was thought most appropriate—one by Kennedy himself. I asked "How about *Profiles in Courage?*" The President, with a smile, said in effect that it wouldn't do, as Bobby Kennedy, his brother, had already presented that one on an earlier visit, and that Sukarno did not like Bobby.

We walked around the Oval Office glancing at the books lining the cases, in the hope of coming up with a good idea. The president finally decided that he would autograph to Sukarno his volume *To Turn the Tide*, and this seemed most appropriate as Sukarno had himself "turned the tide" in Indonesia.

We were still concerned that something dramatic was needed to capture Sukarno's attention and engage his favorable consideration. After all, he was not famous for any deep concern about economic matters. It would be necessary to persuade Sukarno to give political direction to Chaerul Saleh, his economic minister, to negotiate a settlement. Furthermore, time was running out—the hourglass was almost empty and something special was needed.

Finally we decided that I should take a personal letter from Kennedy to Sukarno, and that the letter would conclude with a paragraph that Kennedy was asking me, as his friend and adviser, to give Sukarno a personal message. That unwritten message was to be that sometime after Kennedy's coming trip to Europe he would be making a visit to the Orient, to the Philippines and Japan, and that he would also like to come to Djakarta to pay an official visit to Sukarno.

It was all too well known that Sukarno had been greatly miffed when Eisenhower visited India and Japan but omitted Indonesia. We felt almost certain that the promised visit by Kennedy would be highly pleasing to Sukarno and would greatly strengthen our ties with Indonesia as a friendly bastion in the Orient. It would be obvious that such

a visit would be most unlikely if the oil companies were expropriated—
and it would be part of my function in conveying this personal and
confidential message to point out the opportunities as well as the
problems. Mike Forrestal, as a presidential assistant, was invaluable in
drafting this letter, as well as in many of the other important preparations for the mission.

With any country such a presidential visit would be important, but
with Indonesia it could be strategic. Sukarno was a proud and sensitive
man; he often pointed out that Indonesia, with its hundred million
people (it now is more than 150 million) was the fifth most populous
country in the world (coming only after China, India, Russia, and the
United States); he regarded Eisenhower's failure to visit when in the
Orient as a direct snub; and as a new nation, Indonesia (and Sukarno
as its embodiment) took umbrage easily. Indonesia, after all, included
a vast archipelago at the equator, stretching out some three thousand
miles from the Indian Ocean into the South Pacific.

With this Kennedy visit decided upon (to remain secret, except to
Sukarno, until publicly announced by Kennedy), and the letter in my
pocket authorizing me to deliver the significant message privately to
Sukarno, my hope for success began to sprout.

Four companies were involved—Stanvac (composed of Standard
Oil of New Jersey and Socony Vacuum) and CalTex (composed of
Standard Oil of California and Texaco). Each was represented by an
executive vice president or a senior vice president.

The other principal oil company operating in Indonesia was Shell.
As soon as that company learned of the mission, it sought feverishly to
be included. The British Government interceded in its behalf. But all
of us were convinced that their entry could spell doom from the outset.
For one thing, though a British company, it had long been called Dutch
Shell, and the Dutch were anathema to the Indonesia of 1963. For
another, there was the imminent danger of military confrontation
between Indonesia and Malaysia. The British backing of Malaysia
made Shell's presence a separate risk, all its own. On my last visit to
Harriman before leaving, he was on the telephone with the British
Ambassador, who was urging Shell's participation. Harriman was
adamant. It would threaten failure and would not be permitted. In this
conversation I saw how tough Harriman could be. His answer to the
British Government was a resounding "no."

I shall never forget the challenge Harriman gave me at that time.
It was on my mind every hour from then until the mission was

successfully accomplished. He said, in effect, "Wilson, for the sake of our country this mission must succeed. I don't know how it can be done. That is up to you. But you know how to use presidential power— and that's what it will take. I know that somehow you will do it."

One other message I recall indelibly. After I had my last conference with President Kennedy and was leaving the White House by the side door (to avoid the press) I chanced to meet Dean Rusk, the secretary of state, who was just at that moment returning from abroad. He greeted me warmly, with "Wilson, you deserve a medal for being willing to undertake this mission." It was said with the warmth and kindness of a friend, but coming from one so knowledgeable of the problem, it underscored the general view that success was most unlikely.

Accompanied by Walter Levy and Abe Chayes, I flew from Washington to New York and thence by Northwest Orient to Tokyo, by way of Alaska. In the motorvan at Dulles, on the way to the plane, I noticed that one of the White House press corps sat down immediately opposite me and asked at once where I was going. I feared he was discovering something about the mission. Secrecy was being studiously maintained. I gave a vague, noncommittal answer and countered with a question to him as to where he was headed. He told me with delight that he was starting a pleasure trip to Europe. Until we parted company I plied him with questions and found him eager to tell me all about his trip instead of asking me anything further about my trip. His mind was not on official business. I heaved a sigh of relief.

On the flight to Japan all three of our group were buried in documents and memoranda in further preparations. When the plane put down at Anchorage, Alaska, we took a breather for a short stroll together at the airport. Walter Levy at one point turned to Chayes and me and with a twist of dry humor said, "Well, when this mission is over, if Sukarno turns you down, the people who say Marshall lost China to the Communists will say Wyatt lost the rest of the Orient. Maybe they'll let the two of you come back as far as Alaska, though, and open up a little law office in Anchorage." With a sinking feeling in the pit of my stomach, I fully realized the hazard his comment had underscored.

On the plane I spent the next several hours poring over the last document that had been handed to me just before leaving. It was a confidential biography of Sukarno—in great detail, with all of his elements of greatness, in fact everything about him, warts and all. It was fascinating. It is general knowledge that such a paper exists on most of the world leaders, but this was the first one I had ever seen. It is, of course, of great importance that such histories be prepared, and no doubt all countries do the same about our leaders as well. I had never met, nor even seen, Sukarno, and yet I was shortly to negotiate with him on matters of the greatest importance. I needed to know all about him. The outcome of my personal sessions with him would determine whether negotiations would proceed at all, and, if so, when and where they would occur, and the attitude with which his representatives would approach the complicated, heretofore unsolved and unsolvable problem. While he was the elected head of state, he had dissolved Parliament the year before and now had become the "President for Life". He held undisputed and virtually unrestrained power. His blessing would, in effect, tell his ministers to find a way to do it; his disapproval would confirm the expulsion of the oil companies, the expropriation of their properties, and the likely move of Indonesia into the Communist orbit.

Oil was then a buzz word in international affairs. And it would be a natural for the militant Indonesian Communists to link oil and "Yankee Imperialism" to fuel an inflammatory uprising.

All this made it vital that I develop and carry forward the best possible approach to Sukarno as a human being—but a human being who at the same time was the head of state with almost absolute power.

Negotiations are most propitious when the parties know each other, when they can strike the same wave length. Nuances can then be most important. The Sukarno life story gave me many of the advantages of a long personal acquaintance, and helped me shape my approach.

Thought of all of this again emphasized to me the absolute necessity of keeping the mission on a "good offices" basis and of avoiding as far as possible even the appearance that the American Government was acting as the negotiating agent of the oil companies. My official instructions stated "the United States national interest is your paramount consideration." They emphasized that I was not to "negotiate" for the oil companies—merely to "lend good offices". Of course, all that amounts—very clearly—to State Department vernacular to get the job done, to see that expropriation is avoided, to keep the oil flowing to the West, but without becoming the instrument or agent of the companies. This sublimation of "negotiating" into "good offices" struck me as not unlike Antony's speech in Julius Caesar, when he proclaimed he had come "not to praise him," while all the while extolling and praising the great Julius Caesar.

In the days to follow, I found myself on endless occasions disavowing the role of a negotiator and repeating the charming, nebulous, and ambiguous phrase that I was there on a "mission of good offices"—I proclaimed it in the private session with the oil company executives, at the opening of the private session with the Indonesian oil people, at the outset of my presentation to Sukarno, at the briefing sessions with the press in Tokyo, in presiding over each negotiating session between the two groups of oil experts, and, of course, again at the public signing ceremony at the conclusion.

Sensitive to this difficult role—to get it done, but not to do it—I was eager to learn all I could about Sukarno in order that both my personal and my official approaches to him might somehow create the affirmative atmosphere that would be essential to any chance of success.

I not only read avidly the fascinating story of Sukarno's life but reread it and pondered the possibilities of the coming session. I needed to establish complete rapport from the outset, for without his personal interest and approval no factual or economic argument would prevail. All this had been tried by the experts for two and a half years, but the result had been Regulation 18—threatened expropriation and expulsion.

The document of Sukarno's life was not a dry history lesson. It was life filled with revolution, imprisonment, love, ambition, and human foibles. Few paperbacks could approach the drama that riveted my undivided attention as I flew over the Pacific to Japan! From time to time, I would stop my reading to make notes and jot down ideas both for my formal and my informal presentations to Sukarno. The document I had been given was excellent, and vital to my purpose. It gave me a perception of identity with the man I must convince. Relationships and dispositions became clear. Some of his conduct seemed utterly inconsistent with his powerful position, when gauged by western standards, but it all fell into place when considered in the mosaic of his country and the milieu of his times. Some of it was so personal and revealing that I felt almost like a prying voyeur as I read it. But it gave me understanding of the man and his great achievements, as well as a sensitivity to many aspects of the Indonesian problems and people.

As I completed my reading and analysis, pencilling my last notes, we descended into Tokyo. It was midnight Sunday; we had left New

York Saturday afternoon at five. The nineteen hour flight was ended, the International Date Line had been crossed, our frenzied preparation was coming to an end. In keeping with the secrecy of the mission, the embassy had been instructed to avoid any display on our arrival— merely to transport me to the American embassy. The moment I arrived at the embassy, I asked for the marine guard. I did not want to take the slightest chance that my document about the life of Sukarno could, accidentally or otherwise, fall into anyone's hands or—heaven forbid—be discovered among the papers or in the possession of the American Presidential Emissary. With a receipt from the marine guard for the treasured document, I went to my room at the embassy and found a personal note of welcome from Ambassador Edwin O. Reischauer.

The following morning, without any breather to accommodate jet lag, I was awakened early by a telephone call from a Japanese-accented attendant at the embassy telling me that the *New York Times* was on the phone and wanted to talk to me. That made for a nervous beginning. A news story at that time, before an appointment had even been specifically made with Sukarno, was the very thing that might enable the Communists to pull the rug from under the mission. But the fact that he had discovered my presence in Tokyo and that I was staying at the embassy was a tribute to Abe Rosenthal, who then represented the *Times* in Tokyo. He had diagnosed the location of the pressure point and was pressing. I avoided the call, ate a quick breakfast and walked down the hill through the embassy garden to the chancery to seek the counsel and assistance of Ambassador Reischauer. I introduced myself to my host and confided my problem. He called in Nat Thayer, his press attaché. In due course, it was arranged—negotiated, you might say—that in consideration of an exclusive interview following my first meeting with Sukarno, there would be no advance speculative story. I might add that Rosenthal's responsible handling of the negotiation earned my admiration—I was pleased, not surprised, that he has since become the managing editor of that great newspaper, the *New York Times*.

During that Monday, conferences were held with Ambassador Reischauer and the embassy staff who were to work with us. An appointment was made with Sukarno for eleven o'clock Wednesday morning. We were informed he would allot at least two hours for the presentation, and this was encouraging. He would not dismiss it with a brief session. Chayes and Levy joined me for both lunch and dinner at the embassy with the Ambassador and his charming and intelligent Japanese wife. Mrs. Reischauer asked me at lunch if I would like a typically Japanese dinner, as she had learned it was my first visit to the country. She went personally to the market to select the various components for this very special meal—certainly very special to me.

At dinner Ed Reischauer—one of the ablest ambassadors we have ever sent to Japan—informed me that the Imperial Hotel, the Frank Lloyd Wright landmark, had that day been closed down for the first time in history because of an epidemic of amoebic dysentery. But President Sukarno had decided to stay with his retinue and send out for his food. The result was that the Imperial Hotel, in its entirety, became the personal residence of Sukarno and his ministers and attendants.

On Tuesday, the 28th, we continued with further conferences and cables. Although my instructions called for me to invite the oil company executives only after obtaining favorable assurances from Sukarno, and then to conduct the negotiations in Djakarta, I prevailed on the oil executives to start for Tokyo, on the outside possibility that something might be accomplished before Sukarno left Japan the coming Sunday morning. I have always believed that many solutions can best be achieved under the pressure of time—solutions that might otherwise flounder and fail if permitted a more leisurely cadence.

Ambassador Jones arrived in the afternoon from Djakarta and the four of us (Jones, Levy, Chayes, and I) put our mission together at dinner that evening at the Okura Hotel. There were also conferences with the British about the problems of Shell. In order to be close at hand for the negotiations, Levy, Chayes, and I moved over to the Okura, and my embassy room was then occupied by John Glenn, the astronaut, and his wife, who arrived that day for an official visit following his epic-making circling of the globe in outer space.

After having dinner with my cohorts, I put together the notes for my presentation to Sukarno. There was no time to prepare a formal document. Nor did it seem to me wise. There were neither rules nor precedent for the session that was to occur. I did not know what Indonesian officials might be present, or how many. It was not like an argument in court or to a commission—forums with which I was familiar. And yet in a way, it was. It would be a personal presentation to Sukarno, but presumably in the presence not only of our mission but of several of Sukarno's ministers and certainly his staff. Even that was speculation and would be determined at the last minute by Sukarno. What I was to say should not only persuade Sukarno to give political

Presidential Emissary Wyatt with Ambassador Howard P. Jones and President Sukarno

direction but also be convincing to his oil experts and whatever confreres might surround him. I decided to try to obtain a personal, private session with Sukarno first, and then to make the official presentation under more formal circumstances, with the full group present. By the time I retired late Tuesday evening, I had completed my plan and penned my outline on a small pad.

On Wednesday morning, our team of four plus Mr. Zurhellen from the embassy went to the Imperial Hotel just before eleven o'clock. As there were no hotel people remaining on duty, we were met at the door by one of the Indonesian attendants who conducted us to Sukarno's private quarters. Ambassador Jones was an old friend of Sukarno's, as he had been the American representative in Djakarta for five years. He introduced me and my two consultants, Levy and Chayes. No interpreters were necessary as Sukarno was proficient in English. In fact, Sukarno and his ministers were fluent in half a dozen languages.

Seeing that there were quite a few Indonesian officials in the room,

I immediately asked President Sukarno if I might have a private word with him at the outset. He readily agreed and we retired to an adjoining room. I asked Ambassador Jones to accompany me. Sukarno ordered coffee for us and then turned to me. After some preliminary comments, I presented him with President Kennedy's personal letter. It was fascinating to watch his reaction. He proceeded to read the letter half aloud, following each word with his finger as he read:

May 25, 1963

Dear President Sukarno:

I have asked my old and trusted friend, Mr. Wilson Wyatt, to meet with you in Tokyo on a matter of urgency.

I think you know from our previous correspondence and from my brother how strongly I feel that the United States can play a useful role in supporting the vigorous efforts you are making in building the Indonesian Nation, so that it may fully and independently play its important part on the world stage. I have watched with respect and hope the manner in which you have been leading your country in recent weeks to grapple with the problems of its internal economy.

Recently I have been told that negotiations with two American oil companies have come to a critical stage. Since the foreign exchange earnings from oil are of such vital importance to Indonesia's economy, I have asked Mr. Wyatt who is one of my close political advisers and who shares my warm regard for your country to consult with you as my personal representative on means of insuring that the negotiations result in agreements which will contribute to Indonesian economic stabilization and development. Mr. Wyatt has made himself familiar with all aspects of the oil negotiations, and particularly with the political considerations which are of such overwhelming importance.

After consulting with you, Mr. Wyatt will be available to continue discussions in greater detail with the responsible officials of your Government, and I hope you will encourage him to do so.

I feel sure that Mr. Wyatt's mission of good offices will be helpful to both of us. I hope that you will speak to him as frankly as you and I have spoken to each other, and I assure you that I will be reading his reports with great care.

Aside from these weightier affairs, Mr. Wyatt has a personal matter to discuss with you on my behalf.

Sincerely yours,
JOHN F. KENNEDY

As Sukarno came to the last intriguing paragraph, he looked to me expectantly. I told him that President Kennedy was soon to make an official trip to Europe and that in the fall of the year he planned a visit to the Orient, to Japan and the Philippines. On that trip, he would like to visit Sukarno in Indonesia. Sukarno was instantly exuberant. He confirmed our belief about his reaction to Eisenhower's failure to come to Indonesia by saying that President Eisenhower had visited Japan and India but not Indonesia, which was—he reminded me—the fifth largest country in the world. I replied that Kennedy would be visiting not only Japan and the Philippines, but also Indonesia. Sukarno then exclaimed, "He must come for two weeks. I will show him all over the country. I want him to see Bali, Sumatra, and even West Irian, since he helped us resolve the West Irian problem. And in Djakarta," he said "millions of people will turn out to welcome President Kennedy—more people than he has ever seen before." The letter and its message were clearly pleasing to him.

Sukarno then inquired "commitment?" I cautioned that it was not a commitment but a definite statement of intention, and that it should be kept in confidence until the two presidents should determine the exact time of the visit and make their own public announcement. Sukarno was so clearly pleased that I felt great progress had already been made, even though the negotiations had not begun.

This private session lasted some twenty minutes. We then returned to the adjoining room to meet with the larger group, which included Chaerul Saleh, the minister of basic industry and mining, Dr. Subandrio, the foreign minister, Johannes Leimena, the deputy first minister, the Indonesian ambassador to Japan and, of course, the members of my team, together with various functionaries.

Sukarno invited all of us to be seated and then turned to me and asked me to proceed. My primary purpose continued to be that of establishing rapport with President Sukarno, since his political direction to Saleh was clearly the first and perhaps the most important hurdle. Knowing from my recent reading on the plane to Tokyo that Sukarno's four heroes of history were Lenin, Washington, Jefferson, and Lincoln, I studiously avoided all mention of Lenin but drew a bond in common by speaking of the other three. I stated that just as George Washington was the father of our country, so also was Sukarno the father of modern Indonesia. I recalled that Thomas Jefferson was the founder of the Democratic party, the party of President Kennedy and my own party, and that he (Thomas Jefferson) had written our Declaration of Independence, just as Sukarno had written the Indonesian declaration of independence. I commented that Abraham Lincoln, a great hero to all Americans, was born in Kentucky very close to my home city of Louisville.

I then proceeded to tell him of President Kennedy's friendship, and of his respect both for President Sukarno's historic leadership and for the Indonesian people and their thirst for freedom. I drew the parallel that we had had the same thirst for freedom, and that we had realized our independence through revolution, just as his country had done. Mindful of his vast and varied archipelago and the Sukarno motto, "Unity in Diversity," I spoke of the similarity to the motto of my home state of Kentucky, "United We Stand, Divided We Fall."

As I watched Sukarno's facial expression, I could see that we were, indeed, beginning to establish rapport. When I reached the oil problem, I emphasized that as Kennedy's Presidential Emissary, I was on a mission of "good offices" but not to negotiate in behalf of the oil companies, nor could I offer any inducement in the form of additional assistance to Indonesia. I stated that with proper development of its vast resources, Indonesia could become "the Middle East of the Far East" and a truly great power. We were anxious to cooperate and assist Sukarno in building "the Golden Bridge" to the future—a figure of speech often used by Sukarno in his oratory.

I then came to the delicate line between pressure and persuasion. For this, Ciceronian ellipsis seemed most suitable. I pointed out that President Kennedy's ability to continue the existing assistance programs (Agency for International Development grants and assistance, the Food for Peace program, Export-Import Bank, other development loans, and the like) would depend on both public opinion and congressional support. I was sure that Sukarno, as a political leader, would understand that. He nodded agreement. I told him that I was not there to argue the Clay Report, which spoke favorably of Indonesia as an American friend, but required "fair treatment" of American enterprise and that Indonesia refrain from "international adventures"—both as prerequisites for continued assistance. I correctly assumed he would interpret these references to the Clay Report as a caution about his attitude toward Malaysia in the then pending difficulties.

Nor was I there to argue the Hickenlooper Amendment, which would suspend assistance in the event of expropriation of American properties without fair compensation. But I did point out that both public opinion and congressional support would be heavily influenced by each, and that, in effect, I was appealing to Sukarno as a political leader to assist President Kennedy in the political problems which faced him in his desire to continue the existing assistance.

I stressed the urgency of time. I mentioned the June 15 deadline of Regulation 18. (But privately I knew that there was an even greater hazard in the June 15 date, as the American oil vessels in their journeys around the world's ports had already been instructed, confidentially, to bypass Djakarta after that date.) Anticipating that Saleh might agree to postpone the deadline in his Regulation 18 (and he did do just that) I stressed that the immediate urgency was the congressional hearings dealing with the foreign assistance programs, which would commence the following week. A failure of agreement in Tokyo would be most hurtful. Even a delay would be negative. Only a solution, only an agreement, would be favorable—both to public opinion and to congressional concurrence.

At the conclusion I referred to the Kennedy volume I had presented to him and expressed the hope that Sukarno would "turn the tide" and help us build that "Golden Bridge" to a great future. In all, I spent about twenty-five minutes.

I then presented Walter Levy as a world-renowned oil expert to make some observations on the prospects for Indonesian oil if given effective development. This took another fifteen or twenty minutes. He was very convincing. Then there were brief remarks by Ambassador Jones, Chaerul Saleh, and Dr. Subandrio.

At the conclusion, Sukarno said, in effect, what do we now do to carry this forward? His attitude was completely positive. It was clear to all of our team, and to the Indonesian coterie, as well, that Sukarno was giving the go-ahead.

But I knew that all of this would still be fruitless, or at least of short duration, unless the spirit of cooperation could be carefully structured into a specific and equitable agreement—fair both to the companies and to Indonesia. I suggested that I had asked the oil companies to send their senior principals to Tokyo, that they were on the way, and that if it met with Sukarno's approval, negotiations could be undertaken the next day.

Sukarno indicated that he was ready to meet with the oil companies himself, but I thought this unwise as I knew that a great deal more time, and hard negotiations, would be required to structure a sound solution to the complex problem. I suggested that the oil specialists should meet first, and then report the results back to him. He was delighted and asked his ministers to work out the arrangements and proceed. I was

convinced the battle was half won. Now to build the structure, and
there I was fortified with two experts, Chayes and Levy. The whole
session lasted until almost 1:00 P.M. The Indonesian ministers alertly
followed their leader's cue. They were extravagant in their praise of the
American approach.

That afternoon, at 2:30, I met for an hour with Abe Rosenthal of
the *Times*, joined by Nat Thayer and Abe Chayes. The session went
well. At four o'clock our team returned to the Imperial Hotel to spend
three and a half hours making plans with Leimena and Saleh. Our first
negotiating session was scheduled for the following day, Thursday, at
eight in the evening. This would give the oil company executives time
to conclude their flight into Tokyo, as at my request they had already
proceeded most of the way and were awaiting word.

At the afternoon session, the Indonesians seemed to retreat from
the morning's enthusiasm by stressing that there could not be one
iota of compromise by them. In my optimism, and knowing of
Sukarno's pleasure over the prospective Kennedy visit, I interpreted
their negative assertion as a negotiating posture. Again I emphasized
that I was limited to a mission of "good offices," and could neither
negotiate for the companies nor negotiate any assistance programs.
They invited me and our team to join the next evening's session and
I readily agreed.

At eight, our team met the diplomatic and American press for a
briefing session at the chancery, working through interpreters.

Thursday morning, from ten to twelve-thirty, our team met with
the oil company executives at the chancery. We reviewed the situation
and told them of what we conceived to be the progress that had been
made. They had met with so many disappointments in their dealings
with Indonesia that their failure to share my optimism was understandable. Furthermore, I couldn't tell them, of course, of the proposed
Kennedy visit; that was to remain, literally, a state secret. They took
the adamant position that there was no room for so much as one iota
of compromise. I replied sharply that if that was indeed their position,
we might as well terminate the mission. After all, President Kennedy
had not dispatched a personal representative halfway around the world,
flanked by the general counsel of the State Department and one of the
world's leading oil experts, only to be told by our own side that the
matter was non-negotiable. They quickly realized that I meant it and
became much more conciliatory. At the conclusion of our meeting the
oil company representatives invited our team to be present at the

negotiating sessions to "lend good offices" and we again agreed. After the session, one of the oil executives said to me privately that it was well I had been so frank, direct, and positive with them, and he thought I could now count on their cooperation.

That evening, twelve of us gathered at eight, in the offices of Permina, the Indonesian oil enterprise, for the first negotiating session. Both sides asked me to preside. I opened the meeting by urging both groups at the table to proceed on the premise that it was not a question of *whether* we could agree, but *how* we could do it. I pointed out that I was present with my team at the express invitation of both sides. The evening was launched in an atmosphere of great cordiality. In addition to my "good offices" team of four, there were four Indonesians headed by Minister Chaerul Saleh and the four senior principals from the American companies. We ended the session at midnight with a feeling of hope and a conviction that initial progress had been made. The next session was scheduled for the same hour the following evening. In the meantime, both sides were working intensely on facts and figures needed for the next meeting.

Friday morning at eleven, accompanied by Ambassador Jones, I went to the Imperial Hotel to deliver to Saleh a memorandum requested by the Indonesians, giving a summary of the various assistance programs then in effect from the United States to Indonesia. I had repeatedly made it clear that just as I could not negotiate for the companies, I had no authority to negotiate or promise any additional aid. This fact made them interested in reexamining the nature and extent of programs then in effect—programs that would clearly be threatened by a breakdown in the oil negotiations. Fortunately, Abe Chayes and the Embassy staff, with information rechecked with Washington by cable and telephone, could and did prepare the requested memorandum early that morning.

As Jones and I entered the Imperial Hotel, a staffer who had been sent to meet us at the door took us not to Saleh, whom we had come to see, but to Deputy First Minister Leimina who had arranged the diversion to his room. After preliminaries, he turned to me and said that an oil agreement would cause serious political repercussions in Indonesia and that to alleviate the situation in his country he hoped—and he said this with an ingratiating smile—that I would make "a grand gesture," something "in the neighborhood of $400,000,000 of additional assistance from the United States."

I could not conceal my amazement. His request flew directly in the face of my often-repeated assertion that I had no authority to negotiate or offer additional assistance, just as I had no authority to negotiate for the oil companies. I declined this astounding request as politely as possible, but very categorically. I then showed him the memorandum we were taking to Saleh and explained it. He was, to our consternation, obviously surprised to be reminded of the extent of the already existing programs. We then proceeded to our intended visit with Saleh to review the memorandum with him and leave a copy for the Indonesian foreign minister, Subandrio. At the end of this session Saleh said to me, "The sword play will continue this afternoon. It will be very interesting."

We learned that Sukarno rarely met on matters of national importance without the presence of both Saleh and Subandrio, as each was a known contender to succeed Sukarno. Accordingly, as soon as Sukarno agreed for me to meet him in Tokyo he sent for Subandrio, his foreign minister, to join him in Tokyo where Saleh, the economic minister, was already present.

We had a late luncheon with the American oil executives to discuss the Shell problem which was becoming critical. The British were pressing for entry to the sessions or for direct and parallel negotiations. We agreed things were going too well to chance such a change, and part of the afternoon was spent convincing the British Embassy and Shell. To make our adamant position more tolerable, Shell was kept fully advised at every step, both by our team and by the American oil executives.

Friday evening, again at eight, we met at the Permina suite of the Okura Hotel for our second negotiating session. Meetings started early that morning were now to continue for thirty-six hours until Saturday evening.

By five in the morning, it appeared agreement had been reached on almost all major issues. The London *Economist* reported "Realism came with the dawn; for the negotiating teams on both sides, the night must have seemed to have lasted nearly three years." There was no longer any attempt to perfect final language on all of the details, even though there was no detail that did not have serious economic significance. It had become our objective to develop a document well described as "Heads of Agreement," in which every important issue would be addressed even though in broad general terms. If such a document could receive Sukarno's concurrence in Tokyo, we were willing to hope that it could be expanded later into the final hundred-page document that would be required to conclude the arrangements in lawyer-like nicety and precision.

We did not adjourn at 5:00 A.M. but merely recessed, with the request by Saleh that the oil executives return in two hours with a draft document.

Throughout the marathon negotiations, the Indonesians would "borrow" Walter Levy (with the knowledge and permission of the rest of us) to counsel privately with them as to the effect of various provisions, and just as often the Americans would closet themselves with Levy. Our expert had such clear vision and such objectivity and integrity that the final agreement was fair and equitable to both parties—and as a lawyer I had long since learned that mutuality is the best, and almost the only, adhesive to hold together any long-term agreement.

During the interval for the drafting I had a long session with Saleh. Since it appeared we were about to reach a meeting of minds I again expressed the hope that Shell would be permitted to join the agreement, and pointed out why this could be important to Indonesia as well as to Shell. He replied that he needed the approval of Sukarno and would get back to me after the next session between Sukarno and Tunku Abdul Rahman, of Malaysia, scheduled at nine. Obviously, Shell's fate now depended on the avoidance of the threatened Malaysian confrontation. I was anxious to have Shell included, both as a matter of equity and out of appreciation for Shell's cooperation with our request that they stand by and await the outcome of our negotiations.

I called Tim Wilkinson, the Shell managing director, though it was five in the morning, and told him that the situation was developing favorably and that it was a good moment to meet Saleh. Thoughtfully, Wilkinson had expressed the hope that he might meet Saleh informally in advance, so that he would not appear to be greeting him for the first time at the signing ceremony, should it develop that Shell could be included. Not surprisingly, I found Wilkinson awake, fully clothed, and ready to bounce from his room to ours at a minute's notice. He had stayed up all night, hoping for favorable developments and for a personal meeting with Saleh.

The draft was completed and returned to me for delivery to Saleh at nine—an hour or so late, but a remarkable work at that, in view of the sweep of the agreement. I have never ceased to marvel at the extent to which everyday human foibles present themselves in major affairs as certainly as in everyday life. Soon after the delivery of the draft, one of the American executives rushed back to me apprehensively with the confession that they had made a $10,000,000 error in one of their calculations. I spoke at once with Saleh and the figure was corrected. While it was important, all things are relative, and it presented no problem.

During the night the companies advised me that they would require Sukarno's personal signature. Without his express sanction they did not believe the Indonesians could be counted on to keep the agreement. Their previous transactions with lesser officials had left them saturated with distrust and disenchantment. With the companies this became an absolute sticking point. I approached Saleh. He dismissed the request with the comment that, of course, Sukarno as the head of state could not be asked to do any such ministerial act—the answer was an emphatic "no."

Chayes and I conferred as to what might be done, as this had become a last-minute but potentially tragic stumbling block. We formulated a plan: ask President Kennedy and President Sukarno to agree to issue simultaneous statements of approval. President Sukarno could hardly decline, if I could offer him a simultaneous statement from the president of the United States. This would put the approval on a high-level basis and would be a public commitment.

I slipped into a side room at the Okura while the negotiations were still in progress. It was around four in the morning. I got Averell Harriman on the overseas telephone in Washington just as he was about to depart for the ANZUS Conference. I gave him a brief draft of a proposed Kennedy statement, and the concept of the plan. He liked it and agreed to take it up with the president at once. The statement was telephoned back to me in a revised form, which I feared would not accomplish the purpose. Chayes and I redrafted the paragraph, as well as the statement I wanted from Sukarno. Back to the phone again—but with insistence that the statement not be further altered. This time, success; the White House approved our draft.

I then met privately with Saleh and told him that President Kennedy was so pleased with the coming result that he would be glad to join President Sukarno in the release of simultaneous announcements of approval, Sukarno's from Tokyo and Kennedy's from the White House. I gave Saleh the two suggested statements. I checked with the American oil executives and found, as I had hoped, that they would be entirely satisfied with such a procedure. The public statement from

Sukarno, as a part of an orchestrated public signing ceremony, would clearly constitute a commitment by Indonesia.

Soon, Saleh returned with Sukarno's complete approval. He would be glad to join President Kennedy in simultaneous statements of approval. He gave authority to Saleh to read Sukarno's statement as part of a public ceremony. All of this took place between four and ten on Saturday morning while the specifics of the Heads of Agreement were taking tentative, final form.

At eleven, the full group met again. New problems had surfaced. Redrafting was required. At eleven-thirty, Saleh informed me that the Malaysian confrontation had been avoided in the final meeting (just ended) between Sukarno and the Tunku and that Shell would be permitted to join the agreement. At once I informed the overjoyed Tim Wilkinson. It was a deserved reward (he was later knighted by the Queen) for his and the British restraint and faith when they had so eagerly and, in fact, insistently sought direct negotiations. After all, Shell was the largest of the Indonesian oil operations in 1963.

Subandrio invited Jones and me to lunch with him from one to two in order to perfect the plans for the public signing that evening. A minor point of human interest developed in the course of the luncheon. The foreign minister turned to me and commented that at times the American press, particularly *Time* magazine, had been unfair to his chief. (Mentally, I recalled an item in *Time* that referred to Sukarno's playboy antics, and with a double entendre, contained a line to the effect that he liked going to Paris which he was "prone to enjoy.") Subandrio expressed the hope, in view of this new accord between our nations, that I might prevail upon *Time* to give Sukarno better treatment. As a long-time lawyer for elements of the press I knew how completely unavailing would be such a request. I edged out of that as best I could but with no promise of relief.

The ceremony was scheduled for 6:00 P.M. in a public room at the Imperial. The Embassy notified the media. All afternoon, drafting and redrafting went forward. At 5:15, it developed that one element was still in dispute. Abe Chayes joined the group and assisted them in resolving it. At 5:45, accompanied by Ambassador Jones, I met again with Sukarno in his private suite with Leimena and Saleh present. Many photographs were taken and a very happy mood prevailed. I asked Sukarno how he came to know so much history and to be so fluent in so many languages. He replied, "It was all those twelve years I was in prison under the Dutch. I used my time to read and to learn."

Presiding at the signing of the oil agreement. *At left:* Indonesian Minister Chaerul Saleh and oil expert Walter Levy; *right,* Ambassador Howard P. Jones.

Chayes and Levy joined our session at six and told me the final draft had still not arrived.

At last, at 6:15, the draft arrived and we left Sukarno and filed into the public room, which by then was packed wall to wall with reporters, photographers, interpreters, television cameras, and recording machines.

As Kennedy's Presidential Emissary, I sat at the center of the table and conducted the session. On my left were the Indonesian ministers, on my right Ambassador Jones and the five oil executives—four Americans and Shell's Wilkinson.

Following my statement, I called on Minister Saleh. After opening remarks, he read Sukarno's statement:

It is very much gratifying that agreement has been reached between Minister Chaerul Saleh on behalf of my Government and the Oil Companies.

I am confident that this agreement will serve as one of the provisions for the national development of the vast oil resources of Indonesia for the benefit of our people in the years to come.

I have asked President Kennedy's Special Emissary Governor Wilson Wyatt to convey to the President my very best wishes and my thanks for the constructive role he and Ambassador Jones and their associates have played in extending their good offices to help resolve the outstanding issues in these negotiations.

Sukarno—1/6 1963

I then called on Jones and a spokesman for the oil group, and introduced Levy and Chayes. In order to assure the nonapplication of the Hickenlooper Amendment, the oil company statement included, at my request, a significant phrase that the agreement was "fair and equitable":

Executives of the oil companies stated that the negotiations completed today in a friendly atmosphere have resulted in an agreement which is fair and equitable to both parties and should operate over the years to the advantage of both Indonesia and the companies.

H.W. Page, Vice President, Standard Oil Company (N.J.)

Paul V. Keyser, Jr., Executive Vice President, Socony Mobil Oil Co., Inc.

Harvey Cash, Senior Vice President, Texaco, Inc.

Frederick Boucke, Assistant to the Chairman, Standard Oil Company of California

H. Wilkinson, Managing Director of the Shell Group

Saleh and the five oil companies then signed the original five-page "Heads of Agreement," and the public ceremony was over in a scant thirty minutes. In the words of our assistant secretary of state for Far Eastern affairs "We had not made history, we had avoided history." It was later acclaimed as "preventive diplomacy." All of us then retired to another room for the signing of copies for all parties.

The ordeal was over. With a feeling of happy success, I took my team out to dinner at a Japanese restaurant—the first time in my six-day stay in Tokyo I had been anywhere other than the Embassy, the Okura, and the Imperial. What had started with a phone call from George Ball to Louisville two weeks before, and continued in Tokyo at a frenzied pace for almost six days, was now done.

I called home and gave Anne the joyous news, "mission accomplished." I probably have never been more completely tired, or slept better, than that night.

The attitude of the oil companies was quickly reflected in the following letters to Averell Harriman:

June 1, 1963, from Augustus C. Long, Chairman of the Board of Texaco. "I think we have once again stopped the move of Communism and our great country, I believe, has been extremely fortunate in the outcome of these discussions. . . . My associates and I are convinced that if you had not taken such a great interest in this problem, and if you had not been willing to devote so much time and effort, the United States would have lost this part of the world to the Communists and the companies would have lost their properties."

June 3, 1963, from R. G. Follis, Chairman of the Board of Standard Oil of California. "After many years of dealing in problems involving American oil interests around the world, I can think of no case when Government support was more effective nor more skillfully timed and coordinated."

June 13, 1963, from A. L. Nickerson, Chairman of the Board of Socony Mobil Oil. "Mr. Paul V. Keyser, Jr., who represented Socony Mobil in the Tokyo negotiations, has given me detailed reports of the meetings and he has consistently praised Governor Wyatt for his skillful leadership and his dedicated efforts to bring the discussions to a point where the Heads of Agreement could be signed. In fact, Mr. Keyser's reports indicate to me that dispatching a special Presidential emissary to the sessions made the crucial difference, and that we have here an especially significant example of effective coordination between government and business in the national interest."

The London *Economist* summarized the situation:

And if the West had been unable to do business with Indonesia, chances for Malaysia, and for pro-Western government in South-East Asia, would have been the more in jeopardy. For the international oil industry, the agreement has perhaps another lesson: that companies and their host governments can from time to time agree on deals that are sensible to both, even when the two sides start from positions that originally seem quite unacceptable to each other.

On Sunday morning following the signing, I returned to the Imperial Hotel at 7:45 to see Sukarno off on his flight to Europe. Again he and I talked briefly of the coming Kennedy visit to Indonesia and he urged me to come with Kennedy, never dreaming that the tragic assassination in Dallas would intervene to prevent it. Jones and I joined Sukarno's motorcade to the airport where I received from Foreign Minister Subandrio a personal letter from Sukarno to take back to President Kennedy.

Sukarno's letter conveyed his complete happiness with the agreement and concluded with an interesting reference to the promised Kennedy visit:

Tokyo, June 2, 1963

Dear President Kennedy,

I thank you very much for your letter of the 25th of May, 1963, which has been handed over by your personal representative, Mr. Wilson Wyatt. In addition to the letter, during the talks with Mr. Wyatt, I am confident about the useful role the United States can play in supporting the economic rehabilitation which we are now giving the highest priority.

I wrote this letter a few hours after the signing of the agreement between my minister and the American Oil companies. I must say that it is a very fast work and certainly your personal adviser, Mr. Wyatt, assisted by Ambassador Jones and Mr. Walter Levy are of great assistance in finding the best solution for both parties.

I thank you very much for sending Mr. Wilson Wyatt to me, who is not only a trusted friend but also an able negotiator determined to find a solution.

With regard to the personal matter which you mentioned in your letter, I am looking forward to seeing that it will happen very soon.

Sincerely yours,
SUKARNO

The British prime minister, Harold Macmillan, followed promptly with this hearty agreement in his letter of June 4 to President Kennedy:

I have been very glad to hear the news from Tokyo that the American and British oil companies have been able to reach a satisfactory agreement with the Indonesian Government, and I have admired the skillful way in which your Envoy handled the preliminary discussions with President Sukarno and his Ministers, which were needed to bring about this happy result. I am most grateful for the efforts which were made on behalf of the Shell Company and for the success with which an important British interest has been protected. I hope you will pass on my warmest thanks to both Mr. Wyatt and Mr. Harriman.

And the next day President Kennedy summarized the situation generously in the following letter:

June 5, 1963

Dear Wilson:

Two weeks ago I asked you to undertake a most delicate and urgent mission of good offices to President Sukarno and other officials of the

Government of Indonesia in connection with critical negotiations between the Indonesian Government and American oil companies operating in that country. You accepted promptly and the result has been an outstanding success. An agreement satisfactory to both sides has been achieved after negotiations in which you played an indispensable part.

In putting aside your own concerns on short notice and in taking on this delicate and urgent assignment you have performed a most important service in the national interest. I am grateful to you.

Sincerely,
JOHN F. KENNEDY

On the plane flying back from Tokyo to the United States, Abe Chayes, with tongue in cheek, said to me, "You made one mistake. You did it too quickly. You should have waited for the gunboats to be coming down the Yangtze—then all the world would have known the real difficulty and extent of the problem. Now they'll never know it was touch and go." For my part, I was superbly happy that it was successfully over.

On my return to Washington I reported to the White House (President Kennedy, National Security Adviser McGeorge Bundy, and Mike Forrestal), to the State Department, and to the Foreign Affairs Committee on the Hill. At the White House McGeorge Bundy welcomed me with the happy words, "I am glad to see you return bearing your shield, not on it."

When Averell Harriman accompanied me to the Oval Office to meet with President Kennedy he confided, "These Kennedy boys are tough. First, they send you on this impossible mission to Sukarno, and today they are sending me on an impossible mission to Moscow—to try to work out a ban on nuclear testing." History soon recorded the success of his mission in the signing of the Nuclear Test Ban Treaty.

Following my return to Louisville I wrote Averell Harriman that Ambassador Jones, Walter Levy, and Abe Chayes had worked with me so harmoniously, so effectively, and so enthusiastically that each of them separately, and all of them jointly, were indispensable to the success of the misson at every step of the way.

Several months passed and there were disturbing reports that the Indonesian and American lawyers "holed up at the Waldorf" were having trouble translating the five-page "Heads of Agreement" into the hundred-page final document. The Communists were increasingly troublesome in Indonesia. On the 16th day of September a mob of five

At the Oval Office after the negotiations; standing, Counsel Abe
Chayes and oil adviser Walter Levy

thousand Communists stormed the British Embassy in Djakarta. With
that news my heart sank. The very next week Jim Bell called me from
the State Department. I feared it was a request to fly to Indonesia to
undertake to re-do the agreement. To my intense relief, he said, "The
final agreement was signed at seven this morning, our time (7:00 P.M.
their time), in Djakarta."

Since 1963, sweeping changes have taken place in Indonesia but the oil arrangement has lasted to this day. It provided fair treatment for both sides and incentives for each to continue. *Fortune* in its article on the Indonesian oil negotiations, stated: "Both sides have good reason to be gratified by the settlement!" The Indonesians gained the local pumps (important because they now could carry Indonesian, not American or British, names) and certain other facilities—but all for fair compensation. The oil companies gained exploratory, development, and export rights for thirty years. Indonesia's vast oil resources have been successfully developed and Indonesia, at the crossroads of the Orient, has remained in the Western orbit, friendly to the United States.

Chapter 9

Atlantic City and Chicago

In December, 1963, Ned Breathitt became governor at the end of the Combs-Wyatt administration and I returned to Louisville to spend full time with my law firm. As my four-year term of office as Democratic national committeeman from Kentucky lasted through the next presidential convention, I continued to perform the light duties incident to that office. Anne was serving as president of the Democratic Woman's Club of Kentucky and her political activities that year greatly exceeded mine. We were both chosen as delegates-at-large to the 1964 Democratic National Convention at Atlantic City. The convention was so completely controlled by Lyndon Johnson (who had succeeded to the presidency on Kennedy's assassination the previous November) that there was never a question from the outset as to the nomination of the presidential candidate—nor, really, as to much of anything else. Actually, the only question to be decided was who would run for vice president. And even as to this, everyone knew that Lyndon Johnson would select his own vice president and that the convention, without question, would confirm his selection.

Some three months prior to the convention my old friend Hubert Humphrey was speaking in Louisville to the Young Democrats and I had been asked to introduce him. After his speech that evening he asked me to come to his hotel room to discuss the coming convention, and we talked late into the night. He was then a significant member of the Senate leadership (majority whip) and was extremely effective. He had been almost solely responsible for persuading Senator Vandenburg, a leading Republican, to take cooperative action on a major matter of foreign policy. He was still as energetic and dynamic as ever, but he was not as shrill as he had been in his younger days (as the

Wilson and Anne Wyatt as delegates-at-large, Atlantic City, 1964

leading supporter, for example, of the inflammatory civil rights plank at the 1948 convention twenty years earlier) and he had developed the ability to get along well with "the other side of the aisle."

Senator Mike Mansfield, one of the most lovable and admirable people ever to serve in the United States Senate, was the majority leader. Many people (myself included) thought that Senator Mansfield was growing tired of the position and would happily have relinquished it to Hubert Humphrey, of whom he was very fond. Against this background, Hubert and I had a wide-ranging discussion. Hubert then asked me very frankly if there were certain things that I might do to help him get the vice presidential nomination. I told him I was not close to Lyndon Johnson, who had always opposed not only Stevenson but Kennedy as well. At one time, back when I was housing administrator in 1946, I had gone to Austin, Texas, at the request of the new and upcoming Congressman, Lyndon Johnson, to assist him in his campaign for reelection. I had done so gladly and at that time we were quite friendly. With the coming of Stevenson on the national scene, however, and Lyndon Johnson's loss, first to Stevenson in 1956 and then to Kennedy in 1960—with the Stevenson and Kennedy people always in opposition to him—our paths had parted.

My advice to Hubert Humphrey that evening was to seek the majority leadership. I pointed out to him that it was a position with continuity in office, that it was a post of great significance in determining and shaping national policy, that the Senate was a milieu in which he performed extraordinarily well, that he was admired on both sides of the aisle, and that—at least in my opinion—Senator Mansfield would probably be absolutely delighted for him to take the toga.

Hubert acknowledged the logic of this argument. But then, with that boyish openess so typical of Hubert, he said, "But, Wilson every morning when I am shaving and look at myself in the mirror, I say, 'Hubert Humphrey, you know damn well you want to be Vice President.'" That ended the discussion and I told him, of course, that I would be glad to be of assistance to him in the ways that he had asked.

Hubert was very appreciative when people he thought would be helpful to him in his standing with Johnson spoke up in his behalf. I have an idea, however, that Lyndon Johnson had pretty well decided at the beginning that he would choose Hubert Humphrey, but only after making it perfectly clear to everyone, including Hubert Humphrey, that he and he alone controlled the decision.

Holding out to the very last moment, Lyndon Johnson finally

announced that he was asking Hubert Humphrey to take the place on the ticket as vice president, and the convention dutifully complied.

It was ironical that this time when there was least to do I was attending the convention not merely as a delegate-at-large but as Democratic national committeeman from Kentucky, and that, as Anne was also a delegate-at-large, we were serving in the unusual capacity of a husband and wife team. There were really no decisions to be made and none of the usual significance in the convention process. By and large the convention was merely an occasion for meeting old friends, attending parties, and fulfilling dutifully the office of delegate. The next convention would be very different.

Following the 1964 convention Johnson was elected in a landslide over Senator Barry Goldwater, and the Great Society program—essentially the program devised by Kennedy—was rapidly enacted as the result of Johnson's extraordinary skill with the Congress. But the Vietnam War grew and expanded and became Johnson's albatross. Its objective was never well understood or widely supported, but as casualties mounted and the American involvement multiplied, much of the country and most of the youth clamored for an end to the hostilities. Throughout his entire four year term Johnson continued to defend his position and became the personification of what was probably the most unpopular war in American history. Obviously sensing his situation Johnson announced he would not be a candidate for reelection.

In July, 1968, the month before the convention, I became fully conditioned for the later controversies in Chicago when I served as chairman of the Kentucky Democratic Convention. Humphrey was clearly my choice for president, as we were old friends, going back to the days when he was mayor of Minneapolis and I was mayor of Louisville. Although Johnson had been extremely effective in bringing Kennedy's program into legislative enactment, he was extremely—even emotionally—unpopular because of the Vietnam War. Humphrey, in his race for the presidency, gained greatly from his position as vice president, but he also lost greatly because of his vice presidential loyalty to Lyndon Johnson.

Normally the Kentucky convention goes forward quickly and ends in a brief hour or so. But because of the emotional tension over Vietnam, I was determined to give full hearing to the McCarthy-

With Hubert Humphrey and Bert Combs, 1964

McGovern-Kennedy opposition to Humphrey, not only in the belief that this was the fair thing to do but also because I thought a completely open convention would lessen the tensions and animosities and keep the party together for November. The convention lasted seven long hours, the lengthiest in recent Kentucky history. It was attended by 2,228 delegates, most of whom stayed to the bitter end. The final tally was 41 delegates for Humphrey to 5 for McCarthy, but there was no steamroller at any time. The leaders of the McCarthy opposition expressed appreciation of the fairness with which they had been treated throughout the lengthy and at times tense and electric proceedings.

The following month I went to the national convention as a delegate-at-large from Kentucky and a member of the Platform Committee. This was the convention of the Chicago street riots; the convention when the president dared not seek renomination or even attend; and when Hubert Humphrey was nominated over Eugene McCarthy amid the emotional convention strife caused by the Vietnam War.

At the outset Hale Boggs, who was chairman of the Platform

Committee, asked me to serve as a sort of de facto vice chairman and to help him shape a platform on which Hubert Humphrey could run. This responsibility, to team up with Hale Boggs in the drafting of the platform, added a major interest to the laborious services that are attendant on the task of platform writing.

Our committee held public hearings at the Statler Hilton Hotel in Washington on Sunday, Monday, Tuesday, and Wednesday before the convention opened, then flew by chartered plane to Chicago for discussions and drafting, which lasted from Thursday through the following Wednesday at the Sheraton Blackstone Hotel. Congressman Boggs named twenty of us to a drafting subcommittee with the responsibility for preparing the final language of the platform. Ten very solid days of work had finally produced a platform of 20,000 words.

To achieve consensus from a large and varied group, many of whom are strong personalities with widely divergent views, is always a challenge—and there are always a few difficult prima donnas. I noticed, for example, that there were several members—and significant political figures at that—whom we would invariably lose when it was announced there were television cameras outside the committee room for purposes of interview. Not surprisingly, they were the same members who contributed least to the work of the committee. Although there was no great secrecy about the formulation of the platform, there was at one point considerable excitement when an electric "bug" was discovered in the meeting room, suspended from a television camera on the floor above. The committee ceased its proceedings until the eavesdropping bug was removed.

Among the interesting figures on the Committee were Senator William E. Benton, Connecticut, publisher of the *Encyclopaedia Brittanica*; John J. Gilligan, later Governor of Ohio; Ella Grasso, later Governor of Connecticut; Governor Roger Brannigan of Indiana; Kenneth O'Donnell and Ted Sorenson, from Kennedy's White House inner circle; Senator Wayne Morse, Oregon; Senator Claiborne Pell, Rhode Island; Governor Philip Hoff, Vermont; Senator Jennings Randolph, West Virginia; and Senator Clinton Anderson, New Mexico. Senator Benton, in one of his many unpublicized acts of generosity, provided the literary drafting services of the author Sidney Hyman, who was an old friend of mine as he had been a Stevenson speechwriter back in the 1952 campaign. He filled the very important function of undertaking to make at least good grammar and, at times, good literature, out of the conclusions of the committee.

Needless to say, the most important and the most difficult issue was the shaping of the plank on Vietnam. Finally, there developed a real cleavage. The Kennedy forces, which were then backing McCarthy, not only preferred a somewhat different plank on the Vietnam war, but decided as a matter of deliberate strategy to create an issue and carry forward a major division and debate. They had decided to make the Vietnam plank the test of forces between Humphrey and McCarthy on the Platform Committee.

One of my Kennedy friends on the committee, Kenneth O'Donnell, who had been President Kennedy's appointment secretary, and who later became the unsuccessful Democratic nominee for governor of Massachusetts—took me aside at one point and said, "Wilson, we have concluded that we must have a debate between the McCarthy and Humphrey forces and we have decided to make the issue the Vietnam plank." I appreciated his candor though I regretted their decision. Actually, I think there is no question but what we could have achieved a statement of consensus on this plank just as he and I had done on many other issues, had there been a mutual desire to do so. Our positions were really not that far apart. But the McCarthy-Kennedy forces thought they saw a political advantage in capitalizing on an asserted difference of opinion on this emotional issue, even at the likely cost to the Democratic ticket in November. This was undoubtedly strengthened by the fact that Johnson's position on the Vietnam War was extremely unpopular and under serious attack. This was Hubert Humphrey's Achilles' heel, as he was under the disadvantage of running for president as Lyndon Johnson's vice president, and was therefore under the Johnson cloud.

The reasoning of the McCarthy people was clear. The American forces were bogged down in an unwinnable war far off in Asia. France had failed before us. Now the superpower, the mighty United States, was failing similarly. We were losing our first war. Casualties were high. Young people all over the country were demonstrating against the war. Many were becoming conscientious objectors; many others, in support of their convictions, fled to Canada to escape service; college campuses were in turmoil over the issue. The thousands of patriotic young Americans who endured the hardships of jungle warfare were heroicly defending principles that had become blurred and were not well understood. What was the purpose of the war? Why were we in it? What could we possibly accomplish? The answers were not clear. Nevertheless Johnson had pushed on in his effort for victory. Humphrey as his loyal vice president had not spoken out against the president's position. McCarthy had pitched his New Hampshire primary campaign on the Vietnam issue and astonished the country with his strong showing. He was now seeking to preempt the anti-Vietnam War position as his trademark and ride it to a Democratic nomination for the presidency. Thousands of young people were demonstrating on the streets of Chicago throughout the convention in an effort to influence the decisions of the delegates. Any plank now put forward by McCarthy in opposition to the committee's position would almost automatically be supported by the "doves" even though its provisions were less defensible (as we contended) than the committee's plank, supported by Humphrey.

We put our Vietnam plank in final form and the McCarthy plank was drafted by a group of his adherents captained by Theodore Sorenson, President Kennedy's favorite speechwriter and the author of the bestseller "Kennedy," the chronicle of the Kennedy Administration. Senator McGovern (four years later to become the Democratic nominee) and Ted Sorenson called a special press conference near midnight on August 23 for the purpose of announcing their opposition plank.

When the two opposing planks came before the Platform Committee for debate the following day, Hale Boggs, without any advance warning and just before the issue was to be debated before the 110 members of the full Platform Committee, said to me, "Wilson, I want you to handle the debate for our side." Since I was not a professional in foreign policy, I would have much preferred that the issue be handled by Senator Benton as a former assistant Secretary of State, or by one of the others, but Hale as Chairman had made his decision. I hastily scribbled notes for my argument and the debate went forward before the committee, with Ted Sorenson carrying the debate for the McCarthy side.

I argued that the basic objective of our plank was to end the war in Vietnam; that while ours supported the peace talks then going forward in Paris, the minority plank took no note of them; that ours called for stopping the bombing in North Vietnam in a framework of protection of our troops in the field, while theirs provided less protection for our forces; that ours provided for a negotiated withdrawal from South Vietnam of *all* foreign forces, while theirs was more limited; and that theirs would impose a coalition government on South Vietnam, omitting all mention of elections and self-determination, whereas ours looked to a government of Vietnam chosen by the people in an election open to all major political factions.

It was the exciting highlight of the platform sessions. When the roll was called we carried the day in the committee by a majority of 62 to 35. The majority of the committee was clearly committed to Hubert Humphrey and completely in accord with the majority plank, which committed our party to ending the war. I was delighted that we had won and felt that we had a very reasonable plank. I was really surprised that the McCarthy-Kennedy plank had not included any provision for a popular vote and self-determination by the Vietnamese people, whereas we had a clear-cut provision calling for self-determination. I later learned that after the two platform planks had been publicly announced, the McCarthy-Kennedy forces gathered for a hasty night strategy session where the main question was whether they should remedy their oversight by making an amendment and inserting a self-determination provision. Apparently it was decided that it was too late to do so without embarrassment and that an amendment under those circumstances would make it appear that their plank had not been well thought through at the outset.

Finally the total platform was adopted, including the Vietnam plank supported by the majority, and my duties were over. On the day the platform was to be placed before the convention, I was catching up with a few phone calls and reviewing some papers in my hotel room. Naturally, I was going to the convention to hear Hale Boggs present the platform, but I had every confidence that the matter would go well.

Then, suddenly, the McCarthy-Kennedy forces called for a major debate on the Vietnam plank before all 2,600 delegates in the International Amphitheater and for a roll-call vote. They were going to dramatize the issue to the very end. As I was about to leave the hotel for the convention hall, I had a telephone call from Senator Ed Muskie. He asked me to join him and Senator Walter Mondale in riding out to the convention. I readily agreed to do so and joined them in the limousine. Senator Muskie told me that the reason for calling me was that he wanted me to help him line up people to speak to the convention in behalf of the Platform Committee on the Vietnam plank—which had become, then, the Hubert Humphrey plank. We talked about various names as we drove to the convention hall and agreed that each of us would undertake to get in touch with the ones on our list just as quickly as we arrived at the convention. Since the debate was scheduled to take place in very short order—we then thought it would be almost immediately—there would be no time for anyone really to make preparation but we wanted to make a showing of strength by having significant party leaders speak in behalf of the plank. Senator Muskie talked about how he would conclude the debate and outlined the argument that he would make. I then asked him, in all innocence, "Who is going to open the debate." In considerable surprise he said, "Oh, didn't you know? Hale Boggs decided that you should open the debate." This was literally the first I'd heard of it. Fortunately, I still had with me my notes from my spur-of-the-moment defense of the platform plank before the committee and started reviewing them at once as our car neared the hall. So far as we knew, it would be a matter only of an hour at most after we reached the convention hall until the debate would actually begin.

By that time it had already been labeled by the media as "The Great Debate." And it was to be carried nationwide on television before an audience of millions. Once again, I had a lesson in how things happen at conventions—so often at the last minute, so often without opportunity for advance preparation and, therefore, always with great excitement.

Ed Muskie, Fritz Mondale, and I lined up various speakers for the debate and finally had an excellent list. The McCarthy-Kennedy forces also had a very imposing list to support the minority plank. I remember very well asking one leading figure at the convention to participate with us. He said he was willing to do so but would appreciate it as a great favor if we would excuse him as he was a candidate for reelection and would like to be spared participation in such a controversial issue.

Hastily and nervously, I reviewed my pencilled notes while Hale Boggs was walking to the rostrum to open the presentation of the total platform to the convention. Just at that moment a note was passed to me from Hale Boggs to the effect that he had reversed the order and that Senator Muskie would open the debate and I would give the concluding argument. Needless to say, I was greatly relieved. This gave me much more time to consider what I would say—and an opportunity to hear the other debaters before presenting the concluding speech. Senator Muskie and Kenny O'Donnell opened the debate for the two planks, and Ted Sorenson and I gave the summations. It was an exciting presentation and became the high point of the convention, for the ending of the war in Vietnam was clearly the most significant issue before the American people.

When the hour-long TV debate was concluded and the vote taken, our plank carried the convention by a majority of 1,567-3/4 to 1,041¼.

Addressing the 1968 convention on the Vietnam plank

This settled not only the Vietnam issue for the convention but the presidential nomination as well. The Kennedy-McCarthy forces used this vote as the test of their maximum strength. They knew that even some of the Humphrey forces would side with them on the Vietnam plank. Although the minority plank was soundly defeated the Vietnam issue had been dramatized to an emotional pitch. The insistence on the debate had placed the Johnson albatross on Humphrey's shoulders. Considering the breathtaking closeness of the Nixon majority on election night one can very properly wonder whether the staging of this issue in such a dramatic and emotional fashion did not constitute the final bar to the Humphrey presidency. Soon after the vote on the platform Hubert Humphrey was nominated on the Democratic ticket to oppose Richard Nixon.

On the way out to the convention I told Ed Muskie I hoped Hubert would select him as his vice presidential candidate. Modestly he indicated he would not be displeased, but he had received no word from Humphrey nor had he sought the office. I was delighted when, on the following day, Hubert asked the convention to nominate Muskie for vice president.

Hubert Humphrey wrote me on September 18, the month after the convention: "The Viet Nam debate was probably the most informed, intelligent and thorough debate on a crucial national issue in modern convention history. The plank agreed to by the majority calls for pursuing an early end to the war and seeking a settlement which will recognize the rights of all people of Viet Nam."

George Wallace of Alabama bolted the Democratic Party and as presidential nominee on a third party ticket drained away nearly 10,000,000 votes. Despite this setback and a lame start from the strife-torn convention in Chicago, Hubert Humphrey waged a vigorous uphill campaign which was almost successful, but on election day he lost to Richard Nixon by less than one percent of the vote.

When the next presidential convention rolled around, in 1972, I declined the invitation to serve as a delegate. It seemed to me that the drawn out, fragmented primaries had taken over and that the convention had lost much of its significance when so many delegates had become committed long before the convention was called to order. No longer did the convention furnish a tribunal for the development of a national consensus through the process of negotiation, through the exchange of ideas among leaders, and by the vote of the delegates in light of all that happened up to the time of the balloting.

But as I recalled the many exciting incidents of the seven conventions in which I had participated I could testify to the truth of Vergil's Aeneas when he told his sailors in the midst of a perilous storm, "Forsan et haec olim meminisse juvabit"—and it is, indeed, pleasing to remember these things.

Chapter 10

Return to the Hearthstone

The foregoing chapters concern only a fifth of the more than half a century since my school days. The other four-fifths have been spent in the pursuit of my profession from my days as an individual practitioner to our present firm of more than a hundred lawyers. I have always been most grateful to my partners for their tolerance of my periodic excursions into public life, and I am deeply pleased that they share with me the conviction that participation in the public sector and in volunteer service is not only the privilege but indeed the special obligation of any successful lawyer. Our managing partner, Gordon Davidson, and three of our "graduates"—David Jones and Wendell Cherry, the founders of Humana, the giant hospital company, and J. David Grissom, the chief of one of Kentucky's principal banks—epitomize this principle. Despite their heavy responsibilities in private life these men have given most generously of their talents in leading a wide range of very significant cultural and public endeavors. I have observed that communities almost invariably prosper and develop in rather direct proportion to the dedicated efforts of strong citizen leaders.

Following the oil negotiations with Sukarno in 1963, I had been told that President Kennedy, after his anticipated reelection, had two other missions in mind for me—both intriguing and probably both impossible. One was to go to Kashmir to undertake a rapprochement between India and Pakistan, the other to South Africa to undertake to ease the restrictions of apartheid. These were indications of the breadth of Kennedy's international concerns and his belief in what it might be possible for the United States to accomplish through lending its good offices to the solution of many of the world's problems.

But it is never necessary to go to far-off lands, to peoples far away, for new mountains to climb and challenges to meet. The ones on which we can do our best are often to be found on our own hearthstone in furtherance of the ancient oath of each Athenian youth to leave his city better than he found it.Throughout my four decades of private professional life it has been a great pleasure to work with friends and fellow citizens on everyday problems that confront all of us in our home communities. And in public life, when I was mayor of Louisville years ago and worked with mayors of other American cities, large and small, I was impressed with the similarity of our problems. Whether the place was New York or Louisville or Hazard, the difference was only one of size, not of nature.

When I served on the Board of Trustees of the University of Louisville back in the 1950s we were confronted with the question of racial integration—the same question that faced almost every other university in the country, for that was before the Supreme Court decision that mandated the end of segregation, the end of the "separate but equal" doctrine in education. With the collaboration of Louis Lusky in our law firm, I prepared a brief on the question and concluded that the Kentucky statute that mandated segregation was invalid and that our continuance of the municipal college for black students and the rest of the university for white students was an unconstitutional separation of the races. I presented the brief to my fellow trustees but found them initially almost aghast at the idea.

In due course one of the members of the board, thinking he was playing a trump card against the proposal, suggested that if I would just talk to the deans of the various colleges I would find how opposed and upset they and the student body would be. In view of that comment, I suggested we have a joint meeting of the trustees and the deans for the purpose of a frank discussion of the whole idea. This was readily agreed to. A special session was held at which we went around the table and asked each dean to express his views. What followed was dramatic. Without a single exception the comments were : "Our students are for it; we have been wondering why it has not been done before; we see no problem; what are we waiting for?" They were unanimous. It was another one of those surprising developments in life when it turns out that the facts are the exact opposite of a widely held and unquestioned assumption. The result of the conference was that the board reversed its position and voted to end segregation, close the municipal college (the black school), and integrate the university. Dr. Philip

With President Jimmy Carter on appointment as chairman of the Sixth
Circuit Judicial Nominating Commission in 1979

Davidson, the president, worked out the transition very carefully, and
it went forward without a single untoward incident.

Some years later when I served on the Board of Trustees of
Bellarmine College, Kentucky's largest private school, I found the
educational challenge equally interesting. As I had the opportunity of
viewing the situation from the vantage point of board chairman of each
of the two schools, I could appreciate the unique manner in which the
public school and the private school complement each other and benefit
the total community—each has its own special benefits to confer. And
the Louisville public has shown its generous concurrence by contributing more than twelve million dollars to Bellarmine under Dr. Eugene
Petrik's leadership, at the same time that a successful fund drive of
even larger proportions has been carried forward for the University of

With Governor John Y. Brown, Jr. and former governor Ned Breathitt
on receiving the Governor's Distinguished Service Medallion in 1980

Louisville by Dr. Donald Swain. As we have moved headlong from the
industrial age into that dominated by information, knowledge, and
technology, there is not only a general awareness of the transition but
an avid eagerness for the betterment of our institutions of higher
learning.

In the area of development and in maintaining their very life,
nearly all cities have problems and opportunities that are remarkably
similar. During the 1970s most cities in the United States were
threatened; there was an exodus to the suburbs, the center city was
rotting at the core. And so it was with Louisville. I had the good fortune
to serve as president of the Louisville Area Chamber of Commerce at
the same time that my partner Gordon Davidson was president of the
Louisville Central Area and my son Wilson W. Wyatt, Jr., was
executive director of that organization (the guiding planner of the
downtown revival). It gave us a special opportunity for close coordination of plans for the renaissance of the downtown area and to join the
private sector and the public sector through cooperation with the
mayor, the county judge, and the governor. In a period of less than
fifteen years a total of a billion dollars has been invested in rebuilding

The founders of Leadership Louisville: Maurice D.S. Johnson, Wilson
W. Wyatt, Sr., and Barry Bingham, Sr.

the hub of Louisville's wheel, and former doubting Thomases are now
among the most devoutly converted. It has been a beautiful fulfillment
of a public-private partnership. Either without the other would have
failed, but the joint effort has remade a city both in structure and in
spirit.

In every renaissance all things seem to go well as the yeast of
successful change permeates the entire community. The fund drives
succeed, new leaders spring up, and the normal quarrels over turf are
diminished by the expansion of opportunity and the general climate of
progress. One of the satisfying developments in this zestful period has
been the birth and development of Leadership Louisville. I joined with
two others who had also just "retired"—Barry Bingham, Sr., the
publisher of the *Courier-Journal* and *Louisville Times*, and Maury
Johnson, one of the state's major bankers—in creating this organiza-

tion for the training of talented young leaders who have already shown their concern for the public interest. And more recently I have had a similar pleasure in launching Leadership Kentucky under the auspices of the Kentucky Chamber of Commerce.

There is a great wealth of talent and knowledge to be tapped from the ranks of the "retired," who can apply the experience and the contacts of a lifetime to the many opportunities for service in the area of the public interest, while still proceeding at a more leisurely pace than the frantic rigid regimen of dawn to midnight. When I attended a recent early breakfast meeting—contrary to my present wont—I told my confreres that it was the earliest I had arisen since I vacationed in Zermatt and got up to watch the sun rise over the Matterhorn.

I have always been impressed with Cicero's hopeful philosophy in "De Senectute"—that each advancing year of life should be more satisfying than the ones that have gone before. And so I have found it.

Index